PRAISE FOR *Catch and*

"Our understanding of politics and politicians is vastly improved when a legislator shares his innermost recollections of his work in Congress. Such accounts are rare outside the occasional prominent party leader. Their value is immeasurably heightened when the writer is a perceptive and gifted writer. Les AuCoin's *Catch and Release* is a memoir that all students and scholars of Congress will value for honesty, acumen, and skillful storytelling."

> —John A. Lawrence, author of *The Class of '74: Congress After Watergate and the Roots of Partisanship*

"Les was an amazing congressman. Now he shows that he's a master storyteller, too. This gripping personal history is sprinkled with humor and suspense and lyrically told."

> —Pat Schroeder, former US Congresswoman, presidential candidate, and president of the Association of American Publishers

"Once upon a time in American politics, there was room on Capitol Hill for spirited compromise, principled Republicans, and champions of the have-nots. Les AuCoin lived to write about them, and damn well."

> —Steve Duin, longtime *Oregonian* columnist

"*Catch and Release* is evidence of AuCoin's writing talent as well as his powers of observation. In this memoir, he exudes a sense of purpose that startles us, because we live in an era defined by cynicism, indecent values and greed."

> —Steve Forrester, former publisher, *The Daily Astorian*

"A brilliant memoir, timely and relevant. Historical figures great and not so great come alive on these evocative pages. Fascinating."

> —Robert J. Mrazek, award-winning author of *And the Sparrow Fell, A Dawn Like Thunder*, and other books

CATCH AND RELEASE

Catch and Release
AN OREGON LIFE IN POLITICS

Les AuCoin

Oregon State University Press   Corvallis

Cataloging-in-publication data available from the Library of Congress.

∞This paper meets the requirements of ANSI/NISO Z39.48-1992
(Permanence of Paper).

Oregon State University
OSU Press

Oregon State University Press
121 The Valley Library
Corvallis OR 97331-4501
541-737-3166 • fax 541-737-3170
www.osupress.oregonstate.edu

*For Sue, Stacy, and Kelly
and my granddaughters, Morgan and Jacky*

And for Charley and Rascal, two good dogs

Contents

Photo galleries on pages 77–84 and 165–172

Preface

This is not a chronology. Like the western rivers I love, my storytelling sometimes doubles back and splits a time or two before it resumes its course. Fateful first events launched my story. My journey sculpted it. Parts of the politics I lived were light and funny. Others changed the course of history in the best and worst ways. All parts of that experience show up in these memories.

With my eighteen years in Congress behind me, I followed Wallace Stegner's advice and returned like a salmonid to the western waters of my birth. There, I turned to fly-fishing to replenish my soul. I still thrill to a bent rod and the glitter of a rising form at the end of my line. At that moment of connection, the fish brings me, a visitor, into his realm, and I am transfixed. Using but a twist of feather and a shard of metal, I have mimicked life from within his world. The hookup is the trout's gift to me, and I honor it with delicate handling. Cradling his body facing upstream, I let him fill his gills until, revived, he beats a return to nature.

The act of catching and releasing squares with life as I've lived it. As a kid growing up fatherless in Central Oregon, a career in America's corridors of power was beyond my imagination. I caught a life a boy like me wasn't expected to catch; yet, when the time came to let go of my work, I like to think I released it reverently for having held it in hand at all.

Catching and releasing. Succeeding and letting go. If anything, the ethos works better in life than in fishing. All we can ever do is toss out the best cast we can—that which we can control—and relax knowing that what happens next is entirely up to the fish. The following stories describe some of the prizes I've caught and released in my time. Not all releases were voluntary. I recount times when I snarled my line, too, and what lessons they taught me.

Mine is the story of the eldest of two sons of an abandoned mom who was our sole means of support from the 1940s to the dawn of the '60s.

Despite my modest background (perhaps because of it), I managed to climb the ladder of national politics. By the time I left public life at fifty, an age when many politicians are just getting warmed up, I was the senior member of Oregon's US House delegation, a Democratic whip-at-large, and an official congressional observer to the Strategic Arms Reduction Talks (START). I debated nuclear arms control with officials of both the Reagan administration and Moscow's Supreme Soviet, helped double Oregon's wilderness lands, led the charge for access to abortion, helped open the way to official relations between the United States and the People's Republic of China, and secured funds for the largest public works project in Oregon history—the Portland metropolitan area's light-rail system. I was in my forties when the *Oregonian* described me as "Imaginative and persevering . . . Oregon's most powerful congressman and one of the most influential members in the Pacific Northwest."[1]

In some measure, a memoir is a violation of a fly-fisher's unspoken code, which disdains any description of one's prowess or bad luck. But I exempt myself here; I recount these stories not on trout water but in my writer's den, living in retirement with Sue, my lifelong wedded partner, mother of my children, putter-upper, and inseparable companion.

In telling the stories that follow, I hope to show that to live is "to have and have not." Most of us experience both on our journey. However, the best work of one who holds political power is to narrow the gap between having and having not. Such labors distinguish civilization from survival of the fittest.

While my political passion still burns strong, I turned in my congressional ID long ago and picked up a fly rod on my native soil. Now I picture myself perched on the soft grassy bank of a western river, tracking tufts of cottonwood floating against a flawless sky. I'm fascinated by the memories I'm about to tell, sweet and sour alike, as, one by one, the rush of water carries them past me one more time.

Acknowledgments

First, I give thanks to Sue, my wife of fifty-four years, for her unerring suggestions about how I might approach this work. Her ideas were astute and true, as was her advice in the years I sat in the Oregon State Legislature and the United States Congress. As her husband and father to our children, I hope I have in some measure repaid her love and support.

I am deeply grateful to my former press secretary, John Atkins, my primary editor. An exquisite writer and former columnist at the Corvallis *Gazette-Times*, John knocked the barnacles off more than one passage in my early drafts. Time and again, he remembered nuances and details I had forgotten with the passage of time. To work with my friend again after all our years together on Capitol Hill was a memorable gift.

Author and teacher Molly May of Bozeman, Montana, helped me understand the memoir form and gave splendid advice about showing, not telling. Her alchemy helped me see the past as if it were covered with dew.

Bob Crane, as readers will discover, has been a major influence in my life as a friend and former congressional chief of staff. I am indebted to him once again for his critique of the manuscript and his deft suggestions.

No author should be without a gifted researcher. For two years, Heather Thomas, a House reference librarian at the time, combed the *Congressional Record* for votes and quotes and found obscure documents with meager help from my aging memory. She deserves a medal with an oak-leaf cluster. My friend and urban thinker Rick Gustafson helped me relive the complex politics involved in the development of the Portland metropolitan area's light-rail system. Doing so must have equaled some of his toughest struggles during his presidency of Metro, the only directly elected regional government in the United States. I also owe a debt to Tom Barrows of Salem, Oregon, who volunteered to search the catacombs of the Oregon Legislative Records and transcribe the tape recording of Oregon state representative

Stafford Hansel's historic 1973 speech on legalizing marijuana. I owe a debt beyond measure to Cheryl McLean, my talented copyeditor, who steered me away from troubled water again and again and caught my errors with gentleness. Errors that remain are mine, alone. My friend L. Norman Johnson, one of the wise men of western forest ecology, reminded me of several truths, as did Dr. John Lawrence, my friend of four decades and author of one of the seminal books on the modern Congress, *The Class of '74: Congress After Watergate and the Roots of Partisanship.*

Finally, I wish to thank every one of my congressional aides who, over the course of eighteen years, made my goals their own and worked so diligently that I often had to tell them at night to go home. I could not have done my job without them. They are among the finest people I've known; I think of them as part of my extended family and try to spend as much time with them as I can.

1

Tears and Roses

I was a tall congressman and almost always dressed in my body armor, a jacket and tie. With dark hair and a smooth face, I struck many pundits as tailor-made for Oregon's First District, the state's "silk stocking" district, dominated by downtown Portland and suburban Washington County. But the foundation of my actual childhood was quite different and informed everything that would follow.

One night in 1946, when I was four, my mother's anguished cries shook me from my dreams. "No, Eddie!" she wailed outside my bedroom. "How could you?!" I thought it was a nightmare. Creeping to the door in footie pajamas, I heard my father's voice pleading for calm. Then I opened the door to a scene so shocking I still see it today. My mom, thin as matchsticks, her face flooded with tears, was pounding on my father's chest as his big hands squeezed her wrists while she writhed to break free. The hour was late, but his white dress shirt and tie told me he had just come home.

"What are you doing?" I bawled, collapsing to the floor. Mortified, my parents knelt to lock me in their arms. Rocking with me on the linoleum tile, they apologized over and over and told me they loved me more than anything else in the world and that everything would be all right.

But for we three, nothing would be all right again.

Up to that moment, I had known harmony in our little place in Vancouver's McLoughlin Heights. My parents had rented one of several hundred bungalows, many of which had been built for workers at Henry Kaiser's wartime shipyards across the Columbia River in Portland. In my mind, life was a bright, multicolored painting on a plate-glass window, adorned with flowers and bright green grass and the image of my family picnicking alongside a placid blue lake.

Like a brick, my parents' confrontation shattered that window. The world was suddenly capricious, capable of turning on me when I least expected it. I became increasingly wary and insecure. Instead of the stable dad I thought I knew, my father proved to be an addicted gambler. That night, he had been fleeced yet again at a poker table in Portland. This time, he lost the family savings.

My mother, Alice AuCoin, was grief-stricken. She was one of four daughters of the Darrar family of Madras, Oregon. Life on their homestead had imbued her with the frugality and discipline common among dryland farming families who scratched out a living coaxing wheat from Jefferson County's high desert. She could not comprehend my father's behavior. His recklessness frightened her, but she wanted the marriage to work.

After several days of talks, my parents agreed to a make new beginning. At the age of twenty-seven, my mom wanted to believe my father's promises to amend his ways and work us out of debt. She loved him. Christened Francis Edgar AuCoin in Tenants Harbor, near Portland, Maine, and older by four years, he was the most charming man she had known—tall, articulate, well-read but self-taught, worldly in his way. They had met working together at the Trailways depot café in Bend, Oregon. He was the exotic new cook with dusky French-Canadian good looks, an easy laugh, and a taste for music and fun. He turned the head of more than one waitress, and it didn't take him long to sweep the cute redhead, my mother, off her feet. They eloped to Coeur d'Alene, Idaho, where they wed on September 17, 1941.

In Vancouver, their "new beginning" collapsed within a year. My father walked out, leaving my mother in debt with two young boys to support. My brother, Leland, was a year and a half old.

In a letter left on the kitchen table, my dad wrote that he was bound for Alaska to cook for hundreds of men employed by a government contractor. In the wake of World War II, the north country offered jobs and generous wages, thanks to hundreds of millions in US military spending against America's next perceived threat—the Soviet Union. The War Department was expanding and fortifying air bases, constructing new ports, and engineering the Distant Early Warning Line, or DEW Line, a radar system to detect incoming bombers from the Red Army. The economic boom fired my father's imagination; he dreamed of Alaska's second gold rush and its fast money.

I can't say what he thought his departure would mean for his wife and two sons or how sincerely he even thought about us. I found his farewell letter after my mother died in 2002 and keep it now in a safe place to preserve it for the generations who follow me.

October 30, 1947

Dear Alice,

This is a difficult letter to write, because it will undoubtedly hurt you. However, I want to give you the best and I have never been able to do so working for cheap wages. The more I would try to correct things the deeper I became involved in gambling.

So I am going to ship out to Alaska. I can send you my weekly paycheck and I know you will do more with it than I ever could. It should be about $135.00 weekly by Feb. 1st. You should be able to do all the things you have wanted to do and get all the things I want to you have with this amount. I shall depend on your good judgment in everything.

You know I shall miss you and the boys. I shall write faithfully and hope you will answer promptly as I will be worried as to your welfare. I hope the stake I make up here will ensure our financial security.

I know you will be lonesome but let's make a game of it. We have a goal to reach and I know *you can save*. You know I have the ability to earn it. I should make $10,000 with overtime in less than 8 months. Eat good, watch out for colds, be careful of fires, etc. & you should be OK. I would like to make enough so we could buy our house & maybe a small café in a good town. But it will be up to you to decide what to do with the money; I will abide by any decision you make.

From week to week you will have to pay something on our debts but it won't take long before you can get your washing machine, etc., clothes for the kids & yourself. I'm going to Adak, Alaska for Drake Puget Sound Co. I will try later to get a movie camera thru the PX so you can keep a pictorial record of the baby. I have yours and the kids' picture here in front of me and I can't help but think *what a lot I owe* you and them. This is my chance to do it; this means the boys' schooling and everything we have tried for and failed to accomplish so far.

I want to prove to you my love is sincere and make a real home for you and the boys. Will you write promptly and send whatever encouragement you can? Keep well, don't worry, write often and remember I am doing this for you and the boys.

God bless you and keep you and them. With a heavy heart,
I'll close.
Lovingly yours,
Eddie

The nape of my neck bristles when I read these words. Aside from my father's implausible math, if he believed it at all, no letters ever arrived from Alaska.

Or paychecks.

Or telephone calls.

My mother retreated to Redmond, Oregon. An aunt and uncle housed us there while she found work clerking at the local Safeway. Eight of us, three adults and five children, managed to live together for several months in a three-bedroom house on the corner of Twelfth Street and Dogwood Avenue across from the John Tuck Elementary School.

I'll remember forever the kindness of the aunt and uncle who took us in: my mom's sister, Jeanne, and her husband, Kenneth. My mother did not tell me where my father had gone, just that they had divorced.

Sometime later, a false spring arrived.

My dad showed up at my aunt and uncle's house. The circumstances are a mystery to me. My mother never discussed it, and the grown-ups have all since died. My guess is that he came to Redmond from Alaska either under the force of law to discuss child support or to explore a reconciliation.

Soon he was off again for good and couldn't be found.

Before he disappeared, he left a memory that puzzled me all the way into manhood.

One evening, he called me to his lap in the living room to sing in his rich tenor while my aunt, uncle, cousins, brother, and mom looked on. It felt good to be in his arms again. The song was something about roses. Then came a lyric that made me burst into tears and race across the living room to the comfort of my mom. For decades, I remembered only the trauma of that moment, not the cause. Now and then, I wondered what it had all been about. But in boyhood, such thoughts are fleeting. There are games to play, trees to climb, bugs to catch.

In 1993, during the last weeks of my congressional career, I reflected on my life of 50 years. When my thoughts came around to my childhood, I was jolted by that half-remembered moment in my dad's lap. It was gauzy with age. Finding myself at one of life's crossroads, it was a good time to answer the puzzle. I reached an aide at the Congressional Research Service. A once-popular tune? The late forties or early fifties? Something about roses? A bouquet? Could he identify the song and find the lyrics?

The researcher called back the following day. As he spoke the stanza, I finally understood its knifelike effect. It was the opening refrain of Eddie Arnold's 1948 hit, "A Bouquet of Roses." I took the lyric to mean I had somehow broken my father's heart and that, like petals falling from the flowers, we were destined to part.

My dad probably chose the first song that came to mind. Then again, he did leave. Forever.

I struggled for years to realize I was blameless. Getting to that point was difficult for a boy who felt like an amputee.

When we moved out of my aunt and uncle's home, my mother rented an old sixteen-foot trailer house at Ivan Ivanovich's trailer park on the north side of town. There, she cooked meals on a small propane stove. I can't stand the smell of the gas to this day. Lee and I slept in the bed that lay sideways at the rear. Mom slept on the sofa. She didn't have a bed of her own until I went off to the army fifteen years later.

In the 1990s, James Carville, a Bill Clinton political advisor, uttered what he thought was a clever sound bite. "Drag a $100 bill through a trailer park," he said, "and there's no telling what you'll find." It was his way to demean Paula Jones, a woman with a limited education who had accused Clinton of unwanted sexual advances. But Carville blasphemed a whole class of women, including my mother, who would have loved to keep my brother and me in new shoes. In Carville's calculus, that would make her trailer trash.

We moved from our rented trailer when mom traded her grocery job for waitressing at Stockton's Café, a popular spot on Main Street that specialized in Chinese-American food. Waiting tables offered better pay, plus tips. A single extra dollar meant a lot because my father had reneged on child support.

I suppose you could also say we moved up. Mom rented a one-bedroom house on Fifth Street, unpaved at the time, with a lawn and two huge trees, a weeping willow and a honey locust. Lee and I turned a backyard shed into the Tombstone saloon. Our silver dollars were leaves stripped from the towering locust. With whips from the willow, we took turns being the matinee cowboy, Lash LaRue. For a time, our place was idyllic. Then, when I approached adolescence, I recognized its unsightliness. Shingled with dung-brown tar paper, the house sagged for lack of a foundation. In one corner of the yard, the septic tank emitted a faint odor. Redmond's town center was only half a block away, but to reach it I had to walk across the graveled alley and past the rear of the Piggly Wiggly grocery with its boxes and cans of garbage on the other side of our back fence.

From the time we moved in in 1950, Mom cooked on a wood-burning stove for the next ten years. Even in the heat of late summer, she would can fruit and vegetables. She worked the six o'clock shift at the café and hired live-in babysitters to watch over my brother and me. Lee and I slept in the bedroom; Mom shared her fold-out bed in the living room with the babysitters. None of them lasted long. They were women in their twenties, not long out of high school if they had finished at all. I remember Dorothy, a fun-loving, leggy woman. Sometimes she partied late into the night on Saturday to the music of Wes Tittle and His Tri-County Boys at the Redmond Air Base. When she returned, she inevitably disturbed my mother's sleep. Dorothy's replacement, Pat, was withdrawn and never smiled and left after a month or so. Searching for and keeping good help weighed heavily on my mother.

When I turned eight and was attending fourth grade, Mom felt, after a long talk with me, that she could forego sitters and count on me to awake to an alarm clock, help dress my five-year-old brother, and walk to Stockton's Café, where she took our breakfast order. Then I'd walk Lee nine blocks to the home of a good family with a stay-at-home mom and make it to school on the other side of town by eight o'clock. Mom's daybreak shift ended at two, so she would retrieve Lee and be waiting for me when I got out of school. Commenting on my duties, relatives would say, "Leslie, you're the man of the family now." They meant well, but I always took their words as a stabbing reminder of my fatherlessness.

It was 1950. North Korean forces invaded South Korea; Puerto Rican nationals tried to assassinate President Truman; and Senator Joe McCarthy of Wisconsin launched his witch hunt. I was only dimly aware of these or other world and national events. We couldn't afford a newspaper, and we tuned our old Zenith radio not to the news but to the *Jack Benny Program* or the *Gillette Cavalcade of Sports*. I listened in heartbreak when Ezzard Charles defeated heavyweight champion Joe Lewis. Our dinner table did not crackle with discussions about books or the world at large. They tended to revolve around Mom's workday, my school day, and how well I had filled the kitchen wood box.

One day in 1956, a call came from Los Angeles. Person-to-person for my mother. The man was an acquaintance of my dad. My father was hospitalized with rectal cancer and yearned to see us before he died. His friend would pay all expenses. My mother would have none of it.

She said, "Over these years, we could have died a thousand deaths, and Eddie would not have known. Tell him I'm sorry, but he made the decision to drop out of our life. We accepted it. Now he must too."

Listening from the living room, I thought Mom was being cruel and told her so. She sat down with me to explain how his abandonment had made her feel that she'd been played the fool. After that, I felt better about her. As for my father, I felt no loss. He was never mine, really.

Francis Edgar AuCoin died alone in Pasadena, California, on August 18, 1956. He was forty-six.

Weeks before his death, he wrote from St. Vincent Hospital in Los Angeles. I've saved that letter too.

Dear Alice,

You have known through the years that our love was the real thing. When I lost you, I lost everything in the world. I have paid for these wrongs. Fear, sickness, lonesomeness and continued failure have dogged my life.

During these years, I have had to figure out why a man does what I did to you and the boys. I blame it on a broken home, a drunken father. Hating all, the beatings and other pains from childhood, I wanted my kids to love and respect us. So I gambled to make a big killing. Of course, that didn't happen.

Now I have a blockage in the veins of both legs and serious rectal cancer. Please find it in your heart to forgive me and send me some snapshots of the boys and yourself—the ones I have are thumb worn.

Please pray for me. Please understand I love you and the boys. The things I remember.

Lest we forget,

Eddie

It's hard to know what Mom thought because I found it after her death. Maybe she saw it as a dying man's words of atonement. Or a lonely man ruing a love gone dead. Or a frightened man trying to balance his mortal accounts? Mom died having not mentioned the letter. I was contemptuous of it and its cloying protestations. However, I understood more clearly what gave my mother her steely determination to make it all by herself with her boys. A grifter had dealt her a bad hand, but by God, she would play it until the last card fell.

Years later, fate would give me more information about Francis Edgar AuCoin, and I would be able to make more sense of him and his choices. In the meantime, father hunger would haunt me throughout my boyhood years and beyond. In the sixth grade, I registered for school for the first time without my mom's help. Miss Axtell, a teacher, took down my information. When she came to the dreaded question, I froze.

"Father's name?" she asked.

Everyone in line heard her. I couldn't hide.

The awful truth sucked the wind from my chest. I whimpered, "I don't have one!"

Miss Axtell stared at me.

A knowing mother leaned in from behind. "Leslie's mom is the sole custodian."

I could have kissed the woman.

2
The World Begins to Turn

Maybe one needs bad times to appreciate good ones. By my senior high school year, my oversized feet had waited long enough to square with my newfound height. My six-foot, one-and-a-half-inch frame was an engraved invitation to varsity basketball. At the season's end, my Redmond Panther teammates voted me the team's most valuable player. The Associated Press gave me an honorable mention in its all-state team lineup.

Peer acceptance followed.

But, alas, not good grades. At the time, fear of failure worked against me. It became a self-reinforcing spiral. My mediocre marks led my teachers to develop low expectations for me. I met their expectations.

It would be unfair to foist responsibility for my underachievement on my family. It's true that I never saw my mother crack a book. It's also true that when her eight-hour shift at the café was over, she was dog-tired and had to run our household. With a grade school education, she couldn't help me in my early struggle with parts of speech, verb conjugation, or algebra. But her love of music took us to almost every high school concert. Later, with a secondhand instrument, I won first-chair clarinet in the eighth-grade band. To promote reading, Mom walked my brother and me to the public library on Seventh Street where old Mrs. Ward, with her grave countenance, issued us library cards. My love of books started there with the Hardy Boys and baseball fiction.

Then, in my senior year, something remarkable occurred.

My charismatic journalism teacher, Della Bell, handed back the first assignment of the fall. My paper was marked with a big red A, my first. Throughout the year, her As kept rolling in. I must have had a flair for journalism. In the spring of my senior year, Mary Brown, publisher of the weekly *Redmond Spokesman*, needed an acting sports editor. She asked Della if she knew a student who could step in through the summer. Della picked me.

Soon a whole community was reading my thoughts in print. I was a somebody, and I liked it. I decided to become a sports writer. To boost my career, I enrolled at Pacific University, where Professor Clifford Rowe had built a powerful journalism department. He got me Friday and Saturday night work at the sports department of the *Oregonian,* the state's largest daily, where I took prep scores phoned in from around the state and wrote one-paragraph game stories.

The mix of sports, journalism, and the ribald humor of some of the state's best sports writers enthralled me. For this, the paper actually paid me! By summer, I had done well enough to win full-time work filling in for vacationing staff reporters. By fall, though, my early sophomore grades told me I simply was unprepared for college. With my father's failure in mind, I had to do something radical to arrest my slide. I needed an environment with structure and discipline.

So I joined the army in the fall of 1961. I would hate jumping to the orders of grunting sergeants, but the military's demand for discipline transformed my life. The draft was still on during these years. Barracks life put me in the company of college graduates, men with almost no education at all, and virtually all types in between.

I admired the college guys. They were interesting, had sophisticated tastes in music and books, and many were great raconteurs. As draftees, they had launched their civilian lives before their Selective Service number came up. Their career stories intrigued me. I also befriended men with no college education, of course, but their lives outside the army were built around a narrower field of view. I was cultivating a taste for the life of the mind.

I started putting away half my monthly salary to build a college fund. For hours, I scribbled conservative estimates of my grade point average, semester by semester, to see how high I might go by the time I graduated. I wrote to Professor Rowe at Pacific University, who promised to readmit me on probation. Five years later, I would graduate as a dean's list student.

Even better, I would fall in love with a woman named Sue, a fellow member of the class of 1960 at Redmond Union High School and one of the most popular girls in school.

My world felt right.

3
Sue, Me, and the Summer of 1964

Sue Swearingen had transferred as a sophomore from Salem to Redmond Union High in 1958. She was an instant star, becoming a song leader, president of the pep club, and queen of the prom. As a senior, she won the Faculty Cup, awarded for outstanding extracurricular leadership.

Given that a few hundred students attended our school, you might assume Sue and I were well-acquainted. You'd be wrong. Throughout our high school years, I can't recall us having a single conversation. When we'd pass each other in the corridor, my knees would turn to Jell-O. Sue cringes when I mention it, but here's the truth—her round, liquid eyes, warm smile, and kindness made her one of the most drop-dead attractive girls in school. Upperclassmen virtually fell over themselves to date her. The mere thought of asking her out never occurred to someone like me. She was beyond reach.

But in the summer of 1964, when we were twenty-three and twenty-two years old, Sue and I would make up for lost time. I returned home from "Being All I Could Be" in Europe, gripping my army discharge like a sacred scroll I dared not lose. I didn't know Sue had just returned from several months of hitchhiking through Europe and England. That summer, she was helping her folks turn the Tumalo Emporium southwest of Redmond into one of the most popular family restaurants in Central Oregon.

Still wearing Army khakis, I stepped off the bus at Redmond's Trailways depot. At last, I was a civilian again. Undulating in the Central Oregon heat, the branch office of U.S. Bank loomed over me across the street, although not as high as I remembered. Across from the bank stood the venerable Rogers Clothing Store, where I had bought my high school letterman's sweater and mom, my Sunday church suits.

At the moment I disembarked, Mary Brown, the diminutive owner of the *Redmond Spokesman,* spotted me through her office window from across the street. She stubbed out her cigarette and reached for the phone. On the walk home to Eleventh Street, I could barely wait to bathe away the long road home from military duty. I hadn't seen my mom for two years, but when I walked into my house, she was breathing so fast she almost forgot to welcome me.

"Mary Brown called," she exclaimed. "She wants you to phone back!" History was about to repeat itself.

Mary was losing her news editor. When she saw me at the depot, she thought Providence had smiled. Would I fill the job until returning to college in the fall? As they said in the South at one of my army postings, I jumped on the offer "faster than a toupee in a hurricane."

A week later, I put out my first issue of the paper without losing one advertiser or getting sued for libel. I was giddy.

In the army, I had placed feature articles in the Louisville *Courier-Journal,* the Nashville *Tennessean,* and *Stars and Stripes,* major publications, all. However, nothing in my young life topped writing, editing, and laying out a whole newspaper—in my hometown. With the edition on the streets, I sat at my desk reflecting on the sweetness of life. Then Mary called to me. She had an assignment. My run of good luck was about get even better.

"You know the Swearingen family, right?" she asked. "You and Sue, weren't you in school together? Well, they've opened a restaurant down in Tumalo. I've eaten there—it's excellent. Why don't you do a little feature? Could help with ads. Here's the number."

Kathy, Sue's mom, had taught at Redmond High when we were there. I also recalled her father, Marshall. He reminded me of a Marlboro man with his manly mane of white hair.

On the morning of the interview, Marshall and Kathy greeted me at the Emporium before the restaurant opened for business. Never one to miss a promotional opportunity, Marshall didn't want customers distracting from the grand tour.

"Sue's going to join us," Kathy piped. "She helped us get up and going. I just phoned her; she's running a bit late." They had to know their daughter's bright charm wouldn't hurt my write-up.

While waiting for Sue, we examined the restaurant's rare bottle room and an assemblage of antiques, including a block cheese cutter from the nineteenth century. We were discussing the old-fashioned soda fountain when Sue rushed in, embarrassed, murmuring that time got away from her while picking wild daisies.

Well, of course she would have been picking daisies! I thought. I pictured a storybook brunette stepping gently through a dew-laced meadow. Marshall and Kathy melted away to let the former classmates take it from there.

Sue surprised me with her warmth. Here was a beauty unlike any of the self-absorbed lookers I'd met while seeing the world as "An Army of One"—a well-adjusted, friendly person with no airs. Among Sue's many attributes, she was a fellow liberal, a passionate Democrat, and she had paged at the Oregon Legislature. By the time the tour ended, we realized that she had been hitchhiking through Europe while I was stationed in Germany. We compared notes on Vienna, Munich, and Heidelberg. Sue admitted she had actually carried my army telephone number in her address book. A classmate, Ruthann Hartley, had given it to her. That Sue didn't use it was no surprise—why would a swan bother with a merganser?—but I ribbed her a bit about it anyway. Sue accepted my humor with her million-dollar smile.

When the interview ended, I sat behind the wheel of my '54 Chevy, trying to remember walking back to the Emporium's parking lot. In the passenger seat lay my notes. I was relieved they were still with me. Back at the office, I wrote the article. The clipping is still among my papers. The piece pleased Mary Brown. More importantly, it thrilled Marshall and Kathy Swearingen.

As the summer unfolded, Sue and I crossed paths often. At parties, we would steal a chat together—Europe, politics, music—and a quick jitterbug or two. Sometimes we forgot who we arrived with. Soon we were dating. In the following June, we were wed. At last, I had found two ways of being that I wanted to keep and not release: doing purposeful work and sharing a life with the best person I had ever met.

4

How I Became a Politician

It started in the army, but I didn't know it then.

My road to political office would reveal itself in stages.

In 1963, the Pentagon shipped my mechanized infantry battalion— men and armored fighting vehicles—from Fort Benning, Georgia, to Sullivan Barracks in West Germany, a former Wehrmacht post located 150 miles from East Germany between Mannheim and Heidelberg. I became a member of the Second Battalion, 87th Infantry Regiment, a World War II unit in the storied but now inactive Tenth Mountain Division. There, I was introduced to foosball, German beer, and potential peril from the Warsaw Pact forces mustered across the border.

JFK's handling of the Cuban Missile Crisis and his "Ich bin ein Berliner" speech had inspired me to subscribe to multiple news magazines to sate my growing appetite for politics. I was mapping plans to become a political journalist.

One November night, when the plaintive sound of "Taps" had faded over Headquarters Company, my comrades and I were readying for the next day of duty. Some men were toweling off after a shower; others wrote letters or polished boots and brass or tended to other tasks. A couple of GIs squatted over a footlocker in the middle of the bay, hurrying against lights-out for a quick round of Hearts. On Armed Forces Radio, *America's Top Twenty* wafted through the barracks.

Then came the incomprehensible. Dallas? President Kennedy? No, not Kennedy! We gathered around the radio, waiting for an update from Parkland Memorial Hospital. So little was known. Vice President Johnson might have suffered a heart attack. Governor Connelly might have been hit too. I was hoping against hope for the president. The voice of Walter Cronkite returned, normally so calming, but not now, not this time. I still hear his words:

"From Dallas, Texas—the flash apparently official—President Kennedy died at 1 p.m. central standard time, two o'clock eastern standard time, thirty-eight minutes ago." I steadied myself against an upper bunk. Rudy Gevorkian, a guy from South Philly built like an NFL lineman, stared at the radio through a flood of tears.

Dead? But that vigor!

Cronkite, again: "Vice President Lyndon Johnson has left the hospital in Dallas, but we do not know to where he has proceeded. Presumably he will be taking the oath of office shortly and become the thirty-sixth president of the United States."

No one moved from the radio until correspondents began to recycle what was known about the gruesome wound, the shot or shots, and the First Lady. Gradually, men drifted toward their bunks. The order for lights-out was never so welcome.

By the following Monday in battalion headquarters, the mug shot of a stereotypical pol had replaced JFK's photograph on the chain-of-command board. The switch seemed hasty, disrespectful, unduly methodological. LBJ looked like a ward heeler from the fifties. I tried to force myself to admire peaceful succession as provided by America's Constitution.

It was a heavy lift.

On the day after the murder, a Saturday, I had gone on a day pass to the city of Mannheim. A copy of the front page of a daily newspaper, *Mannheimer Morgen,* was posted on street-corner kiosks. JFK's photograph, bordered in funereal black, stretched across six columns under the banner, "KENNEDY ERMORDET" (Murdered). I stood amid thirty or forty men and women in the pale chill of morning. No one moved or said a word. They stared at the news. As a relatively unfledged twenty-one-year-old, I had no experience with history turned upside down. Nor had I realized how one leader could touch so many lives and lift so many hopes. It all seemed so wrong, so untrue. I could almost feel the weight of the world's loss.

Who, if anyone, would pick up the baton?

Fast-forward four years, to 1967. In Forest Grove, Sue and I had staked out a pleasant life where I worked as Pacific University's public information director and won awards as its college magazine editor. Our daughter, Stacy, two, and her brother, Kelly, one, utterly fascinated us. However, we detested Lyndon Johnson and his dirty war in Vietnam. When TV news reported that an obscure Democratic senator with a gray countenance had filed for president, I called out to Sue, "Honey, we at least have a candidate."

Neither of us had heard of Eugene McCarthy, the antiwar senator from Minnesota, but in him we saw a way to express our opposition to the war. We joined a local group of McCarthy volunteers who were already organizing Washington County, at the time a suburban-to-rural area due west of Portland. Before long, we were deeply absorbed in grassroots politics.

Of the two of us, Sue was the one with political experience. Her parents had been close to Oregon's major Democratic politicians. The late Senator Dick Neuberger and his wife (and successor), Maureen, and ex-governor Robert Homes and his wife, Marie, were her parents' frequent houseguests. Her folks also were on familiar terms with Senator Wayne Morse. Sue's mother had been active in the Portland League of Women Voters at the height of its influence in the fifties, and her dad was a former president of the Oregon Farm Bureau. Sue practically grew up on liberal Democratic politics. Paging in the Oregon House of Representatives left her on good terms with dozens of state legislators.

By 1968, the presidential campaign heated up when LBJ dropped out and Robert Kennedy stepped in. Sue and I stayed loyal to McCarthy, who alone had challenged LBJ when no one else wanted to. We became volunteer campaign managers for the Minnesotan's western Washington County operations. We organized door-to-door canvassers, the distribution of lawn signs, street corner volunteers wearing sandwich boards, and carpooling to rallies in Portland. We lined up homes in Forest Grove and Hillsboro to bunk and feed University of Washington students for a weekend when they came in busloads to canvass for McCarthy. I escorted Hollywood actor Tony Randall through the Hillsboro business district and drove Myrna Loy from Portland International Airport to the county Democrats meeting. At a Hillsboro store, a man trying on shoes told Randall he was for Nixon. "Well," Randall responded, "I hope your shoes pinch your feet!"

On May 28, McCarthy defeated Kennedy, 44 to 38 percent in the Oregon primary, the first time a Kennedy had lost an election. By then, Sue and I had become seasoned campaign operatives, acquainted with an army of liberal activists. We had a long list of tested volunteers and their telephone numbers.

One week later, we watched the shocking television coverage of Bobby Kennedy's assassination in California. Next came the police riot at the Democratic National Convention in August, and in November, the most unthinkable result of all: the election of Richard Milhous Nixon. An added insult was the defeat of Oregon's senator Wayne Morse in the general election. The antiwar hero had lost his bid for a fifth term to a little-known but covetous Oregon state representative named Bob Packwood.

Ironically, Oregon's antiwar Democrats might have abetted Morse's general-election defeat. In scores, we had volunteered hours to McCarthy or Kennedy, not the senator, to avenge the war crimes of LBJ. Morse seemed safe. He seemed to think so, too, until the end. Oddly, Kennedy's campaign didn't help Morse, either. The besieged senator had maintained a studied neutrality in the primary. But in the closing weeks, the RFK campaign unilaterally listed Morse on its delegate slate to the National Democratic Convention. The late Ron Abel, Morse's campaign press aide, wrote that the Morse campaign headquarters was subsequently inundated with angry protests by McCarthy voters who thought Morse had betrayed his word.[1] Morse's interparty wounds were manna for Packwood in his general-election upset of the old warrior.

The 1968 general election exacted an especially bitter toll on young opponents of the war. With high hopes, we had helped force an incumbent president out of the White House and felt sure a new president would end the fighting in Vietnam. In the end, we had to release our dreams, our heroes, and our ambitions to face a worse future with Nixon, Agnew, and Packwood than before we began. Politics, however, moves in cycles even when it seems certain to have reached end times.

Sure enough, thanks to a visionary group of liberal twenty- and thirty-somethings, our dismay didn't last long. They had conjured the idea of an annual weekend political conference, starting at Timberline Lodge on Mount Hood in 1969, where crestfallen McCarthy and Kennedy activists and others from across Oregon could spend a weekend debating issues, building alliances, and inspiring each other to keep driving for progressive causes. They called it Demoforum. The organizers[2] gathered names of activists from around the state and solicited funds from wealthy liberals to finance stipends for those who couldn't afford the price of admission and lodging. In the six years of its existence, it would produce a new generation of Democratic leaders. Among them were two governors, a presidential cabinet member, an Oregon secretary of state, two US congressmen, a state attorney general, and scores of mayors, city and county leaders, and state legislators, including two Oregon House Speakers and two majority leaders.

For Sue and me, Demoforum was an elixir. The setbacks of 1968—after
all of our liberal exertions—had left us depleted. But when the lively gathering of kindred spirits concluded, we drove down the mountain jabbering
nonstop about issues, careful to use our newfound knowledge of Roberts
Rules to maintain order all the way home to Forest Grove.

As election year 1970 came around, Sue and I kept an eye on the local
weekly for a new campaign to manage. One by one, Republicans declared
their candidacy for an Oregon House seat that had been vacated. There were
two sons of prominent businessmen, a suburban mayor, a public relations
man, a fellow actually named Bud Wiser, and Jess Mason, a radio agricultural
commentator who claimed to be "a farmer outstanding in his field." None
were impressive, except for the mayor. He was Bud Kyle, a man with name
familiarity from previous races. He looked formidable.

We were still searching for a Democratic candidate when I made a
trip to Chicago for Pacific University. Setting my bags down in my room,
I thought about Al Urbanavičius, a Lithuanian-American and close army
friend who hailed from Chicago. Eight years earlier, Al and I had been
buddies and coworkers at the public information office at Fort Campbell,
Kentucky. I had been a writer, he a standout army photographer. It would
be a treat to rekindle our friendship. As I thumbed through the phone book,
I could picture Al, a scarecrow of a man with a bobbing Adam's apple and
glasses as thick as pop bottles.

Not one Urbanavičius in the book.

Who was that other guy from Chicago? The barber we liked with a
bunk across the barracks bay? Tony something. He and Al might have
crossed paths when they returned home. What was Tony's last name? Started
with an S, I knew. Some good that did in a city of three and a half million. I
wrestled with my memory for hours before I somehow dredged it up.

Scafini! Tony Scafini!

Grabbing the phone book again, I found no Tony or Anthony among
the Scafinis, who numbered into the hundreds. Maybe I could find a parent. I ran my finger down the pages of the directory and started calling, cold
turkey. After many dry holes, I struck the mother lode at last. Tony's mom
told me her son was now a cop in a suburban town. When I reached him,
Tony told me he had lost track of Al but had heard something about him and
Playboy magazine. It made sense. As a photographer, Al was an artist.

I called the magazine. "We have no one here by the name of Urbana-vičius," the receptionist said. OK, I explained, I was just taking a stab at locating an ol' army buddy. She paused and asked for my name and number. *Why name and number?* I dared not hope, but I gave her both. Minutes later, Al called me. He was now Alexas Urba and for years had been shooting centerfolds for Hugh Hefner. At our breakfast the next day, I saw that the transformation was complete: my friend wore contact lenses, bell-bottom trousers, and thick mutton chops that nearly reached his chin. After a tour of the *Playboy* offices, which was, um, scenic, we went to Al's home. It was an old warehouse he'd turned into his private studio with space for up-and-coming artists who had caught his eye. His living space was a loft that hung over half the lower floor. Following our reunion and a million resurrected memories, I never saw Al, or Alexas, again. But as a memento, he gave me a two-by-three-foot copy of a stirring photograph he took of JFK addressing army troops during the Cuban Missile Crisis, when both of us had been dispatched to other military installations and placed on high alert. To this day, the photo has not been published. It adorned my office wall throughout my years in Congress and now hangs above my desk in my writer's garret.

The inscription reads, "JFK. Cuban Missile Crisis—Savannah, Georgia, 1962, US Army photograph." Signed, Alexas Urba. (Alexas died November 10, 1989, at the age of 46.[3])

On my flight home, I passed up dinner and gazed down at a carpet of clouds. The reunion and JFK photo had jolted my senses. Shards of memory flashed across my mind—a race riot in Nashville, Nixon's bogus "secret plan" to end the war, a polluted river that caught fire near Lake Erie. It had come to this. After the heady, hopeful politics of 1968, I thought the country was about to jump the rails.

As I thought about my life, I could see that politics, not journalism, quickened my pulse. No longer would it be enough to report political news or manage campaigns. And there was that Oregon legislative seat. Could I run for it? Why the hell not? Most of the Republicans running were walking clichés. I wanted to influence events myself, ones worthy to be remembered. When I told Sue, an activist at heart, she immediately agreed to the race. We knew Washington County had been solidly Republican since the 1936 FDR landslide. No matter. We were on fire and had the names of McCarthy volunteers and had mastered a style of door-to-door campaigning for which the county was unprepared.

Sue's familiarity with incumbent Democrats in the legislature was a huge help. Senator Ted Hallock, Senator Jason Boe, House Minority Leader Harl Haas, and Representative Frank Roberts gave me shrewd advice on messaging, tactics, and fund-raising. At a Democratic House reception to introduce new faces to lobbyists, Sue, having been a page for two sessions, easily introduced me around. Although I was a long shot, Sue put our race on their radar screen in a way I could not have done alone.

Two months later, with the aroma of fresh coffee in the air, men and women crowded shoulder-to-shoulder around the dining table in our little rented home on College Way in Forest Grove. Card tables filled the living room, each occupied by four or five volunteers. There was just enough room to squeeze past each other to reach the bathroom. If anyone had come for dinner, they'd find no room to lift a fork.

It was the improbable nerve center of my first campaign. I was running on the issues of clean air and water, consumer protection, property tax relief, and land-use planning. Of course, I remained an advocate for peace, racial justice, and economic opportunity, but I knew to focus on the topics foremost on voters' minds.

Our household buzzed with volunteers folding letters, addressing envelopes, and stuffing them with my final pitch for support. My mom, fifty-four, had driven over the Cascade Range from Redmond to help out, and she started each day baking cinnamon rolls by the dozens for campaigners who poured into and out of the house. When not baking, she would sit at the dining table, a string of postage stamps dangling around her neck, a sponge in hand to moisten them, happily chatting up her table companions while affixing postage to the mailers. A young volunteer stacked finished letters in bins, which would require multiple trips to the post office before the work party ended.

Seasoned observers saw the Republican primary as the main event. I was unopposed in the Democratic primary, a fact that didn't demonstrate my electoral chops so much as the haplessness of the Democratic organization. As a candidate, I was a twenty-eight-year-old unknown with an unpronounceable surname and I hadn't held any office whatsoever.

Emerging as the primary election winner on the Republican side was the veteran campaigner, Mayor Kyle. In my primary, given the choice between no one or me, voters opted for me.

Early summer brought news from Thailand. My college pal, army private Bob Crane, had kept up a subscription to his hometown paper, Forest

Grove's *Washington County News-Times*. When he read that I was running, he wrote that he would soon be discharged but wasn't expected back on the job at the New York *Daily News* until after the election. He would work for me if I could use him.

Use him? *Use* him? By return mail, I named him campaign manager.

I had met Bob in 1964 at Pacific University when I had returned from the army, reenrolled, and started dating Sue by long-distance. My friendship with him blossomed on campus when we studied journalism together and talked politics. After college, Bob developed the best organizational skills of anyone I knew, honed on the rough and tumble New York City politics he covered as a reporter at the *Daily News*.[4] He would be a manager I could trust completely.

His arrival in Forest Grove hurtled the campaign into boost phase. We were opposites in social graces, ideaphoria, and attention to detail, but we became each other's stronger half in a partnership that would last through my years in the US House and my US Senate race in 1992. He was chief of my congressional staff for twelve of my best years and is still my closest friend, one who always has my back.

Stubborn, brash, and indefatigable with a canny attention to detail, Bob quickly imposed structure on our organization. He set up a network of precinct captains to motivate and inform our volunteers. By the end of the primary campaign, our workers numbered more than three hundred.

The betting line for the 1970 November general election touted Mayor Kyle as the prohibitive favorite. Although his abrasive ambition annoyed some movers and shakers, he moved with relative ease within the local merchant and moneyed classes. His campaign mirrored ones Republicans had run for decades almost by rote. Billboards went up along virtually every highway, several local newspapers lauded the candidate's leadership. Rotary, Kiwanis, and other civic groups offered time at their dais. Republicans were accustomed to running the county and saw no need to go off script.

In other words, they had Bob and me right where we wanted them.[5]

He had quickly picked up what Sue and I had learned from the McCarthy campaign about the art of asymmetrical ground politics. With Bob running the war room, I walked to five thousand homes in my primary campaign and would reach five thousand more in the general election. Voters seemed taken with the idea that a candidate had arrived at their door to ask for support and answer their questions. After a day at the office at Pacific University, I would walk key neighborhoods from five o'clock until my legs got rubbery around seven-thirty, typically the time families sat down for dinner. On weekends, I was glad to hear the roar of a football game on TV in someone's living room. "Who's winning?" I'd smile when the homeowner came to the door. It was a great way to break the ice. My Saturday-Sunday regimen went from eleven in the morning to seven at night. For eight months, March to November, my meals were the brown-bagged sandwiches Sue packed. If I caught the sweet smell of freshly cut grass, I'd jokingly approach the homeowner to ask if she or he needed a hand. That usually brought a smile. At a screen door, I once met a housewife in her bra and slip. "Read this," I stammered, shoving a flyer into her hand before rushing down the block.

Sue knocked on the doors of some twenty-five hundred additional homes. Once, she worked a Hillsboro neighborhood with a man named Don, an elderly volunteer from the Retired and Senior Volunteer Program, or RSVP. At one house, a homeowner snarled at Don at the door, "I've been waiting for you SOBs!" he yelled. With that, he punched the old man in the face. Sue, one block away, was incredulous to see Don shuffling back toward her with a bloodied face, holding his broken glasses. She told him to turn the guy in, and he did. After the election, the AuCoin camp was elated to learn that Don won damages against the ogre.

That episode was the only act of violence our canvassers encountered. Their work was arduous nevertheless. It also was central to every aspect of our operations. When voters said I had their vote, our volunteers scribbled a 1 next to their name on a computerized walking list that contained addresses from the County Elections Office. Friendly-but-cautious responses deserved a 2. Neutral was 3. Unpleasant attitudes or a hard-core Republican merited a 4 or 5, respectively. We ignored the 4s and 5s for the rest of the campaign.

As the race progressed under Bob's guidance, supporters concentrated on the 1s, 2s, and 3s. They looked up phone numbers and called the 1s to recruit them as volunteers. The callers reached 2s and 3s to ask them about their issues and concerns. If the voter responded, we promptly mailed them a position paper on their subject of concern. Our organization began to grow. By November, we had a veritable army of canvassers, mail-stuffers, telephoners, and homeowners willing to take an AuCoin lawn sign. Bob stayed in almost daily touch with individual area captains to encourage volunteers who were engaged in politics for the first time.

My opponent's lawn signs showed up gradually over several months and soon became part of the landscape. We stored our homemade signs until the last two weeks of the campaign. Then, using the addresses of voters who had agreed to post them, two-person teams with pickups loaded with signs and sledgehammers fanned out across the county on a single Saturday morning to plant them. Overnight, as if by magic, my bright yellow and deep blue signs covered the county. They seemed to jump out on every block. A gaping Pacific University professor told me, "Les, I think you actually might win." I couldn't tell if he was pleased or apoplectic.

We were on a roll. Having saved our advertising budget, we ran half- and full-page newspaper ads in the last two weeks to reinforce the shock value of the lawn signs.

When the returns were counted, we won by twelve points, 49.5 to 37.6 percent. At our election-night party at the home of early supporters David and Sandy Lowe in Forest Grove, the volunteers went wild. As the county's leading vote getter for any office,[6] I was suddenly noteworthy and got prominent media coverage. Two years later, I won a second term, and Democrats chose me as House Majority Leader, the number two position in the Oregon House.

In contrast to the often ugly media spectacle of contemporary American politics, I often think about our little house on College Way and the big medicine we created there. It wasn't just that we won an upset victory. It was that every volunteer knew exactly how his or her work fit into the mosaic. Each owned part of my victory by dint of effort and had a hand in issues that mattered to them. They had bonded together at work parties around dining room tables. They attended twenty-five-dollar spaghetti feeds in church basements; they handed out flyers at the Sausage and Sauerkraut Festival in the Dutch village of Verboort just north of Forest Grove; they worked the phones and fanned out in neighborhoods to knock on doors. There was esprit in what they did together. Many of them remain friends to this day. As the decades advanced through my nine terms in Congress, I felt delight when greeting a constituent to hear, "You came to our door."

5
I Passed Through Jim Crow's Door

In subsequent campaigns, I continued to walk sylvan neighborhoods in communities like Beaverton, Hillsboro, and Tualatin. The squeals of children at play and laughter of neighbors at backyard barbecues made the world seem serene. I contrasted those scenes with army memories of racially charged Nashville, Tennessee. More than any other experience in my life, the racial violence that once engulfed me there was the reason I was in politics and canvassing these precincts.

Fourteen years earlier, I had spent a weekend at the YMCA in downtown Nashville. My army pass from Fort Campbell was good for three days. On this and other leaves, I often joined Vanderbilt University students to register blacks to vote.[1] But on this weekend, I wanted a respite, the nourishment of a good book, solace from barracks life, and an escape from the barking ignorance of certain sergeants. ("Irri-*goddamn*-gardless, soldier!")

Early on my first morning at the Y, I awoke to odd slapping sounds outside my open window. I looked down on the street to see a dozen black kids running pitter-pat in twos across the sun-washed pavement. They looked to be nine or ten years old. The girls' gleaming patent leather shoes set off their pink and white chiffons. The boys wore their Sunday-best dark suits and bow ties. Adorable. As the children crossed, two well-dressed twenty-something men ran along with them, shooting wary glances up and down the street. One led the way, the other brought up the rear. Seconds later, everyone disappeared around the corner. The scene made me smile yet seemed odd. I couldn't imagine where they were going because it was Saturday morning, not the Sabbath. Seventh-Day Adventists, maybe. But why the wary looks? I didn't know.

I glanced at my watch. *Eight o'clock.* Time for breakfast downstairs.

I pushed my grits aside and enjoyed an extra coffee while browsing through the *Nashville Tennessean*. Before long, good weather lured me out for a stroll around town. Although Fort Campbell was but sixty miles to the north, this was my first trip to poke around the Athens of the South on my own. Besides voter-registration work, every other visit had been a nighttime foray into the honkytonks in Nashville's Printer's Alley. The alley was the dry city's block-long oasis of private clubs where anyone could buy a one-night "membership" to quaff liquor until three in the morning.

A few blocks north of the Y on Church Street, a crowd roared. A parade, probably. But no. I rounded a corner and walked into the rear of a white mob. Up in front, screamers were straining forward against a police rope, jeering. When I squeezed through to see the source of the rage, my jaw dropped. The children who had awakened me stood frozen, wide-eyed, their backs pressed against a brick building, trapped by hundreds of angry whites roped off at both ends of the street.

But—?

Why—?

You don't know what a racist mob is until you're inside the belly of it and it seizes your gut, makes your skin burn, and drives you dizzy. You are swept into an otherworld where there is no reason or mercy, only rage.

The sudden roar of a car engine rose above the pandemonium. A pink Thunderbird smashed through the yellow police line. Four young white greasers in ducktails rolled down their windows as the driver sped toward the children and jumped the curb. My mind finally caught up with the scene before me: *They were going to kill the children!* The kids jumped clear. The T-shirted driver swore. Slamming the car into reverse, he threw up a cloud of burnt rubber. From the middle of the street, he shifted into first and gunned it again. Once more, the T-Bird flew over the curb. A little boy was moving too slowly. One chaperone pulled him to safety. The other reached for the handle on the driver's door.

The dirtbag at the wheel pulled out a hunting knife with a blade at least a foot long. Baring his teeth, he waved it at the young black man. "Want some o' this, nigger?" he snarled. The chaperone jumped back.

Only then did the police arrive to disperse the crowd. To ensure their safety—finally!— cops put the children and their escorts into a paddy wagon and drove off. No one arrested the Thunderbird thugs for their attempted murder. The crowd melted away. I was left standing on the sidewalk, knees knocking, trying to comprehend what I'd just seen.

This wasn't Nashville's worst period of racial violence. Three years earlier, many hundreds of students from the city's four major black colleges launched waves of demonstrations, including sit-ins. Their passive resistance to police beatings and mass incarcerations prompted black ministers to stage a boycott of downtown stores. Beatings and arrests continued until the jails overflowed and finally the befuddled Nashville mayor appealed for the end of racial discrimination. Nashville became the first in the South to at least begin desegregating.

To begin, however, is not to finish. It took the passage of the Civil Rights Act of 1964[2] to abolish official Southern apartheid. Racism, however, remains America's open sore. Coupled with the contemporary rise of white nationalism, racism is putting at risk the political progress of the sixties and beyond.

For years, the specter of that day in Nashville would well up in my mind like an uninvited visitor. Now it visited me again, more than a decade later, as I walked door-to-door through these serene and predominantly white Washington County neighborhoods, searching for votes. My mind wandered back again. I remembered getting off work early at Fort Campbell and dropping into the Enlisted Men's Club for a couple of cold ones to slake my thirst in Tennessee's humid heat. It was only a few weeks after the nightmare in Nashville. I was on my second beer when the radio behind the bar carried a special announcement from the White House. President Kennedy was about to address the nation from the Oval Office with what would be perhaps the greatest speech of his presidency.

Kennedy announced that he had nationalized the Alabama National Guard to force George Wallace away from the entrance to the University of Alabama. In defiance of a federal court order, the governor had blocked the admission of two blacks, Vivian Malone and James A. Hood. Alabama was the only state that had not integrated its education system.

The president's opening was measured, almost administrative. Then he found words that spoke directly to me:

> We are confronted primarily with a moral issue. It is as old as the
> scriptures and is as clear as the American Constitution. The heart of
> the question is whether all Americans are to be afforded equal rights

and equal opportunities, whether we are going to treat our fellow Americans as we want to be treated.

If an American, because his skin is dark, cannot eat lunch in a restaurant open to the public, if he cannot send his children to the best public school available, if he cannot vote for the public officials who represent him, if, in short, he cannot enjoy the full and free life which all of us want, then who among us would be content to have the color of his skin changed and stand in his place? Who among us would then be content with the counsels of patience and delay?

In just fourteen minutes, JFK gave voice to all my feelings from Nashville's streets. I have never shaken off the message of Nashville or Kennedy's summons. It is to fight to heal racism, America's original sin. It was that summons that propelled me to keep fighting for civil rights, including the legal and economic rights of Native Americans in my congressional district. Since the 2016 election, the message has become especially salient, having belched up, as it did, a new level of racial violence, jingoism, and xenophobia into the highest level of American politics.

We may fail to become the nation JFK imagined, but I will live my life trying for it. It's the only way I want to live.

6

House Majority Leader at Thirty-One

For some reason, voters often give control of the Oregon Legislature to the party that loses a landslide election for the presidency. In Richard Nixon's wipeout of McGovern in 1972, Oregonians followed form. They elected Democratic majorities in both the state senate and house for the first time in ten years. In the house, Democrats seized the majority on a wave of newly elected young Democrats. These twenty- and thirty-somethings were grounded in the civil rights and anti–Vietnam War movements. They didn't agree with the credo, "Don't Trust Anyone Over Thirty," but they had little patience with the status quo or old guard members of the House Democratic caucus.

At thirty-one, I was close in age to most of the talented newcomers. I had won reelection by smashing a veteran Republican chairman, 60 percent to 40, in the only reapportioned district that pitted two house incumbents against each other. (Once again, I was indebted to Bob Crane, who took a leave-of-absence from the *Daily News* to manage another victory that caught the attention of Oregon's political leaders.)

Coupled with my relative youth, my show of electoral muscle led several incoming freshmen to urge me to run for house Speaker. One of them, Earl Blumenauer of Portland, was particularly convincing. Earl had exceptional strategic gifts. He also was a natural bridge to other young Turks. In brainstorming sessions at my home and working the phone, he was tireless. (Twenty-two years later, in 1994, those same gifts would send Blumenauer to Congress, where he is a veteran member of the powerful House Ways and Means Committee.)

With but one week before the house Democrats were to meet in Salem to select their leaders, I barely had time to savor my reelection. All day long, I placed calls to corral votes.

At the party caucus, my votes held strong while two veteran legislators were eliminated. On the third and final ballot, it came down to Dick Eymann of Springfield or me. Dick, a veteran legislator and tax policy expert, edged me out by three votes. By acclamation, my colleagues voted me Democratic Majority Leader, the number two position in the legislative party. Looking back on it, I feel damned lucky I lost. I was thirty-one, in my second term. I shudder to think of the mistakes I might have made. However, as the party's floor leader and chair of what was inarguably the most powerful committee (State and Federal Affairs), I handled some of the hottest political potatoes of the 1973 session.

The 1973 legislative session was criticized at the time for lasting longer than any session in history. But its true measure is the many groundbreaking laws it enacted, which has earned it the reputation as one of the most progressive legislative sessions in history.[1] It created public employee collective bargaining; passed Oregon's first-in-the-nation statewide planning bill; enacted open public meetings, open records, and conflict-of-interest laws; set up the Portland area's Metropolitan Service District, the first regional local government in the nation; proposed the use of gasoline taxes for mass transit; rewrote the landlord-tenant laws; issued $200 million in bonds for affordable housing; and proposed a sweeping reform of public schools to equalize educational quality for every child, whether in the richest city or the poorest town.

Then the legislature fashioned the jewel in Oregon's crownlike reputation for groundbreaking policy: it removed criminal sanctions for possession of small amounts of marijuana, the first state in the nation to decriminalize the drug. It predated by more than forty years the complete legalization of pot.

Just as remarkable was the man credited with the law's passage—a conservative Republican pig farmer from rural Hermiston, Oregon.

With a chiseled jaw and a reputation for rectitude, the legislator Stafford Hansel could have passed as an old-time prairie preacher. This made him a perfect candidate for the Interim Committee on Alcohol and Drug Abuse. House Speaker Dick Eymann and I needed his conservative gravitas on the panel. The sagaciousness of our selection would soon reveal itself.

Led by Stephen Kafoury of Portland, the committee dug deeply into the problem of addiction in Oregon. Immediately, the idiocy of the existing law was apparent. Alcohol abuse was more dangerous than marijuana, yet alcohol was legal and ubiquitous while pot possession was criminal.

When the committee met to vote, it opted to legalize pot in amounts of up to eight ounces. Each of us knew the moment was momentous. Kafoury broke the silence that fell over the room. "OK," he said impishly, "now who's going to carry the bill [to the house floor]?" Everyone chuckled. Some members shifted in their chairs. This hot potato was a real baker.

"How about Staff Hansel?" someone quipped.

The lawmakers erupted in laughter. Coupling marijuana and Staff Hansel seemed as apt as linking Billy Graham to a fifth of Wild Turkey.

But the pig farmer stunned us all. "I'll do it," he said. What ensued was a political moment uncommon even in that golden era of Oregon politics, when pols tended to solve problems rather than weaponizing them for partisan gain.

As he opened the floor debate, Hansel announced that he had no personal ax to grind. "I'm kind of a square," he confessed, revealing he hadn't had so much as one alcoholic drink for twenty-four years or a cigarette in twenty-five. "[But] I support this bill," he declared. "The issue should be faced by this legislature and by every legislature in the United States." [2]

The old warrior took exhibits out of a shopping bag and displayed them on his desk. Bottles of hard liquor clinked against each other as he arranged them. Near them, he placed a pound of coffee, a stimulant once banned in some European countries. Elsewhere he placed bottles of aspirin and other over-the-counter pain relievers easy to abuse. He pointed to a pack of cigarettes, a bottle of beer, and a bottle of wine. All were legal to sell. For each exhibit, Hansel recounted their toxicity if consumed to excess. He reported the statistical results of their often-devastating impact on American society. He cited a presidential commission report on marijuana, research studies, and statistical data.

Next, he held up a marijuana cigarette—possession of which was then a class C felony punishable by a fine up to $2,500 and five years in prison. With a voice ringing with authority, he cited findings from the presidential commission that concluded, "Marijuana is a rather unexciting compound of negligible toxicity at the dosage usually consumed in this country."

House members sat spellbound. "Those who hang their hat on continued illegality seem to do so not on any sound research, but rather fear of some research that might be done in the future. Unlike alcohol or heroin," he continued, "marijuana use does not produce withdrawal symptoms; it has not been shown to cause insanity, produce genetic damage, [or] lead to crime or violent behavior."[3] That being so, he asked, why should we "criminalize a large part of our population, leaving many with a record that will be the only blotch on an otherwise law-abiding life?"[4]

I am thrilled, still, with Hansel's courage and leadership. However, it was 1973, and outright legalization of any amount of pot was political over-reach. The House narrowly defeated the bill on June 14. Ruefully, member after member, moved by Hansel, asked Chairman Kafoury to bring up a less sweeping reform measure.

A week later, Kafoury did. He carried a bill that decriminalized pos-session of up to one ounce of pot. It passed, 41–16, on June 22,[5] making Oregon the first state in the nation to make possession a nonfelonious mis-demeanor, roughly the equivalent of a traffic ticket. The consensus of most observers, including Kafoury, was that no bill would have passed without Hansel's dramatic effort.

The sky did not fall when the law went into effect. Now, more than forty years later, Oregon and other states have completely legalized what society once considered the "demon weed."

That day when Stafford Hansel spoke still lives in my memory. It reminds me that in American politics, giants once roamed. Fact-based dis-course transcended partisanship. As unlikely as it may seem in this age, I have to believe both will return.

7
Straight but Not Narrow

In the early seventies, to propose a gay rights law was about as likely as the Columbia River running dry. It was well before the American Psychiatric Association dropped homosexuality from its list of mental illnesses. Before Miami's ordinance prohibiting discrimination on the basis of sexual orientation and before Anita Bryant—the "Come to the Sunshine State" TV shill—led the bigoted backlash that repealed it. It was before Harvey Milk's election to the Board of Supervisors in San Francisco and seven years before the National Democratic Party adopted a platform calling for protection against discrimination based on sexual orientation.

That rare.

To their everlasting credit, however, two of my best friends in the 1973 Oregon legislative session were ahead of their time. Representatives Stephen Kafoury[1] and Vera Katz of Portland introduced a bill that proposed to ban discrimination against gay men and lesbians in employment and public accommodations.

My State and Federal Affairs Committee was the place where bills were assigned for party-friendly action—passage or burial. It was there that Steve and Vera's bill landed.

As with most of my constituents, I had been aware of discrimination against gays, but only peripherally. When the controversial bill landed in my lap, I caught myself wishing it would go away. Then I remembered the blacks whose rights I fought for in the South. What was that about, at bottom, if not to prevent dehumanization and bigotry? I was seized by a feeling expressed years later by Elon Musk: "There are times when something is important enough, you believe in it enough, that you do it in spite of fear." Chastening myself for my initial reflex, I vowed to soldier on.

The house Republican leader, Gordon Macpherson, approached me on the floor. "Les, you don't want to do this," he said.

"Do what?" I had been counting votes on several other bills.

"The queer thing. It's toxic. As a Republican, I shouldn't help you. But you bring this bill to the floor, it could taint you forever."

Other legislators, Democrat and Republican, took me aside to lobby against the bill. As the murmured stereotyping continued, I felt my skin burn, just as it had when I was shunned as a kid in my middle school years.

I decided to air arguments about the bill in a public hearing. My staff went to work on a witness list and a research paper.

One witness, George Nicola, a gay man from Portland, got a haircut and purchased a suit for the occasion. In what was reputed to be the first documented occurrence of a parent speaking publicly in support of a gay child[2], Rita Knapp and Ann Sheppard of Portland gave powerful, heartfelt testimony that surprised my committee with its moral force. They spoke of loving families, familial bonds, their children's good deeds and scholastic leadership. Did government have a right to deny a full life to innocents like these solely because of their sexual orientation?

The witnesses constructed a mosaic of pain and principle impossible for the audience to ignore. I announced a committee vote to be held the next week.

When it came, the roll call fell one vote short. Committee members shot glances at each other.

I paused before announcing defeat, trying to accept bitter reality. Then Sidney Bazett, a Republican from Grants Pass, spoke up.

"Mister Chairman," he said. "Do you need my vote?"

I looked at Bazett in disbelief. He was known as the most conservative member of the legislature.

"Yes, Sid," I said. "I do."

"Then I change to aye."

I could have hugged the old man. He had known my wife, Sue, from the days she had been a house page. We respected each other. "Thank you, my friend," I said. "Thank you so much."

Bazett[3] announced that he would be a nay vote on the floor, but at the moment it didn't matter. Bigness had bested bigotry.

I asked my friend Lloyd Kinsey, a GOP moderate from Portland, to carry the bill on the floor. As the number two Democrat in the house, it would have been counterproductive were I to have led the debate. Kinsey did a first-rate job. The whole debate was high-minded.

The bill, however, died on a tie vote. I was learning that even when the sun, stars, and moon seem in perfect alignment—even then—victory can be elusive. It was a lesson I would not forget. This knowledge kept my expectations in check whenever I threw everything I had into a battle. In politics, if you let disappointment bend your sword, you're through.

As a congressman, I wouldn't give up. I spoke at fund-raising banquets across the country for the Human Rights Fund, the nation's major gay rights organization.

It took thirty-five more years for the Oregon legislature to remedy the wrong. On May 9, 2007, Senate Bill 2[4] was signed into law. It added "sexual orientation"—by then a protected characteristic under Oregon's hate-crime statutes—to several statutes that prohibited discrimination based on religion, age, race, color, sex, national origin, and marital status.

In the years since that first Oregon legislative vote, despite repeated setbacks for human equality, progress has been made. Gay and lesbian Americans may now serve openly in the military, where they willingly put their lives at risk for their country. Meanwhile, the Supreme Court has struck down prejudicial state laws banning same-sex marriage, making that solemn institution available to all.

As this was being written, laws enacted by red states to restrict black voters are being systematically invalidated by the courts as unconstitutional. For all this, barriers still remain for gay and lesbian citizens in employment, services, and housing. A cloud of ignorance has doomed military service of transgender Americans. No legitimate argument exists for such a cruel and self-defeating move. If history is a guide, however, it will be overturned.

8
My First Political Crisis

My work wasn't always sure-footed. In Salem, my most uneven performance involved the epic failure of a bill I introduced to protect consumers who bought homes in what Governor Tom McCall called "sagebrush subdivisions." The steps I took while steering this bill into law and its consequent political chaos can only be understood in the context of a white-hot political environment that boiled up in 1973.

In physical height that matched his legacy, Tom McCall was a sequoia. There was no one like him, nor will there likely be again. In just ten years in political office, he virtually remade Oregon.[1]

McCall inherited a Boston accent from his Massachusetts forbearers.[2] He was gifted with a rage for justice and both eloquence and a common touch. A Republican, he was the mirror opposite of the Ayn Rand disciples of selfishness who dominate the twenty-first-century GOP. In McCall's world, when people and their government locked arms, they could move the Cascade Mountains.

On the opening day of the 1973 session, I sat at my desk, listening to the symphony of the governor's words.

"Today," he said, "we still cling to a belief that reasonable men and women can cure the complex ills of society—and that no problem can elude an enlightened people's search for a solution. . . . The interests of the many must be protected from the grasping few."[3]

McCall and I were graduates of Redmond Union High School some thirty years apart. Our shared roots amused us. Looming above shorter men walking with him, the six-foot-five McCall would spot me in a Capitol corridor and call out, "Top o' the morning to you, classmate!"

Ever the reformer, McCall had his staff approach me in 1973 with a consumer-protection bill for home mortgage purchasers. I agreed to introduce it "at the governor's request," a term of art denoting a gubernatorial initiative. The measure called for a three-day cooling-off period for consumers who bought home mortgages. It was aimed at go-go real estate sales that bilked both in-state and out-of-state buyers. In Deschutes County, alone, a place McCall and I called home, one scam was a development named Whispering Pines, where among other sins there were no pines. Other utopian pitches bilked unwary consumers across the state with fantasies much worse. Ultimately, the bill would trigger a political earthquake, threaten my career, and strain my friendship with McCall. But almost exactly one month before these developments occurred, a political wildfire of even greater significance erupted. It left the charismatic governor crestfallen and morose.

On May 1, 1973, by a 3–2 ratio, Oregon voters smashed McCall's audacious plan to reform the system of funding public schools.[4] I stumped for the measure, as did many Democrats. As a source of funding, it would have replaced local property taxes with a state income tax and equalized educational opportunities across the state.

The Democratic legislature had passed the bill enthusiastically. But from the start, McCall's own party colleagues attacked it. To legislative Republicans, raising taxes on income was political heresy. The war of words between the governor and his legislative party led to a break in relations. When, at the urging of Republican legislators, Oregonians defeated the measure,[5] rumors flew that McCall might switch parties in the following year and run against US Senator Bob Packwood as a Democrat.[6]

I wrote to urge my friend to make the switch, pledging my best efforts to make him at home in my party. It seemed clear that he could clobber the junior senator. In a long letter, I told McCall that if he made the jump, I would work overtime to organize Democrats behind him.

No response came during the next month, during which McCall's first-in-the-nation bill to enact statewide land-use planning cleared the legislature, with my help. I did not speak with the governor during this period. But passage of the land-use bill, one of his lasting legacies, had to have provided balm for the proud man's wounds. It must have pleased him further that a Republican senator, Hector Macpherson, a Linn County dairy farmer, was the bill's chief sponsor.

Soon thereafter, McCall answered my letter:

June 19, 1973

Dear Les:

Your letter means more to me than just about any I have
received ever in my life. And it will mean ever more as the years
pass and I lean more and more on the highlights of my public
career to sustain my spirits in a too-placid harbor.

I was really quite serious in my recent contemplation of
the virtues and drawbacks of the two parties. It was so close a
thing that I was almost waiting for a tie-breaking sign. It came
from those paragons of pygmyism, [Frank] Ivancie and [Blaine]
Whipple, who spoke not without ulterior (and I believe) selfish
motive. And that reminded me that [Vern] Cook also was over
there [in the Democratic Party] and others of a stripe that didn't
make my Neanderthals seem so god-awful.

Then, too, at that moment of closing the door on "what
might have been," I was comforted by a clear, warm reminder of
the other kind of Democrats and Republicans who I could aid
and promote—party be damned—because of their dedication to
statecraft—also, party be damned. You are a front-runner in this
classification, and it is you and the others who are so gifted that
really make the two-party system a useful institution. An institution, I mean, that gains strength on the competition between
people of superior competence to determine who best honors
the call of public service, in the term's loftiest meaning.

Faithfully yours,

Tom[7]

The letter may be the only extant record of how close McCall came to
changing parties and altering the course of Oregon history. I tucked it into
my collection of keepsake papers and returned to the real estate consumer
protection bill with renewed energy.

Our legislation had attracted instant opposition from the housing
lobby, one of the strongest in Salem. To those interests, another layer of
bureaucratic red tape was intolerable.

Consistent with my belief, and McCall's, that no problem can elude
the search for a solution among reasonable men and women, I convened a
series of private meetings with the disputants, the governor's staff, and my

legislative assistants. It was an unusual move, but the only way I knew to keep the adversaries from grandstanding for their followers.

Following weeks of difficult negotiating, the parties agreed to a series of amendments that made them feel better, at least, about a bill they'd prefer had never been born.

I pushed the bill out of my committee without a hearing, a rare move that proved to be a dreadful mistake. However, the commercial interests had come to terms, I reasoned, so why hold a hearing? The measure passed the House, 55–4 and the Senate, 28–2. In support, Representative Mary Burrows of Lane County told the House it might be "the sleeper bill of the session." A "sleeper" is a bill that attracts little attention when being enacted but makes a big impact later. Burrows didn't realize how prophetic her words would be.

At the Senate Rules Committee, Democratic senator Tom Mahoney of Portland was curious. He noted that the bill listed me as its sole sponsor "at the request of Governor Tom McCall."

"So whose bill is it?" he asked.

I said that my staff and I worked with McCall's office and representatives of the affected industries. "I have some pride of authorship here."

The crusty veteran was a friend. He studied the stub of his well-chewed cigar. "If the bill works," he growled, "the governor will get the credit. If it fails, you'll get the blame."

Everyone got a good laugh.

A lobbyist, Dave Barrows, hurried behind me to the witness table. He was the savings and loan industry's man in Salem. Perspiring, he apologized for his last-minute testimony. He had taken a call from the trade association's national office, pleading with him to block the bill— something about a "problem in the secondary mortgage market." To the committee, he could have been speaking Japanese. No one was a housing-finance expert. If there was a problem, why hadn't Oregon's Department of Veterans' Affairs complained? It was the state's largest mortgage lender. I shot a glance at McCall's lead staffer. He wasn't buying it. Neither was I. The committee pushed the bill out for a final vote on the senate floor. McCall signed it into law in June, and the legislature adjourned in July. The bill would go into force the following January.

That September, McCall appointed a new real estate commissioner, M. Jeffrey Holbrook. The man was a realtor. Under Oregon law, he had to be.[8] I drove to Salem to forge a working relationship with him before he wrote rules to put House Bill 2607 into effect. But when I stepped into his office, the atmosphere was as cold as a meat locker.

Holbrook was humorless, arrogant, and rude. "The law's a mess," he grumbled. "I'm going to try to fix it if I can." He had trashed the bill for a half hour before I headed for the door. To suggest we disliked each other would be wrong. *Detested* is more apt. Did McCall know what he had done? I couldn't believe he did.

On November 8, Holbrook irked me further at the Governor's Housing Conference in Portland. He told an overflow crowd he would apply the law to a thousand existing subdivisions. The legislature had never considered retroactive enforcement. Holbrook went further. He quipped, "So far, I've been given a sieve and asked to make a bucket out of it."[9] I was piqued. McCall was silent.

The next bombshell was Holbrook's formal budget request for the new law—almost half a million dollars. He brought the proposal to Oregon's Legislative Emergency Board, a mini appropriations committee that allocates funds between legislative sessions. As a board member, the size of the request staggered me. The governor's staff had suggested the law would have no impact on the budget. Moreover, Holbrook could not specify how he would spend the funds. I used his elusiveness to skewer his empire-building request. The board put off the decision until its December meeting.

Holbrook responded by running to McCall with a letter of resignation. The governor refused to accept it. In a statement, he said, "I share Jeff Holbrook's concern over delays in registering the state's subdivisions, of which he estimates as many as one thousand may be illegal. Whether the commissioner is allowed to have the personnel and financing to meet the obligations of his office could determine the quality of life in Oregon for the next fifty years, perhaps forever."

He added, "My efforts to induce Jeff to stay should not be viewed as an act of defiance or hostility to the house Majority Leader. I have immense respect for both men."[10]

On December 27, the State Emergency Board approved a budget that cut $120,000 from Holbrook's request. Holbrook, however, was no fan of compromise. He charged that the board was "stacked with members who had an axe to grind," specifically naming me. I replied that if other administrators quit when the legislature cut their budget requests, every agency in government would be leaderless.

On January 1, 1974, the law went into effect.

That's when the real political hurricane broke loose.

Secondary market investors refused to buy bundled home loan notes from Oregon lenders. The risk of a buyer opting out of a mortgage had made such investments taboo. Stuck with the mortgage paper they wrote, unable to get replacement capital for new loans, Oregon banks closed their lending windows. Home sales and construction—the state's largest industry—froze.

Builders, realtors, and lenders screamed for my head. Editorials splattered ink all over my intelligence and judgment. At home, Sue was worried about these events, but she urged me to soldier on. It wasn't easy. I was knee-deep in something otherworldly.

My friend Jason Boe, the senate president, stopped me in a Capitol corridor to hand me a sheet of paper. It was a transcript of Senator Mahoney's prediction. Old Tom had been right: the bill didn't work, and I, not McCall, was getting the blame. Boe thought this would cheer me up?

I called for Holbrook's firing. I felt certain he torpedoed the law by adopting harsh and inflexible implementing regulations.

Why couldn't lenders hold new mortgages for three days—the length of the waiting period—before selling them to investors? Asking such a question was like trying to stop a mob to discuss its grievances. In the mentality of a herd, there's little space for individual thought. Individual discretion is subsumed by the crowd; people think and act in lockstep and feed off each other's energy.[11] I wanted it to be over, unaware that it would not be the last time I'd be caught in a political stampede.

McCall remained silent amid the clamor. My feud with his commissioner may explain why. The governor was loyal to his administrators. Still, I felt betrayed. I felt it only fair that Oregonians understood that the bill—good, bad, or ugly—was the work of McCall and me together.

I called a press conference at the Capitol press room. Angry builders and realtors outnumbered reporters by at least three to one by. In evidence were no nooses, but plenty of jeers. I passed out a copy of the bill's title page to remind the media that the governor also owned the bill:

Introduced by Representative AuCoin
at the request of
Governor Tom McCall

"When you call this measure the 'AuCoin Bill,' you're ignoring the governor's responsibility," I said. "I have no pride of authorship. I simply worked with affected industries and the governor's staff to improve Tom McCall's bill." Then Gordon Macpherson of Waldport, the house Republican leader, produced a transcript of what I told the Senate Rules Committee—that I did have "pride of authorship" in the bill.

Ouch!

I was shocked to realize that in my ire, I forgot I had used those words to express my pride in negotiating the final version of the bill. *Cowardice* quickly joined the invective hurled at me.

An unprecedented one-day special legislative session repealed the bill two weeks later.[12] I thought it should be amended to satisfy the secondary-market problem while protecting mortgage purchasers from shams. McCall did, too, and said so. But public opinion demanded a hanging. From the house floor, I looked up at galleries jammed with hundreds of Oregon homebuilders. They wore scowls and red lapel buttons that read, "Repeal!" On the vote to do so, thirteen other defiant Democrats joined me in voting nay. They seemed to respect me for not succumbing to intimidation. That was some consolation, but I was drained. If the law had survived, it would have been a signal achievement for McCall and me. I had to let go of what might have been.

The kerfuffle taught me some lasting lessons. When in trouble, face the music. "Man up"—even if others who are responsible duck out. Writing legislation is public business; it should be done in public, not behind closed doors, even for the best of reasons.

Tom McCall never did accept responsibility for his part in the bill, and we never discussed it. I believe that, having suffered through the tax debacle, the governor had no energy to jump into another caldron. It is not a harsh judgment to observe human nature in our heroes. If anything, human weaknesses make them more heroic. To me, Tom McCall is all of that. More than a lot of politicians I've known, he dared greatly. Sometimes he failed spectacularly. But his achievements still light up Oregon's political skies.

On the day House Bill 2607 was destroyed, Representative Keith Skelton of Portland passed me a quote from Teddy Roosevelt:

It is not the critic who counts; not the man who points out how the strong man stumbles, or where the doer of deeds could have done them better. The credit belongs to the man who is actually in the arena, whose face is marred by dust and sweat and blood; who strives valiantly; who errs, who comes short again and again, because there is no effort without error and shortcoming; but who does actually strive to do the deeds; who knows great enthusiasms, the great devotions; who spends himself in a worthy cause; who at the best knows in the end the triumph of high achievement, and who at the worst, if he fails, at least fails while daring greatly, so that his place shall never be with those cold and timid souls who neither know victory nor defeat.

I admired Skelton, a friend and erudite legislator. His gesture did much to bind my wounds. "Daring greatly" struck a chord.

9
Dialing for Dollars

I decided to run for Congress in 1974, the post-Watergate year. The fallout from my housing bill was all but gone. While the state legislature had provided a good platform for public service, Washington was the venue that counted most in the fight for economic and racial justice, environmental protection, and opposition to the arms race.

To win, I got help from many people. Among them was President Gerald Ford. Ironic, I know. And wholly unintentional. However, his pardon of Richard Nixon, and the Watergate scandal before it, made Republicans more radioactive than they'd been since Herbert Hoover. In Oregon, as elsewhere, GOP vulnerability created openings for young Turk Democrats. Veterans of the civil rights and antiwar movements, forty-eight of us stormed into the US House that year for the first time.[1] I was the first Democrat in Oregon history to win in the state's First Congressional District. At thirty-two, I was also the youngest congressman Oregonians ever elected.

Sue and I had to take a huge financial risk to make the race, unlike wealthier candidates. I quit my marketing job in Portland to stump full-time. With two children, ages eight and nine, we lived for a year off loans and our meager savings. Had I lost, our debts would have been staggering. The private job market valued my labor at about $10,000 a year. That would have been just enough to make ends meet with almost nothing left over to tackle a stack of IOUs. As I look back on it, our hubris stuns me. But we were in our thirties and undaunted.

For a loan, Sue went to the local branch of our bank in Forest Grove. In those days, small-town bankers knew their customers. A person's character was one form of collateral.

The loan officer was considerate. "Sue, what's your joint annual income?" she asked.

"Well," Sue smiled. "It will either be $10,000 a year or $46,000" (the congressional salary at the time).

Both women laughed. Then the banker bet on our integrity, and the loan came through.

That was the last time we saw the banker. I wonder how she felt when we won. She must have known she'd helped our little family make it to Washington, DC, and a vastly different life than the one we had known in Forest Grove.

The geography of Oregon's First Congressional District was another challenge.

It stretched from the urban center of Portland, the state's largest city, to Astoria, founded in 1811 by John Jacob Astor at the mouth of the Columbia River. From there, the district shot down toward California, to the southern border of Benton and Lincoln Counties.

The district was home to electronics companies, Nike, US National Bank, Willamette Industries, Pacific Power and Light, Tektronix, countless nurseries, hops farmers, fruit and filbert orchards, grass-seed growers, commercial fishing fleets, dairy farmers, seafood packing plants, private woodlands, sawmills, coastal tourism meccas, and six colleges and universities.

It was hard to reach far-flung, dissimilar voters with political messages. But my volunteers and I did it in one of the hottest races in the country. We defeated Diarmuid O'Scannlain, Oregon's public utility commissioner, 56.1 percent to 43.9. One reason was that I had boned up on the issues and aspirations of varied local constituencies. It was exhausting but I took it as a vital obligation. In spite of a tight budget, I hired a full-time researcher to develop briefing books. That whiz kid, John Wolf, is a friend to this day. I stole him from the staff of state senator Betty Roberts's Special Joint Committee on Aging. Betty said she forgave me.

My campaign cost was $150,000. Total.

My opponent and I were required to run under a new Oregon law that capped campaign spending at that level for US House candidates.

Contrast that figure with $3.275 million.

That's what Congressman Greg Walden raised in his 2016 reelection in Oregon. Walden's Second District, a great expanse of Eastern and Southern Oregon, is a Republican haven, but he raised an average of $26,000 *more in one month* than O'Scannlain and I did, combined, in two years!

The US Supreme Court had made the difference. On January 21, 2010, in a case called *Citizens United v. Federal Election Commission*, it ruled that campaign spending was "speech" and therefore protected from prior constraint by the First Amendment. The decision opened the spigot to unlimited (and often unreported) campaign contributions in staggering amounts. In 2012, David and Charles Koch of Denver spent just under $400 million in the presidential campaign, eclipsing the amount spent by both parties' nominees in 2002[2]. Sheldon Adelson, a Las Vegas casino mogul, donated $15 million to Newt Gingrich in the 2012 Republican presidential primaries[3] and $35 million to Donald Trump in 2016.[4] These gifts exclude funds through other political committees, often made secretly.

These are tip-of-the-iceberg examples. By 2016, total spending by all federal candidates reached $6.5 billion.[5] In this environment, self-starting, idealistic candidates still manage to win. Doing so, however, is increasingly rare. They deserve our gratitude and respect. And we should ask ourselves what we are willing to sacrifice in time and treasure to help them battle against a tsunami of big-bucks spending.

The *Citizens United* decision came down long after I had left politics. But back in 1976, as I readied for my first reelection to Congress, an earlier Supreme Court struck down Oregon's campaign spending limits. The ruling didn't go as far as *Citizens*, but it did vacate many spending limits in the federal and state laws that governed my first congressional race.[6]

As a direct result, within ten years, I found myself raising almost $1 million to retain a seat that had originally cost me $150,000.[7]

Think of it. *One million dollars for one of 435 seats in the US House.* An increase of almost 600 percent in one decade!

Nationally, from 1976 on, attack ads multiplied because oodles of dollars were freed to fund them. At the same time, voters grew increasingly cynical about the system. The United States ranks twenty-seventh in voter registration, behind, among others, Mexico, Slovakia, Estonia, and the Czech Republic.[8] Do you see a cause-and-effect relationship? I sure as hell do.

These monies do not come from bake sales. Funds from political action committees (PACs), representing special interests, became a major factor in campaign finance. In a free country, citizens have the right to associate with each other and petition their government. PAC defenders say that's all they are. But not everyone belongs to a PAC; besides, the sum total of all the special interests does not add up to the public interest. More troubling is the

Supreme Court's authorization of "dark money." These are unlimited funds from undisclosed donors that serve to reward fund-raising skill more than a candidate's legislative competence.

To come up with funds for my million-dollar campaign in 1986, my top aide, Bob Crane, and I figured I needed to raise about $3,000 a day, excluding weekends and holidays. If I raised, say, only $1,000 on Monday, on Tuesday my goal would be $4,000.

Despite low voter registration, no other democracy in the world spends as much as we do on campaigns.[9] Most of the money buys TV attack ads and viral internet commercials that smear one's opponent. The country's most basic issues are seldom addressed.

In 2016, China claimed much of the South China Sea as its sovereign territory. More than half of the world's annual merchant-fleet tonnage passes through those international waters. Wars have been fought for lower stakes. But in that presidential election year, despite the $4.4 billion[10] spent on campaign TV spots, not one candidate mentioned the subject.

If not our putative leaders, who will tell the people what they need to know? An informed citizenry is what makes democracy work. David Souter, the former Supreme Court justice, mirrored Thomas Jefferson when he said, "An ignorant people can never remain a free people." Souter added that "passive ignorance" and "disgruntlement" could lead to an authoritarian ruler.[11]

Besides its toxic effect on the political process, money takes a toll on the men and women who serve our republic. I experienced the stomach-wrenching realities of major-league fund-raising in 1992, when I decided to run for the US Senate. Dialing for dollars at that level was exhausting and demeaning. My opponent, Bob Packwood, used his chairmanship of the Senate Finance Committee to shake down millions of dollars for his campaign war chest. He often hosted "Breakfast with Bob" meetings for lobbyists. The price of admission: $5,000 a plate.

The chair of the Democratic Senatorial Campaign Committee (DSCC), Senator Chuck Robb of Virginia, promised me strong financial support. But the DSCC's support turned out to be conditional. It meted out funds based on a candidate's personal fund-raising success. Here was a classic chicken-egg dilemma. If the party gave me an early financial boost, my chances of impressing prospective donors were good. But it was hard to impress donors when the party didn't provide significant support.

So I phoned until I thought I'd give myself a cauliflower ear.

Early every morning, my office manager would hand me a two-page list of Democratic donors located around the country. I had one day to call every name.

Making cold calls to strangers takes a boatload of hubris. The calls went something like this:

"Mister Willard! Hi, it's Les AuCoin. Democratic congressman running for the Senate here in Oregon. Senator Robb told me to call you. We've got a helluva race here, and I need to raise..."

"Who is this?"

"Uh, Les AuCoin. A-u-C-o-i-n."

So it went, from seven o'clock until evening. Using a car phone from the second row of the campaign van, I would be dialing before a breakfast speech, while riding to a midmorning newspaper interview, en route to a donor lunch, and even on my way to a debate. Only when I turned in for the night did it end.

For my efforts, the next morning, an aide would thrust a new call sheet into my hand as my van moved out again.

Groveling on the phone felt so odious, I wanted to take a shower. When I left the Congress, begging for money was one big reason I never ran again. As much as I loved my access to some of the country's brightest people, the intellectual stimulation of serious debate, and the satisfaction of influencing American life, I couldn't stomach big money's growing role in politics.

My friend Congressman Rick Nolan of Minnesota memorably described the effects of big money in the *Citizens United* era. Nolan was one of the Watergate Democrats who stormed the Bastille with me in 1974. He went home after six years, then returned to the House after thirty-two years. He retired again in 2019.

"We're telemarketers now," Nolan told Norah O'Donnell of CBS' *Sixty Minutes*. "What happened to democracy?"[12]

O'Donnell wanted to know what the congressman meant.

"Because of all the money," Nolan replied. "Both parties have told newly elected members that they should spend thirty hours a week at Republican and Democratic call centers across the street from the Congress, dialing for dollars."

The call centers are fitted with row after row of narrow desktops. Separated by padded walls, they are sound-proof rabbit warrens. "That's a lot of telemarketing," Nolan said. "Probably more than most telemarketers do."

Simple arithmetic shows the cost of thirty hours a week divided into an annual congressional salary of $193,500 is a little more than half that salary. For a rough sense of how this breaks down, let's assume a member of Congress works the phones ten months a year, that a working month is four weeks, and a typical workday is ten hours. Obeying party leaders means that taxpayers pay $96,756 a year for their representative to work the phones instead of perform official duties.

It has come to this: candidates must raise money like hell to go to Washington to raise money like hell.

There is no destination.

No end.

There is only the next phone call.

It would be one thing if such a fate affected only the private lives of members of Congress. But the public pays the price, too.

The money quest keeps good men and women from running.

Then it creates, if not corruption, "honest graft."[13]

Once, having long since left the Congress, I made an appointment on Capitol Hill to ask a congressman for his help. I was a professor at Southern Oregon University and traveled to Washington to explore available funds for a university project. On the afternoon before the meeting, the man's chief of staff phoned me. It seemed the congressman had just scheduled a $500-a-head cocktail hour for that evening at a nearby watering hole. Could I make it?

Pay to play.

"Sorry," I lied. It was the first time I'd been extorted. "I've made other plans."

"You could send a check," the aide pressed.

My stomach tightened. "The school doesn't make political contributions," I replied truthfully. "And your congressman isn't in my budget." That was also true.

I called the next morning. The meeting was still on. It went smoothly enough. But the university got no help. Nor an explanation.

When I recall this episode, I think of the cynic's line: ours is the best political system money can buy. In 2016, the *Economist* magazine downgraded the United States from a "full democracy" to a "flawed democracy."[14]

Cleaning up this cesspool is harder than one may imagine. But it must start with us, the public. We may not be rich, but we are many. Robert Kennedy was right when he said,

Each time a man stands up for an ideal, or acts to improve the lot of others, or strikes out against injustice, he sends forth a tiny ripple of hope, and crossing each other from a million different centers of energy and daring those ripples build a current which can sweep down the mightiest walls of oppression and resistance.[15]

Such a "ripple" might be a small monthly withdrawal from your checking account to a deserving candidate. If started early enough, regular automatic contributions to can produce a surprising total. Best of all, at the time, you likely won't notice it. We can also ask ourselves how much volunteer time we're willing to give to a campaign. What is it worth to turn America around? A week of our time? A day?

An hour?

The old line is truer now than ever: "Now is the time for all good men [and women] to come to the aid of their country."

10
Voodoo Economics

If unlimited campaign spending created voodoo politics, Ronald Reagan pioneered "voodoo economics."[1]

He called it "supply-side economics." It promised to cut waste. And taxes. And not touch the social safety net. And give taxpayers back $1 trillion. And boost military spending by $4.5 trillion. On top of all that, *voila!*—the federal budget would balance itself within four years.

Faith-based budgeting. Worthy of Oral Roberts. Voters bought the package, though. Offering political cotton candy, Reagan ousted the hapless Jimmy Carter from the Oval Office. By the time The Gipper took the oath of office in 1981, Americans were genuinely fond of their new leader and his sunny disposition. Reagan's plan required no personal sacrifice—if you were among the wealthy who got most of the tax cut. His Gallup Poll popularity stood at 60 percent. Drawing on that deep well, Reagan urged Americans to light up the switchboard on Capitol Hill to demand support for "our" economic agenda. Reagan seldom used the word *my*; it was always *our*.

Americans hit the phones. By the tens of thousands.

One of my constituents driving up Interstate 5 heard Reagan on the radio. He got so aroused, he nearly careened off the freeway.

He believed his president; the rich would invest in factories, equipment, and innovation. There would be a trickle-down effect causing a surge in production that would make America ride high in the saddle again. Lots of jobs, rising wages, lower taxes, and a sound dollar.

My constituent swerved into the Burns Brothers Truck Stop south of Portland. From a phone booth, he reached my receptionist. "You tell that boss of yours," he said, "if he doesn't vote with the president, my wife and I will donate against him the next time he runs. The largest amount possible. Even if his opponent is Mickey Mouse. Or Goofy!"

It was a political stampede.

John le Carré, the British novelist, once mused that "America has entered one of its periods of historical madness."[2] He was referring to the drums of war against Iraq in 2003. But his comment aptly described the hocus-pocus of Reaganomics in 1981. Americans so fervently yearned for change from the Carter years of stagflation[3] that they had little appetite for reason. It was hard to have a logical discussion with even some of my most prominent constituents.

Consider the letter I received from John R. Howard, the president of Portland's prestigious Lewis and Clark College. Using his official stationery, he dropped any pretense of academic nonpartisanship. He wrote that he would use "everything within [his] power" to defeat me if I didn't "support our president's economic plan." Howard avoided policy details. I feel sure he didn't know them. His argument simply was that the nation hadn't tried this kind of politics. Congress had a duty to give it a "try."

I told my receptionist to hold my calls.

At my desk, I fired off a reply. I asserted that Howard's logic astounded me. "We haven't tried Fascism either," I wrote, "but I won't accept that as a reason to try it. I hope, for the sake of your students, that your flawed reasoning doesn't reflect the quality of their learning."

At town hall meetings across my district, I would ask constituents, "What about the deficit?" When the push-back came, I would say, "If you took a big cut in wages, then went on a credit card spree, are you saying you wouldn't end up in debt?"

My arguments went nowhere. Americans were living in an altered state.

Once I got into a heated exchange about Reaganomics with Arthur Laffer, the iconoclastic economist who developed the theory the president had adopted. Laffer, an economist of little previous note, called it supply-side economics.

"Don't worry about deficits," he said, grinning at me across a conference table. "The economic surge from the tax cut will trigger a revenue bonanza. It'll make up for lost tax revenue and pay for the military buildup, too."

I smiled back. "Do you also pull rabbits out of hats?"

Others jumped in. A few minutes later, a man next to me relayed a folded note.

The message, written with a fountain pen in a careful hand, read:

"Les, in the universe of people who think 'supply-side' economics won't create deficit problems, one-third of them are sitting in this room."

I glanced down the table. There sat Alan Greenspan, the future chairman of the US Federal Reserve, smiling at me owlishly. It felt good to encounter a Republican who acknowledged Laffer's recklessness. But they were rare. In the public mind, opposing Reagan was tantamount to defending Jimmy Carter's record of 12.67 percent inflation,[4] 7.15 percent unemployment, and a prime interest rate of 20 percent.[5]

As everyone knows, Tip O'Neill and his loyalists lost the economic policy brawl with Reagan. When the electronic vote closed, I stared at the tote board with a knot in my stomach. From the advance vote count, we knew the outcome hadn't been in doubt. What got to me were the ways we lost.

You'd like it not to be at the hand of a Hollywood actor with little intellectual curiosity. You'd like your defeat not to result in spending cuts that fell hardest on kids who go to school hungry. Or jobless workers in need of retraining. Or the elderly poor in need of medical attention.

You'd also like it if 48 turncoat Democrats hadn't provided the margin of victory.

And you'd certainly like your opponents to know what the hell was in the bill.

They didn't.

No one did. At the time, it was unprecedented. A parliamentary maneuver required the House to vote on it immediately after Republicans and Democratic quislings slapped a fourteen-hundred-page document together overnight. It looked as if it had been patched together with chewing gum, staples, and Elmer's glue. Reagan's forces loaded it with handwritten scrawls, typewriter inserts, scratch outs, and arrows drawn with a felt-tip pen to connect paragraphs. They even left the scrawled phone number of someone named Debbie in the margin of one page.

Someone should have preserved the document in the National Archives: a monument to neoconservative recklessness.

Worse than the budget document's physical appearance were its priorities. It was harsher on domestic programs than any budget since Calvin Coolidge.

Most of the cuts landed on the part of the domestic budget that accounted for only twenty-five cents of every federal dollar. They included: elimination of general revenue sharing with cities, a 60 percent cut in other programs for local governments, and reductions to college loans, legal services for the poor, municipal libraries, housing, child nutrition, public transit, and much, much more.

In spite of the cuts that laid waste to domestic programs, Reagan *tripled* the national debt. It stood at $1 trillion when he arrived in office. Eight years later, it reached $2.9 trillion.[6]

Who benefited from the borrowed money? Military contractors, for starters. From 1982 through 1985, they experienced a tsunami of spending that exceeded what the United States spent in any four years of the Vietnam or Korean Wars.[7] Civilian corporations and the wealthy came next, major beneficiaries of massive tax cuts. It was Robin Hood in reverse. History's largest transfer of wealth—from the middle class, poor, and vulnerable to businesses and individuals at the top of the ladder. Growth in the number of homeless Americans became a leading indicator. On Reagan's watch, some six hundred thousand additional persons lost shelter. Counting the part-time homeless, the number of men, women, and children in the streets grew by 1.2 million.

As I saw my political values savaged, the myth of Reagan's greatness drove me up the wall. They would name airports for him. Even now, they're naming streets and avenues for him.

I have a better monument in mind, a suggestion I read somewhere. Almost every city has park benches where at least one homeless person likely sleeps every night. Each town should name one of its benches in honor of our fortieth president.

David Stockman, Reagan's budget director, was an architect of the president's plan. Not long after he left the government, he had a come-to-Jesus epiphany. In his 1986 book, *The Triumph of Politics: Why the Reagan Revolution Failed*, he ruefully wrote:

> The inflation-battered American economy of 1980 was no more sustainable or viable than is the deficit-burdened economy of 1986. ... The magnitude of the [Reagan Revolution's] fiscal wreckage and the severity of the economic dangers that resulted ... [show that] it was the basic assumptions and fiscal architecture of the Reagan Revolution itself which first introduced the folly that now envelops our economic governance.
>
> The Reagan Revolution was radical, imprudent, and arrogant. It defied the settled consensus of professional

politicians and economists on its two central assumptions. It mistakenly presumed that a handful of ideologues were right and all the politicians were wrong about what the American people wanted from their government. And it erroneously assumed that the damaged, disabled, inflation-swollen U.S. economy inherited from the Carter Administration could be instantly healed when history and most of the professional economists said it couldn't be.[8]

I couldn't express it better myself. For my opposition, in 1982 and 1984 I faced the stiffest reelection challenges of my House career, from a Reagan Republican.

The advent of Reaganomics transformed the modern Republican Party. It became the Tax Cut Above All Else Party. It still is, in the age of Donald Trump, against all evidence that tax cuts, standing alone, accelerate the national debt and do nothing for the middle class and poor. Formerly, conservatives tended to be cautious and prudent, a reflexive force against Democratic interventionism. Reagan's revolution, however, turned conservatives into "candy givers" around tax cuts alone. The likes of Representatives Jack Kemp of New York and Newt Gingrich of Georgia and Senator Phil Gramm of Texas had found a way to pose as the party of the little guy. Gingrich declared that the GOP's aim was to create a "Conservative Opportunity Society." By keeping more of what they earn, taxpayers could get ahead by spending or saving it more wisely than a bureaucrat in Washington. Left unsaid was that most of the benefits went to the superrich, widening the gap between them and the rest of America. Tax cutting became so ingrained in the party's catechism that a neoconservative activist, Grover Norquist, conceived a "no new taxes vow," dressing it up as the high-sounding "Taxpayer Protection Pledge." Even today, all Republican candidates are expected to sign it, and most do, to survive in party politics.

By 2016, with the help of the previous three tax-cutting Republican presidents, the national debt had risen from less than $1 trillion to $19.7 trillion.[9] It was made possible only by borrowing money from our children and from abroad. Republicans *talk* about the deficit crisis. But they never mention that virtually every independent economist says deficit reduction must come from a combination of spending cuts, which the GOP adores, and tax increases, which it loathes.

In 1998, I won a presidential appointment to the governing board of the Federal Home Loan Bank of Seattle. In that position in 2011, I joined fellow directors from across the nation at a national conference in Washington, DC. Collectively, we oversaw our banks' lending policies. Republican senator Mike Crapo of Idaho gave us a fervent soliloquy about the "moral" imperative of cutting both annual federal spending deficits and the national debt. He would have made a good Elmer Gantry. I listened intently with other bank board directors. When Crapo came up for air, I complimented him for his convincing description of the debt crisis. Then, noting that with that year's deficit of $1.2 trillion,[10] one could shut down the entire domestic side of the government—closing homeland security, farm programs, and the FBI—and still leave $596 billion in red ink.[11] With that in mind, and the urgency of the problem that he described, I asked, "Should a tax increase, dedicated to debt reduction, be a part of the strategy?"

His eyes widened at my apostasy. "No!" he exclaimed. "America doesn't have a taxing problem; it has a *spending* problem."

Bumper-sticker wisdom from another drinker of the Kool-Aid.

Crapo's argument was one I heard throughout the years I served with Reagan and George Bush Senior. Like a bad penny, it came back around again in the Republican era of Senator Mitch McConnell, Speaker Paul Ryan, and Donald Trump.

11
People Over Freeways

In the early eighties, two deep recessions sent national unemployment to 9.7 percent[1] and 11.9 percent[2] in Oregon. Cities across the First Congressional District were bleeding jobs and experiencing a steady deterioration of roads and transportation systems. Two cases were Portland, the largest metropolitan area of the state, and, to the southwest, practically its mirror opposite, the tiny rural community of Grand Ronde on the leeward side of the Coast Range in Yamhill County.

In the Portland region, the challenge was to help local leaders gain a municipal rail system that would drive urban planning, stimulate private investment, and create thousands of jobs.

I can't prove it, but in 1981 if Rick Gustafson hadn't phoned me when he did on a freezing morning in Washington, the light-rail passenger network that became known as MAX might never have come into being. The City of Roses and environs might otherwise have become yet another megalopolis sapped of vigor and strangled by smog and sprawl.

I do not claim paternity. Many talented individuals did massive lifting to create the MAX system. Without dozens of them—especially my friends Senator Mark Hatfield, Rick Gustafson, my legislative director Michelle Giguerre, and Dick Feeney, Tom Cowan, and Tom Walsh of the Tri-County Metropolitan Transportation District (TriMet)—it wouldn't have happened, either. I'm just saying that Rick convinced me to contribute my part, which, in the words of TriMet lobbyist and former Congressman Bob Duncan, turned out to be crucial.[3]

Rick's urgent call came a few days before I was to choose two subcommittees to join as a new member of the House Appropriations Committee.

As the executive officer of the Portland area's regional government, the Metropolitan Service District, Rick heard rumors that I might not opt for the Transportation Subcommittee. He had heard correctly; after my first choice,

Interior Appropriations,[4] I was leaning toward the Defense Subcommittee as my second. War and peace, after all, had helped pull me into politics. And that panel desperately needed a national security-minded liberal.

Rick called because Portland and its suburbs, arrayed around the confluence of the Columbia and Willamette Rivers, faced a migraine. Local governments and TriMet had lost an advocate on a congressional committee that was central to their success. Their champion had been Bob Duncan, who chaired the House Transportation Appropriations Subcommittee before suffering an upset loss in the previous May primary.

Duncan's defeat put at risk one of the most forward-thinking urban designs of any region in the nation. At its heart was a light-rail system. It was to be built in part with interstate transfer grants, namely federal funds made available by the city's rejection of the controversial Mount Hood (Interstate) Freeway. That behemoth would have destroyed 1,750 homes[5] in Southeast Portland and sliced whole neighborhoods into islands of isolation. In their vision, however, local leaders opposed to the new interstate freeway saw an archipelago of vibrant urban neighborhoods with walk-to shops and stores, downtown housing to keep the city from becoming a series of empty concrete canyons after five o'clock, reduced automobile emissions in an airshed boxed in by the Coast and Cascade Ranges, better fuel economy, and guided suburban growth that tended to follow rail lines instead of spilling randomly into rich agricultural lands. They saw rail transit running like ribbons through the multicounty region, linking bus transfer stations, bicycle lanes, park-and-ride centers, a fare-free downtown zone, and transit stops at the Oregon Convention Center, Memorial Coliseum, the Oregon Zoo, the Pioneer Courthouse Square, and other attractions. A city, in other words, that put people first.

There was one sticking point. Interstate transfer grants had to be approved by Congress before they could be distributed to eligible cities. To build the entire rail system, additional general funding would be needed. But losing Congressman Duncan as chair of the House Transportation Appropriations Subcommittee might mean no funds at all.

"We've got to have a Portlander on that House subcommittee," Rick told me. "The work of a decade is hanging in the balance. We need you; you're the only Oregonian on the House Appropriations Committee."

"Hey, I'm a fan," I said. "But our own Mark Hatfield chairs the Appropriations Committee in the 'House of Lords.' Can't Mark keep the project going? Hell, the senator was master of ceremonies at Reagan's Inauguration."

"Les, Reagan's people are freeway people. On top of that, other committee members will be pushing for their own states' interests. We need Hatfield *and* you."

I was an enthusiast of Portland's vision. In the 1973 legislature, I had pushed through a ballot measure (ultimately defeated by Oregon voters) that would have diverted some highway money to transit. Making the assumption the light-rail plan was safely on track, I thought I had the luxury to consider the Defense Subcommittee.

Rick's call turned me around.

If Portland stood a chance of being one of the most innovative cities in the country, I wanted to help. Given the project's importance, I chose Michelle Giguere, my able, intuitive legislative director, to staff me. I could move to defense after the light-rail job was done.

Other cities would have killed for a major freeway. After all, expressways reduced automobile congestion, didn't they?

Well, no, they didn't.

Giving new meaning to the adage, if you build it, they will come, more freeways simply invite more cars, and most Portlanders knew it. Like pneumatic tubes, they suck residents out of the city and disgorge them into suburban sprawl. I had been passionate about municipal planning since my days in the state legislature, when I had helped pass Tom McCall's first-in-the-nation statewide land-use planning bill. It required cities and counties to adopt comprehensive growth plans and to consider key planning criteria, such as preservation of farm and forestry lands, before allowing new development.

The new urban vision was a far cry from the plan proposed by Robert Moses, New York's "master builder" of the mid-twentieth century, who favored highways over public transit. In the 1950s, Portland's city fathers and captains of business sought Moses's advice. He proposed a network of freeways that encircled and carved up Portland like a pizza pie. A brilliant legal aid lawyer, Neil Goldschmidt, and other activists rallied to kill a key component of the plan: the Mount Hood Freeway. The rejection was controversial, but in time the public came around. Goldschmidt went on to become a Portland city commissioner, mayor, US Secretary of Transportation, and Oregon Governor. The death of the freeway, perhaps Goldschmidt's greatest achievement, turned out to be the end of freeway mania in the City of Roses.

When Rick rang off, I gazed out my office window to contemplate the epic opportunity within reach of the one-million-plus residents of Oregon's largest metropolitan area. I considered the irony: as a kid three decades earlier, my knowledge of transportation and neighborhoods was pretty much limited to the two-way dirt street I had lived on in Redmond, Oregon, population twenty-five hundred, in the late forties and fifties.

I also savored the prospect of the legislative ballet I could choreograph with Senator Mark Hatfield, Oregon's prominent progressive Republican. Working from the House subcommittee, pulling Democratic votes, I could win approval of parts of metropolitan Portland's light-rail wish list each year. Meanwhile, Hatfield, with Republican support, could legislate other parts of it in the Senate. When our respective subcommittees met in conference to harmonize the two bills, Hatfield and I would then support each other's amendments to win everything we wanted. These were heady days. As our friendship deepened over the years, Hatfield and I would often lunch together in his small dining room near the Senate Appropriations Committee hearing room. There, over soup and sandwiches served from the Senate Dining Room kitchen, we would plan strategy, discuss family life, and trade gossip. Sometimes we'd chuckle at the quip attributed to Hatfield's predecessor at the helm of the Senate Appropriations Committee about allocating federal funds. Senator Warren Magnuson had joked, "I want to be fair—half for Washington State, half for the rest of the country." Mark and I never came close to that measure (neither did Magnuson) but, as allies, we rarely lost a project for Oregon.

Despite the advantages Hatfield and I had with our appropriations seats, I knew our work on the MAX rail system would be difficult. The new Reagan Administration soon made that manifestly clear. It declared a ban on federal funding for new urban rail systems. Shocked, municipal leaders in the Portland region cried foul. Their letter of intent from the US Urban Mass Transit Administration (UMTA) committed the federal government to $60 million in light-rail interstate transfer grants. They assumed they could practically take the agreement to the bank. Now, it seemed to have all the value of a Confederate three-dollar bill.

When it came time for Transportation Secretary Drew Lewis to testify before the Transportation Subcommittee, I was prepared.

"Mr. Secretary," I began, "will the Portland light rail be exempt to your no-new-starts policy?"

"No."

"Even though the local leaders have a letter of intent from your department?"

"That's right."

I opened a dictionary. "Here's the Oxford English Dictionary, sir. It defines a letter of intent, which Portland has, as a 'good faith agreement between two or more parties, usually enforceable by law.'"

Lewis lowered his voice. "Congressman AuCoin, dictionary editors aren't running a country or balancing a national budget."

"No, they aren't balancing budgets," I returned. "Neither is President Reagan, is he?"

Lewis's face darkened. "If you're worried about your funds, the Portland region will be eligible. But not for rail."

My encounter with the secretary forced Metro, TriMet, and their municipal allies into some soul-searching. The reality was that TriMet, then a bus system, was ill-equipped to manage millions of rail or road funds. So the agency reached agreement with local governments to use the interstate transfer grants for buses and park-and-ride stations where the future westside rail line would run. In return, everyone agreed to support light rail later. They were betting that Hatfield and I would find a way to "later." It was a table-stakes wager.

I added an amendment to the Department of Transportation's bill, making the deal legally binding. Senator Hatfield helped me protect the language in the conference committee. Our partnership and friendship helped produce an urban rail system that would be the largest public works project in Oregon history, stimulating $10 billion of private investment and ten thousand jobs. Moreover, it helped Portland become recognized as one of the best transit cities in the United States.[6]

To Secretary Lewis's everlasting credit, his last act as a cabinet secretary was to convince Reagan to make an exception to the president's reflexive antitax dogma. Lewis sold the president on a five-cent increase in the federal gas tax to repair the nation's crumbling transportation infrastructure and backlog of road and transit projects. The $50 billion measure set aside 20 percent for transit. Now Hatfield and I had resources to work with. Our best efforts would have been impossible without that tax.

The senator and I relied on the unprecedented cooperation and imagination of local officials who had formed a policy committee and a panel of technical experts to prioritize yearly financial needs. Having demanded that these entities cooperate and bring to us a common recommendation, the senator and I continued to play Fred Astaire and Gene Kelly in Washington, improvising a legislative choreography that produced some head-turning results.

One of those was how we funded the renovation of the old and only east-west expressway, the Banfield Freeway. When the first light-rail project, a fifteen-mile line eastward from downtown Portland to Gresham, was in progress, local transit leaders sheepishly asked if we could combine the freeway renovation and the light-rail projects into the same project so they would be finished together without interruption. Light rail would piggyback on freeway work under way.

Mark and I enacted the idea into law with an appropriations amendment. It might well have been the first and only time a highway was remodeled with funds designed for rail.

The mid-1980s brought voter approval of bonds to build the Oregon Convention Center, now one of the largest venues of its kind in the Pacific Northwest. Accordingly, at the local governments' request, Hatfield and I added vital funds for a light-rail station there.

With the completion of the Portland–Gresham line, plans for construction of a new line to the west became a local priority. I was excited. Unlike the first line, this project would be wholly within my congressional district. I saw the light-rail link as a way to strengthen cooperation between affluent Washington County and its cities and sister governments in the region, one of my longtime goals. As usual, David Stockman, Reagan's budget director, threw up spending objections. I recalled that Reagan once proposed putting the controversial MX ballistic missiles on rails throughout the Western states to protect them from Soviet attack. To friends, I joked that if we stuck just one missile on the west-side light-rail line, we'd win White House approval in no time at all.

Without a Reagan administration funding request, Senator Hatfield and I wrote a provision into the annual appropriations bill requiring the federal government to partner with local officials in studying the project and beginning preliminary engineering, a precursor to construction. Steps of this kind are not commonplace but, constitutionally, Congress holds the purse strings. It also helps when one of the legislators chairs the Senate Appropriations Committee and belongs to the president's party. Ultimately, the Urban

Mass Transit Administration (UMTA) gave conceptual approval of the line out to 185th Street, in the middle of Washington County. But the approval did not take the line to rapidly growing Hillsboro, the county seat, a fact everyone in the region but me was willing to settle for. The city had an early history of opposition to any form of regional government and, like Gresham, it held an often-unfriendly attitude toward Portland. Hillsboro was a growing exurb twenty miles west of Portland and attracted high-tech investment at a steady clip. Within a few years, the area would come to be called the Silicon Forest, a powerhouse of Oregon's economy. Many merchants could foresee commercial value in being in the light-rail loop. One retailer told me he expected light rail to bring Portland shoppers to his store. I added statutory language to the bill to mandate a federal full-funding contract, naming Hillsboro as the line's terminus.

Remarkably, even after the bill became law, Brian Clymer, the UMTA director, objected to the line. He knew the region was also planning a north–south MAX rail line and evidently resented how much of his budget might go to the Portland area.

I will never forget a to-the-woodshed meeting Hatfield and I set up in his office. We invited then-Governor Goldschmidt to join us in a private meeting with Clymer. The obstinate bureaucrat had the nerve to spell out his objections to two senior members of the Congress and Oregon's governor, arguing vehemently against the law we'd already passed. The heat rose as the meeting went into its third hour. Finally, I picked up the last page of the bill, where the president's signature appeared.

"Does this signature look familiar to you, Mr. Clymer?" I snapped. "I don't know what planet you're from, but here on Earth, this signature represents your marching orders!"

Although we didn't extract Clymer's agreement by the time we broke up the meeting, we knew it was just a matter of time. He hung on for months but finally followed the law.

Now in 2019, I delight to see how the light-rail system has branched out through the region. It runs south to Milwaukie and links downtown Portland to its international airport. Streetcar lines have joined the mix. And as I write this, a new rail line between southwest Washington County and downtown Portland is in the offing. The 2015 survey by *Monocle* magazine named Portland one of the world's twenty-five best in urban livability.[7]

My son, Kelly, and I try to have a father-son weekend each year to watch the play of our beloved NBA Portland Trailblazers. In our first outing, we waited for a taxi after the game to take us downtown to our hotel. Then a MAX light-rail train pulled up at the Rose Quarter station, the same stop Hatfield and I added for the east-side rail line. We rode the train over the Willamette River to the city center within blocks of our lodging. I relished thinking back on my work while watching many of my former constituents taking advantage of it. They were a tossed salad of elderly couples waving Blazer banners, teens talking together nonstop, parents and children finishing a night at the arena, and college-age kids going somewhere decked out in grunge black. Light rail had become such a part of their lives, they would have surely been surprised to hear it almost didn't happen at all.

Some evenings when I'm in downtown Portland, I take a seat for a moment on a sidewalk bench and enjoy the blur of TriMet buses pulling in and out of the transit mall on schedule and trains crisscrossing the streets alongside bicyclists. The sidewalks are alive with pedestrians even at ten o'clock or later. Bistros and pubs are open. Concertgoers spill into the streets.

Watching a city flourish, knowing I had something to do with it, makes me thankful for those local visionaries with whom I worked so many years ago. Some of them are gone. But I still hear their voices; I still see them gesturing and describing their ahead-of-their-time plans.

It makes me smile. Because of their vision and two friends they could count on in Congress, modern Portland is an attractive, livable city that has made great strides in putting people first.

To be sure, the city's explosive population growth in the last twenty years has overtaxed its highway infrastructure, despite mass transit. That's a real problem. But if Portland-area residents still have innovation in their DNA—and I'm betting they do—their region will continue to be a national leader in minimizing asphalt construction and neighborhood fragmentation.

12
The Children of Spirit Mountain

In the summer of 1978, I turned a rented Winnebago into a congressional office on wheels. For two days, my staff and I drove to out-of-the-way rural towns that seldom, if ever, got a visit from a federal representative. My franked mailings told residents the date and time I would show up at each stop. With two caseworkers,[1] office equipment, supplies, a driver, and my district office manager, we set off to visit the public in places like Falls City, Grand Ronde, Jewell, Mist, Amity, and St. Paul, Oregon. Residents of these towns paid taxes like everyone else. I didn't know how or if other members of Congress reached out to residents in similar whistle-stops. But I did know this: these folks deserved as much attention as others who lived in the gated neighborhoods of affluent suburbs.

Residents showed up who had problems with government agencies—missing Social Security checks, lost passports, disputed veterans' benefits—as well as other troubles beyond my ability to help, like missing child-support payments, local landfill complaints, and uncollected trash. Others wanted to know where I stood on issues, so Q-and-A sessions were part of each stop.

One town in particular haunted me—Grand Ronde, a wide spot in the road in Yamhill County. It was located a few miles leeward of Oregon's Coast Range on Highway 18 between McMinnville and the Pacific. Here, about a dozen people stood waiting for me by the side of the road because, with the local schoolhouse closed for the weekend, there was no building in which to meet. They were huddled against a drizzling rain outside a tiny coffee shop. Not far away stood a derelict railroad station. In the middle distance, two mobile homes looked in need of repair. Farther away rose a fog-shrouded peak they knew as Spirit Mountain. If one wanted a picture of rural poverty, misery, and hopelessness, this was it.

I did not know that this place owned a history of heartbreak going back more than a century. For thousands of years, vast stretches of western Oregon and northern California had been home to some sixty different Native American tribes. After the passage of the Land Donation Claim Act of 1850,[2] which validated settler claims in the Willamette Valley, whites poured into the area, triggering escalating conflicts among tribes, settlers, miners, and ranchers—including white vigilante militias that tried to run the tribes off their traditional hunting and gathering grounds.

In 1856, in response to pro-settlement political pressure and racial violence on the frontier, President James Buchanan ordered the army to remove the tribes to a sixty-thousand-acre reservation in the Grand Ronde Valley. Authorities thought this location would prevent the Indians from impeding America's Manifest Destiny to expand across the continent.[3] In tribal history, the forced march is referred to as the Trail of Tears. The government renamed the peoples, the Confederated Tribes of Grand Ronde.[4]

In 1954, in a stated effort to encourage the Indians to become "regular Americans," Congress passed the Tribal Termination Act.[5] The law erased the legal relationship promised to tribes when the federal government broke promises made to end the Indian wars. Tribal people, of course, were not erased. They plunged into poverty, alcoholism, and disease. *Termination* meant axing treaty obligations and social programs that had been promised to Indian nations in return for their lands. Washington, DC, wanted to ignore its historical obligation and "get out of the Indian business."[6]

In the worst of the betrayals, the law severed native peoples from their land, the cornerstone of their identity for millennia and their source of sacred meaning. Senator Hatfield accurately observed that tribes like the Grand Ronde were "ill-prepared to cope with the realities of American society" when the termination act was enacted, and it threw them "abruptly from a state of almost total dependency to a state of total independence . . . [forcing them] to leave the only way of life they had known."[7]

On the day my Winnebago pulled to a stop in the settlement of Grand Ronde, all that remained of the sixty-thousand-acre reservation was a five-acre cemetery where the tribes' ancestors lay. I did not know this history, but I did sense I'd stepped into a landscape of despair. My constituents sought my help with their lost Social Security checks, qualification for veterans' benefits, and other federal government snafus.

When at length my four-wheeled office pulled out and jostled up the road, my staff organized documents they had collected, getting ready for the next stop. At the trip's end, they would intervene to solve the immediate problems my constituents encountered with various agencies. But as the vehicle bumped and swayed away from Grand Ronde, I knew that finding a missing government check would do nothing to attack the bedrock hopelessness of the area—so different from life in upscale Portland and environs.

Change was in the air, though. I just couldn't see it.

Beginning in the 1970s, tribal activism, aided by advocacy groups such as the Native American Rights Fund, began work to restore official government recognition of tribes and, with it, social services and at least some of their historic lands.

The tribes of Grand Ronde joined the effort. In the early 1980s, some two years after my Winnebago visit, a delegation met me in Washington. They sought a bill to restore their federal status and, with it, the benefits their people had been denied for twenty-seven years. I was pretty well beaten up from another tribal restoration bill I had introduced five years earlier and, ignorant of their history, I wasn't thrilled at the thought of running the gauntlet again.

That earlier bill restored the federal status of the neighboring coastal Siletz Tribe, but only after a firestorm of opposition. In that earlier era, "superior Indian hunting and fishing rights" had become an incendiary issue between whites and tribes throughout the Pacific Northwest, triggered by a federal district judge's thunderbolt ruling that Columbia River tribes had an inherent right to fish in their "usual and accustomed places," including off-reservation lands, regardless of laws governing nontribal fishing. No one knew how the ruling would apply outside the Columbia River Gorge. Assuming the worst, sporting groups, state fish and game agencies, and political opportunists flew into a rage that spilled over to my Siletz bill, which died in 1976. Even stalwart liberals opposed me, like former state senator Don Wilner, a member of the American Civil Liberties Union and one of my old allies in the Oregon legislature. My reelection opponent made it a key issue and plastered billboards across the First District that read, "More Fish, Less AuCoin."

Despite the pummeling, I won a second term, 58.7 to 41.3 percent. The following year, when the Siletz entered into a consent decree in federal district court to voluntarily forego potential indigenous hunting and fishing rights, I referenced the decree in a new Siletz bill and moved it through Congress with ease.

The scars from the first battle were fresh when the Grand Ronde delegation came to see me. Hatfield had instantly pledged his support for restoring their federal status. That move did not please me because, despite the tribes' residency in my district, the senator did not give me a heads-up, unusual for him. It pains me now to admit it, but I harbored doubts. Who were these twenty-seven tribes and bands? Not once had I heard of them. Did they have a common history that would merit federal status? What was that history? I assigned the issue to Suzanne Bohn, one the most tenacious but junior members of my staff, to research the historical facts.

I also knew that, as with the Siletz, to have any chance of success, the Grand Ronde had to prepare the ground locally. They had to win endorsements of municipal and country officials, churches, chambers of commerce, civic groups, state legislators, and leaders.

During the meeting, I affected a stern demeanor as I explained these realities. I wanted to test the group's mettle and disabuse them of any thought that the work would be play. They went to work.

While the tribes' members worked the grass roots—meeting with local landowners, businesspeople, and county officials—Suzanne Bohn steadily fed my in-box with information about their history. Through her persistence, I began paying closer attention. Gradually, the tribes' shared history of heartache sank in. I was glad that, despite my early doubts, I had kept an open mind.

Several months later, Grand Ronde leaders proudly returned with their homework. They had agreed to a judicial decree on hunting and fishing. And they garnered endorsements from a majority of civic, religious, and political groups in Yamhill County. It was a first-class job. I pledged my support. A tribal elder, Kathryn Harrison, broke into tears up in the House Gallery when she watched me drop the bill in the hopper. The legwork performed by the Grand Ronde paid off. On September 22, 1983, Congress passed the measure, and President Reagan signed it into law.

With tribal status officially restored, Hatfield and I agreed that economic independence was essential for the people of the Grand Ronde. This meant a reservation. Political reality dictated that it could not be the sixty thousand acres they lost, but it had to be a large enough to foster enterprise and a sustainable economy. We proposed two reservation bills—one of fifteen thousand acres, the other of five thousand acres—to prevent any one bill from being used for target practice.

The tactic didn't work. Lots of local whites wanted no reservation, period.

Across Yamhill county, political fireworks began at once and, with them, no small amount of racism. Bill Jolley, the owner of a local refrigeration business and an outspoken Indian opponent said: "What is now calling itself a tribe appears to be nothing more than a special-interest group seeking unjust compensation." John Hampton, president of nearby Willamina Lumber Company, opposed the withdrawal of forested lands from the federal timber base. It was lost on him that the lands represented a fraction of the area once owned by, and confiscated from, the member tribes. A wood-products industry leader with a bare-knuckle reputation for championing his self-interest, Hampton had designs on the timber to feed his mill a few miles down the road.

The local paper, the *Sheridan Sun,* opposed giving the tribes any federal land. The paper raised ominous questions: Would tribal police drive white hunters and fishers off their lands? Who would have rights to water from Willamina Creek? Constituent phone calls and letters made it clear that Hatfield and I had bought ourselves a piping-hot potato.

No one in the non-Indian community mentioned, and likely did not know, that 40.5 percent of tribal families lived below the poverty level, compared to 7.7 percent of the rest of the state; that unemployment among tribal members was 23 percent, three times the state average; that 42 percent of all tribal adults aged nineteen and older had not completed high school; that 50 percent of tribal homes needed rehabilitation; or that 40 percent of tribal families were not receiving adequate health care because they could not afford it.[8]

I made several trips to the nearby towns of Willamina and Sheridan to discuss the reservation with local officials and citizens. Several opponents—many of them openly bigoted—pointedly asked me, almost as a dare, are you going to just pass a bill back in Washington regardless of local opinion? I wanted to leave the Grand Ronde on the best possible footing with the local white community. That required a local hearing to clear the air before I made any legislative move.

I consulted with Mark Mercier, the tribal chair, on the timber industry's worries about the tribe exporting logs abroad. US law banning raw log exports from federal lands did not apply to sovereign Native American lands. The industry was averse to anything that would reduce the availability of government timber for its mills, especially for foreign export.

Finally, I scheduled the field hearing for August 10, 1987, at the elementary school gymnasium in Grand Ronde.

With local opposition still crackling, I expected a lot of false information to be repeated on the night of the hearing. I instructed Kevin Lynch of my staff to require the attendance of experts of several federal agencies—the Forest Service, the Bureau of Land Management, the Fish and Wildlife Service, the Bureau of Indian Affairs, and others. My seat on the Appropriations Committee that handled those agencies' budgets made recruitment relatively easy. These government officers would sit against the wall to my left, at a right angle to the witness table and the table I would use to run the hearing. They were to be my "truth squad" to answer questions of law when called on.

A couple of nights before flying out for the hearing, I worked in my den in Washington to craft an opening statement. As I did my homework, I envisioned the crowd that would be in waiting: undoubtedly large and possibly unruly. I needed a good opening quote, one that would galvanize the community around the virtue and historic importance of the reservation. Thumbing the index of *Bartlett's Familiar Quotations*, I spotted the name of nineteenth-century army general Philip Sheridan, the namesake of the next town over. *Perfect!* I thought.

Then I turned to the quote. "The only good Indian is a dead Indian."

The omen did not steady my nerves.

The gymnasium was packed when I arrived early for the hearing. As I strode to the front of the gym, rows of constituents eyed me with expressions ranging from mere opposition to barely veiled loathing. The witnesses and the federal agency experts were waiting in place. Up front, I paused behind my table to size things up. John Hampton and his local timber group—panel number two—looked hungry for raw meat. The thought of their loggers being denied access to nearby commercial public timber was, to them, an outrage.

Political inspiration sometimes strikes like lightening. It happened to me that night. Studying the hostile mien of the tribe's opponents, I decided to deviate from the standard procedure in which witness panels testify one after the other. In that format, I knew that immediately after the Grand Ronde panel's opening testimony, Hampton's group and others would find it easy to raise unfounded allegations about the tribe, their intentions, or their use of the reservation, leaving tribal officials helpless to respond until the meeting's end. That would be way too late. I wasn't going to allow it.

"Here's what we'll do," I murmured to Lynch, my aide. "Bring another table up alongside the tribal council's table." His smile told me he knew exactly what I was thinking. I would call up the first two panels to the parallel tables. When first the tribal leaders and then Hampton's group aired their views, I held them in place and went back and forth between them, asking for a response to any assertion made by the other. When a technical or legal question arose, I called on my truth squad.

The tactic worked even better than I'd hoped. Hampton, who fed his mill with timber within the proposed reservation, objected to removing even five thousand acres of Douglas fir from the government's timber base. Turning to the tribal panel, I asked, "Mark [Mercier], you've heard Mr. Hampton's complaint, what's the tribes' position?"

"Congressman, this isn't the first time we've heard about local timber supply," Mark replied. "The tribes have decided to not build a mill of our own for twenty years. We will sell our timber on a sustainably sound rate by closed bid to local timber operators. We would accept this language as an amendment to the bill."

I turned back to Hampton. "Doesn't that solve your problem, John?"

"But the tribe isn't governed by federal laws banning exports," Hampton complained. "They could easily ship off their whole annual harvest to Japan through the Port of Coos Bay. This would still reduce the federal timber base in this region."

"Mister Mercier?" I asked.

Mark's demeanor reminded me of a major-league slugger just waiting to send a line drive over second base. "We will agree to not export logs for ten years," he said. "Now let me tell everyone what it will cost us. In today's market, we would leave $4.5 million on the table. But we're willing to do it to achieve an economic base everyone can live with here in the valley."

On it went, through other witnesses, some with hobgoblin myths easily shot down by the truth squad. The audience began to thin out. Tension, which had seemed ready to burst, waned like air from a punctured balloon.

Then Peter Murphy Jr. stepped forward, the president of Murphy Logging in Springfield, Oregon. I blinked in disbelief when, as an unscheduled witness, he declared support for the reservation. He testified that in the

1930s and '40s, his company was the area's largest employer. "During that time," Murphy said, "70 percent of my company's workforce was Indian, mostly Grand Ronde." Pointing to Hampton and Hampton's timber allies, Murphy said, "We have been in the forest products business for a long time, as have my associates of Willamina, Fort Hill, and Taylor lumber companies. But the Grand Ronde have offered an extremely reasonable compromise, one that should be recognized and appreciated."

The last ounce of the helium had seeped out of the balloon. The gym was virtually empty. I gaveled the hearing closed. In Portland, I celebrated with Lynch and Hatfield staffers. The Grand Ronde would never be have-nots again.

Amid the jubilation, my mind drifted to Spirit Mountain, in Grand Ronde legend the home of strong and powerful spirits, called Skookums.[9] I had heard one speak in the person of the first Grand Ronde tribal chair, Kathryn Harrison, who had traveled to Washington on a red-eye to testify before the House committee considering my tribal restoration bill. She told the committee of the "trail of tears," when the Umpqua, Molalla, Rogue River, Kalapuya, and Shasta people were swept up from their ancestral lands by the government and relocated to the Grand Ronde Valley, only to have their land taken away again and their tribal status terminated.

"Our people have endured much, but they have endured," she testified. "We have walked through twenty-seven years of termination. But like our ancestors, we have continued to hold tightly to those strands of our heritage, mindful of the coming generations."[10]

Today, the Confederated Tribes of Grand Ronde are among the most successful tribes in the Greater Pacific Northwest. Their timberlands produce some $500,000 a year. Their Spirit Mountain Casino, located ninety minutes from Portland, is a major local employer, bringing in millions in revenue a year. Even more impressive is the tribes' big-hearted generosity. The Spirit Mountain Community Fund dedicates six percent of the tribe's casino proceeds to nonprofit organizations in eleven predominately white northwestern Oregon counties in its service area—$74 million in its first twenty years. The fund also has provided more than $5 million in financial assistance to nine other federally recognized Oregon tribes. Working with the American Political Science Association, the tribe also finances two young people a year to study government in Washington and intern on Capitol Hill.

The Grand Ronde's industry and generosity move me deeply. Classic underdogs. Belittled by whites. Thought of as malingerers. They are fulfilling the native tradition of potlatch, a rite in which good fortune is distributed to others. Mychal Cherry, executive director of the tribal community fund, said, "Giving is a way of life for Native Americans, and no matter what we've been through and endured, that will never change; it's who we are."

Part of my heart will always reside with the children of Spirit Mountain.

13
My Alaskan Aleut Cousin

A lame-duck session[1] of Congress can be raucous as a pub brawl or quiet as a crypt. Its hurry-up-and-wait could teach the army a lesson. Usually spilling into December after an election, the session pits holdover members of Congress in brinksmanship over unfinished business—usually a spending measure that must pass before a new Congress convenes. Nerves fray. Tempers snap. Defeated incumbents wander about as vacant-headedly as victims of post-traumatic stress syndrome. Everyone blames someone else for foot-dragging that prevents adjournment for Christmas.

Fortunately, lame-duck sessions are rare. In 1985, I came into one after having defeated my most serious challenger a year earlier. I was exhausted. I wanted out of this hothouse. It was the Advent season, and I wanted to be with Sue and the kids. Out of the blue, I got a letter from my father's niece.

My father's niece?!

My heart almost stopped. Never would I have imagined having a living relative on my dad's side. The woman was Martha Demientieff, an Alaskan Aleut whose husband and family would turn out to be highly respected in the north country. She and Clyde Demientieff, her husband, ran a Yukon River barge service that shuttled cargo into and out of Alaska's interior.

"Your name is unusual," she had written. "When my uncle, Eddie [Francis] AuCoin lived here, he used to talk about his sons, Leslie and Leland, in Oregon. I read about your recent election in the *Anchorage Daily News,* and I wondered if you might be my cousin. If so, would you please let me know by return mail?

Having lived with a black hole for more than forty years, I wasn't sure how or if to respond. I placed the letter on my desk at home. When Congress finally adjourned, I intermittently stole a peek at it. It lay there, staring back at me. The woman's hunch about a family connection didn't appear to be mistaken. Alaska, after all, was my dad's destination in 1947. She knew my

73

first name and my brother's. The nature of her barge business suggested reliability. A service that shuttled valuable cargo for others must have required bonding and a good reputation. Still, if I opened this door, what else would I find?

On the other hand, she reawakened my lifelong curiosity about my father. Mom had told us next to nothing about him. Perhaps the story was too painful for her; maybe he shielded his past even from her.

Finally, I sent Martha a short letter. "We might be related," I wrote cautiously. "Would you kindly send some photographs of your uncle?"

Soon, via return mail, I had a half-dozen photos of my father smiling up at me as I sat on my sofa in the living room. *So, that's how he looked after he left.*

In one picture, he held two part-Aleut girls on his shoulders, Martha and her sister, Mary. Another showed the image of a man Martha identified as her father, Wallace. Still another, taken on the East Coast, pictured a gangly older French-Canadian wearing a cabbie cap and huge shoes. A note stated he was my grandfather, a ship's cook.

I was thunderstruck. The letter told me more about my dad in a few minutes than I'd known in a lifetime. Gooseflesh ran up my arms. A few days later, I wrote Martha to acknowledge that we were cousins, no two ways about it. That led to an exchange of several letters over the next two months.

In February, we planned to meet at Sea-Tac International Airport. I arranged an extended layover on my flight to my district. Martha flew in from Anchorage, a short hop. We met at the airport Hilton for five hours.

Martha about my age, with kind brown eyes. She conveyed a keen intellect. Her gentleness seemed to acknowledge that I might be sensitive that she had known my father better than I. She married Clyde Demientieff, a descendant of Russian and Aleut parents, and helped him found the biggest barge company on the Yukon River. Their son was a banker, their three daughters were housewives. In addition to helping run the family business, Martha got a teaching degree and taught grade school in Holy Cross, Alaska. I described Sue, Stacy, and Kelly and our life together.

I sponged up everything I could learn about my dad. It turned out that every child of Rosanna Coffey AuCoin and William AuCoin of Portland, Maine, had been placed in a foster home after the mother died in childbirth with their ninth child. Our grandfather, William, was a ship's cook whose crew trawled for cod off Georges Bank between New England and Nova

Scotia. He was at sea for weeks at a time and could not look after the children. In 1926, my sixteen-year-old father rebelled against abusive foster parents and ran away with his brother, Wallace, age fourteen. They lived on the lam through the Great Depression.

We could only guess at the compromises, cons, and brushes with trouble the boys might have experienced while on the road in the late twenties and thirties. For years, they must have lived hand to mouth, relying on their wits in hardscrabble times. A footloose struggle for survival at a young age did little to prepare a man to sink a taproot into family responsibilities. I thought of my father's deathbed letter with this new history in mind. Two victims may have resided in my parents' doomed marriage, not one.

To my astonishment, Martha told me that her father, Wallace, also had abandoned her and her sisters for several years. When her mother died, the kids ended up in a poorly funded Catholic orphanage. Food was scarce. Martha chewed smoked salmon into fine pulp to feed her infant sister.

Martha learned most of the AuCoin family history when our respective fathers' last surviving sibling, Mary, located her through the Hall of Records in Anchorage in the early eighties. Aunt Mary lived in Palmetto, Florida. While her health was good, Martha would fly her to Alaska for family visits. Now they corresponded almost weekly. Soon Aunt Mary was writing to me. A correspondence developed among the three of us. I kept wondering why this was happening to me now? All I knew was that I was on the path of my enigmatic father.

After the new Congress convened in 1986, my defense committee work took me to MacDill Air Force Base in Tampa, Florida. The city of Palmetto was less than fifty miles away. Should I go meet Aunt Mary? I was conflicted. Mary, however, was the only person on earth who had known my father from boyhood. I rented a car and took off.

I arrived in town unannounced, so I could cut and run if I got cold feet. The street map told me my aunt lived in a trailer park. I drove through the gate and navigated the curved lanes. Hopes and dread played in my mind. What mattered most to me in those days was time with Sue and the kids and, with my work, I barely had time for them. I dreaded a new family entanglement. I didn't know if it would suck me dry or nourish me. However, I had to learn more about my dad. Even small things would make him more human. What music did he like? Was he political? What gave him joy? What made him angry? What had he hoped to do with his life?

Soon I came upon Mary's trailer sitting among modern thirty-five- and forty-foot behemoths. It was a wee sixteen-footer from the fifties, almost a dead ringer for the one I had lived in at Ivan Ivanovich's park in Redmond. I drove past and pulled over. Inhaling deeply to collect myself, I took in the sweet scent of gardenias. Over my shoulder, lights shone through her window. She was at home. I teetered on a cliff; did I really want to open this relationship? At what emotional cost?

I decided that the meeting would bring me closer to my father than I would ever get in this life. Backing up, I parked and knocked on the door. Mary peeked out from behind a curtain and instantly recognized me. Martha must have shared my snapshots. A short, elderly woman with dusky skin and dancing brown eyes threw upon the door. "Finally, finally!" she cried, hugging me.

From six o'clock to almost midnight, we talked about the harsh life of Depression-era foster homes Portland, Maine. We exhausted every topic we could think of about Mary's original family, her deceased husband, Sue and my kids, and my brother and his daughter. She was only five when her mother died. Then came foster homes. After that, the siblings scattered to the winds. She told me where her parents were buried and the address of the AuCoin family home. She said that in later life she saw my father occasionally, once in San Francisco. He had some problem with his legs. She repeated that he was a wonderful guy, a bookworm and music lover, and handsome. We agreed to keep the letters going. Martha and I would, too, in the short remaining years of each woman's life.[2]

I drove away from Palmetto, grateful for the hours I'd spent there. Mary's years in foster homes helped explain the tangled emotions and yearnings of a childhood my father and his brother had endured before her, before ending it decisively and setting off into the unknown. Did they feel relief, or desperation? Were they frightened? How could they have managed? Although these questions would never be answered, I felt I finally understood my father and his behavior.

I did not forgive him.

I understood him.

That was enough to extinguish the last dying ember of doubt about my worth as a boy.

It had taken a long time.

We—Kelly, Stacy, Sue, and me (left to right)—called ourselves the "Fearsome Foursome." We played together, adventured together—even campaigned together. I nabbed a few days from my working schedule during House recesses for family time. Of the 49 new congresspeople elected in 1974, only a handful remained married. Times spent together helped our family withstand politics' centrifugal force. Photo: Dave Swan

From second grade until my high school junior year, this was my home on Redmond's Fifth Street. Mom, at the back door in this image, gave Lee and me the bedroom and slept on a fold-out couch. She cooked on a wood stove until we moved in 1959.
Photo: AuCoin collection

In one of the few existing photos of my dad, Francis Edgar AuCoin, he introduces me to a holiday gift at our home in Vancouver, Washington. Four years later, my father abandoned my family.
Photo: AuCoin collection

My brother Lee and I get ready to go to church in the fifties. Even on a waitress's wage, mom provided us "Sunday best" clothes to attend church services.
Photo: AuCoin collection

[*Above left*] My first-grade school photo. I attended Jesse Hill Grade School on 827 SW Deschutes Avenue in Redmond. Today, it is the city library. Photo: AuCoin collection

[*Above right*] The first dog I ever loved was a cocker spaniel named Pat. I don't know why we named him Pat and can't remember where we got him. He burrowed under the fence at our cottage on Fifth Street and chased every car that came by. Here, I am in sixth grade. Photo: AuCoin collection

[*Right*] This photograph appeared in my high school yearbook senior year, when my teammates voted me most valuable player. An Associated Press poll of Oregon coaches named me honorable mention on the All-state team that same year.

Les Aucoin, Sr., F
1-yr. letterman

Governor Tom McCall signing the subdivision consumer protection act in 1973. I introduced the measure at his request. After clearing the legislature by a wide margin, it became an explosive issue and presented me with my first political crisis. Photo: AuCoin collection

An impromptu staff meeting in 1975, my freshman year. In the last 10 to 12 years of my career, my office had one of the lowest turnover rates in the House. Photo: US House

Conferring with House Speaker Jim Wright in the late-1980s. I was 47, Dean of the Oregon House delegation, 84th in house seniority, a member of the Democratic whip organization, a veteran of the Appropriations Committee, and an official congressional observer to the US-USSR arms control talks in Geneva. Photo: US House

Congressman Tim Wirth (D-CO) and I testify for increases in federal aid to college students. Higher education continues to be a cause I care about. I serve on the board of trustees at Southern Oregon University, where I taught political science classes following my years in Congress. Photo: AuCoin collection

I introduced candidate Jimmy Carter at a large rally in downtown Portland in 1976. Here, I'm pointing out a sign in the crowd that reads, "We're from Plains, Georgia." Photo: AuCoin collection

Congressman Ron Dellums (D-CA) joined me at Portland's Multnomah County Courthouse for a field hearing on the Nuclear Freeze. In 1993, Ron would rise to chair the House Armed Services Committee. Photo: AuCoin collection

During the 1984 presidential campaign, a downpour turned vice presidential candidate Geraldine Ferraro's notes into mush at a rally in downtown Portland. The weather didn't dampen the spirit of presidential candidate Walter Mondale, though, who shows a laughing crowd what remained of Geri's notes. My role had been to introduce Ferraro. Photo: *Oregonian*

[*Right*] Geri Ferraro and I were pals dating back to our work together in the US House. Her getaway visit to a friend in Cannon Beach, some years after her 1983 campaign as Walter Mondale's running mate, gave us the chance to spend a few hours together in my district. Photo: AuCoin collection

[*Below*] The annual spaghetti feed at Catlin Gable School was a mainstay in each of my campaigns. The event didn't raise a lot of money, but small and even large donors came to count on it. Usually, I had a VIP guest who helped me serve pasta and then pitched my candidacy to the crowd. Here, then-senator Joe Biden serves up his big trademark smile with the pasta. Photo: AuCoin collection

As a nineteen-year-old buck private, I wrote a sports column for the Fort Campbell, Kentucky, newspaper. For extra money, I started writing promotional stories for off-duty work. This led me to a match in Hopkinsville, where an enraged female wrestler chased me out of the ring to the locker room. The audience roared approval when she hurled folding chairs at me. Photo by the late Al Urbanavičius, US Army

In my first campaign for the Oregon House, I walked to 5,000 homes in Washington County, extending my hand to everyone within reach, sometimes with ridiculous results. Photo: AuCoin collection

Our furniture was late for my family's first night in our new home in Washington's Cleveland Park. Sue and I were 34 and 33; the kids, 10 and 9. That first night, the city looked awfully big. Movers delivered our household goods soon after this picture was taken. Photo: AuCoin collection

14
No Protection at Sea

Every March, my schedule looked like a salad tossed by someone on LSD. Coinciding with spring break for schools, hundreds of First District families flocked to the capital for a look at the monuments and a quick photograph with their congressman. They would be joined by delegations from public and private organizations who had something to tell me about how the newly published presidential budget would affect them.

Once I actually met in my personal office with a Soviet nuclear arms expert while outside, waiting to see me, were a US Navy admiral and his entourage. Queued behind them were representatives of a back-home ministerial association, officials of the Washington County Soil and Water Conservation Service, a delegation from the Oregon Parent-Teacher Association, and members of a Native American tribal council.

On another memorable day, I bade goodbye to a group of Oregon state legislators and welcomed into my inner office Admiral Paul Yost, commandant of the US Coast Guard. My reception area brimmed with next-in-lines. Each had a wish list.

I should have installed a revolving door.

Admiral Yost eased his wiry frame into a leather chair across a coffee table from me. I warmed to the guy right away. He was unpretentious despite an immaculate uniform with a chest filled with ribbons. The first admiral I'd met with no entourage.

We chatted easily in my sitting area. I almost always met visitors this way; I eschewed facing them from behind the protective barrier of a desk.

"Commandant—" I started.

"Make it 'Paul.'" Yost smiled. His eyes shone.

"Good to meet you, Paul. How I can help you do your job?"

He took the cue. Over the next half hour, Yost told me that President Reagan's budget had slashed the Coast Guard's request for additional funds to counter drug trafficking and accidents at sea. It was incomprehensible. He needed help.

I lamented the old pattern of short-sheeting the Coast Guard, the only branch of the military tasked to save lives and the only branch not funded through the Department of Defense. You could fund it with the Pentagon's table scraps.

"You realize," I said, "that you're expected to support the president's budget?"

"I'm a new guy in town." Paul smiled mischievously. "Must be naive."

Chuckling, I told him that I had been a fan of the Coast Guard since my former assignment as a freshman on the Merchant Marine and Fisheries Committee. "When you finish your rounds with my colleagues, let's size up how much running room we have to solve your problem."

"Roger," Paul said, with a surprised grin.

"In the meantime, watch your step," I cautioned. "You don't want to get crosswise with those budget bean counters at the White House. They demand tribal loyalty and turn vicious when they don't get it." The commandant nodded and gave me the handshake of a man who had just made a friend.

In turn, the commandant was a perfect friend for me. As it turned out, I really needed one.

At home, forty-nine commercial fishermen from Newport, Oregon, a coastal town dependent on seasonal fisheries, had died in the twelve years leading up to the moment Yost called on me. Any seaman who fell into the frigid Pacific would die of hypothermia within fifteen to thirty minutes, even in protective gear. The nearest Coast Guard helicopter stations were in Astoria, 105 miles north, and North Bend, 85 miles south. A chopper from either base would have to fly more than 550 miles an hour to reach Oregon's central coast in time to save someone in the water. Even if that were possible, and it wasn't, the crew would have perhaps five minutes to extract a dying man from the waves.

I came to learn about these dangers from women who coped with them every day. They were the wives and mothers of the seamen who made up the second-largest commercial fishing fleet in Oregon. Many had lost husbands and sons at sea. All were determined to prevent new fatalities. As the number of such deaths mounted, they organized the Newport Fishermen's Wives, which became a revered institution in the community. They gathered facts, marshaled arguments, and appealed to the Coast Guard high command. Getting nowhere, they turned to me, their congressman.

Their stories of loss and near disaster landed like hammer strokes. I learned how Kenneth Lasseigne, the son of one of the leaders, Sidney Lasseigne, died with two others in the previous year when his seventy-five-foot trawler capsized thirty miles off Newport's Yaquina Bay. The freezing men bobbed helplessly in the icy current while the Astoria-based chopper responded to the SOS. The craft arrived more than an hour later—long after the seamen had lost sensation and might have muttered a farewell to loved ones before slipping unconsciously into the deep.

My Oregon field representative, Chris Pierce, and I spent hours with these gifted, determined women, sipping coffee, taking notes and listening with a knot in my gut to their tales of grief and despair. Seeing their loved ones off to work, they could never know if they would return or if the Pacific would seize them forever. When their men were at sea, most wives glued themselves to the Coast Guard emergency channel.

"Why do they venture out in hazardous conditions?" I asked.

Sidney Lasseigne explained that their seafarers were tethered to capricious fate. "The regulators set seasons based on calendar weeks, not weather reports," she said. "In Oregon, the season for Dungeness crab starts in early December. Even if opening day coincides with a winter storm, most fishermen risk it rather than lose a moment that will never return. Everyone has loans and home mortgages to pay. A trawler starts at a half-million dollars."

That explanation gave new meaning to the Blessing of the Fleet. The annual event features a flotilla of commercial boats sailing out from Yaquina Bay in single file. From each vessel, someone solemnly tosses a flowered wreath into the sea in honor of those whose remains lay below. It is as close as townsfolk can come to decorating the graves of lost loved ones.

I had to do something to limit these deaths. The women and the broader community knew they had won me over because I told them so. I was already forming a plan, but I didn't offer promises. To give hope and take it away would be unconscionable.

A few weeks later, Admiral Yost came back to see me in Washington. It was a matter of days before my Appropriations Subcommittee would vote on the transportation bill with funds for the Coast Guard.

"How much support did you find among my colleagues?" I asked.

Yost sighed. "Everyone loves the Coast Guard, but not enough to fund it."

I played my ace.

"Paul," I said, "I've found a way to fully fund your budget." I had counted votes in come-to-Jesus conversations that congressional colleagues sometimes have with each other when the chips are down. Startled, Yost leaned forward, his bright eyes holding me in his gaze. "That's . . . just amazing," he sputtered. He looked like he might swallow his tongue. "But—"

"Don't worry," I said. "I'll offset the cost by trimming other accounts in the transportation bill. Overall spending will be less than the president's request."

Exulting, Yost seemed to relax.

Pause.

"Now, Paul, I need you to solve my problem."

I told him about Newport. He replied with the standard line. The Coast Guard spread its bases along coastlines as evenly as possible. A new chopper on the central Oregon coast would save more lives, sure, but a third craft would give Oregon heavier search-and-rescue coverage than any other state in the country.

"Paul, I want to solve two problems at once, yours and mine. If I restore your cuts, I want that chopper in Newport. Newport will ante up a lot of local matching funds. Two in one, and done."

That smile again, brightening Yost's creased face.

We had a deal. The seafarers of the central Oregon coast would no longer be so vulnerable to the whims of the icy Pacific. The Coast Guard would be fully funded.

The Newport station is an object lesson. By virtue of my committee position, I could have shoved it down Admiral Yost's throat. Had I done so, I almost surely would have triggered rear-guard hostility, an inelegant result.

The Scriptures say it is better to give than receive.

In politics, it works best to give *and* receive.

15

Reagan, Star Wars, and Caspar Strangelove

Caspar "Cap" Weinberger's comment was mind-bending. Ronald Reagan's über-hawkish defense secretary came before the House Defense Appropriations Subcommittee to explain the premise of Reagan's proposed $4.5 trillion military buildup, the largest in history. In his haughty voice, Weinberger asserted that the administration's strategic doctrine was to prepare the United States to fight and "prevail" in a global thermonuclear war.[1]

"Prevail?" I sputtered. "In an all-out nuclear war, how can you say we would 'prevail'?"

Weinberger gave me a thin smile. "Well, you don't want us to lose, do you?"

Weinberger's fetish for nuclear weapons was right out of *Dr. Strangelove*, the darkly comic 1964 movie about nuclear Armageddon. The word around Washington in the 1980s was that Ronald Reagan's defense secretary never met a nuke he didn't like. The man's shopping list was almost as long as his pale, dystopian face.

I had studied nuclear strategy for years with my legislative aide Bob Sherman, a man with a laser-like mind who had dedicated his life to nuclear arms control.

It didn't take long to see that Weinberger had plenty of ideological company in the administration. Virtually every senior member of the military–foreign affairs team believed the nation could and would survive a nuclear exchange. They wanted to build a civil-defense system—including bomb shelters—to "provide for survival of a substantial portion of the US population in the event of nuclear attack."[2] They did not dwell on the fate of everybody else, the dead and walking dead.

One of many credible scientific analyses estimated that a nuclear war would instantly kill 35 to 80 percent of the American population,[3] poison crops, land, and water with radioactive debris and, according to some scenarios, induce nuclear winter, which would obscure the sun indefinitely. Destruction of our oil refineries alone would wipe out our freight transportation and cause widespread starvation. I tried to imagine "victory" celebrations amid ashes, carnage, famine, and disease.

Long before Reagan's election, our nuclear arsenal was powerful enough to destroy Soviet Russia many times over. To me, the certainty of once-over destruction gets us to deterrence, but more than once gets us nothing more. The only "winning" nuclear war is the one not waged. Reagan's hawks, however, thought real men had to build weapons. Everything they said emphasized a desire to defeat the Soviet Union so thoroughly that our bombs would bounce the rubble inside the Evil Empire. They seemed to forget that in the thirty minutes before our warheads landed, the Soviet's retaliation would bounce our own rubble too.

My differences with Weinberger were not limited to the fantasy of winning a nuclear war. I also helped lead congressional opposition to deployment of a first-strike strategic weapon known as the MX Missile. The intercontinental ballistic missile (ICBM) was to be deployed on railroad tracks with each missile carrying ten large nuclear warheads, known in the sanitized argot of the Pentagon as "MIRVs," multiple independently targetable reentry vehicles.

Strangelove and Co. felt that US security required surprise-attack nukes that would catch the Soviets with their guard down. As one of two arms-control advocates on the House Defense Appropriations Subcommittee, I argued that if we developed such weapons, the Soviets would soon do so too. The history of the Cold War arms race was monkey see, monkey do.

The problem is this: if two superpowers arm themselves with first-strike weapons, one is bound to use them. Like two scorpions in a bottle, stingers poised, one is virtually certain to strike the other before being struck itself and killed. Such a hair-trigger stance by the two superpowers would almost certainly mark the end of the nuclear deterrence that had prevented nuclear war since the dawn of the Atomic Age.

This buckaroo mentality and the crushing spending weight of Reagan's weapons budget had one positive consequence, although entirely unintended: it gave rise to the grassroots Nuclear Freeze movement. It called for a mutual, verifiable freeze on the development, production, and testing of nuclear weapons. It quickly grew from a few usual suspects on college campuses and coffeehouses to a broad political front that included, according to the polls, a large majority of the American people and several former foreign policy officials. Although the labor movement had been rather hawkish during the Cold War, twenty-five national labor unions backed the Freeze, as did the AFL-CIO.[4]

The great advantage of a Nuclear Freeze treaty was that it would protect both superpowers from destruction and eliminate the drive for destabilizing first-strike weapons like the MX.

State legislatures and city councils across the nation voted to formally endorse it. Addressing the US National Guard Convention in Indianapolis, I argued for the Freeze on the basis of national security. I explained how it would not only eliminate the nuclear first-strike threat but would free up funds for much-needed investments in readiness, including pilot flying hours and maintenance of more-likely-to-be-needed conventional arms, including fighter jets, tanks, and Bradley Fighting Vehicles. I got a standing ovation from the men and women in uniform.

Weinberger was having none of it. All this and more were on my mind as he and Colin Powell strode into the cavernous hearing room of the Rayburn House Office Building to tell the public and my committee about another improbable Reagan weapon proposal, the controversial Strategic Defense Initiative (SDI)—"Star Wars," as Ted Kennedy so aptly called it. It was a Buck Rogers scheme—an antimissile ballistic missile system on steroids. Advance word of a successful test intercept of an airborne warhead filled the room with television cameras and a standing-room-only audience.

The administration had spent what amounts to more than $360 billion in 2017-adjusted dollars[5] on Reagan's shield in the sky and other defense systems. Even congressional hawks were losing patience with this budget sinkhole. An intercept, however, suggested that the SDI could become viable, which was exactly Weinberger's purpose.

To the whirl of television cameras, the secretary fluffed his breast like a robin that just enjoyed a worm. "I came to report that an SDI interceptor just hit its target in a test in Hawaii," he intoned.

I read a scribbled note my aide Bob Sherman shoved under my elbow. Bob always seemed one step ahead of Reagan's weapons team. Armed with the same Top-Secret clearance as mine, he was always informed.

Turning to Weinberger, I said, "According to weather reports, Mr. Secretary, this 'hit' happened on a clear, sunny day. You must be counting on the Soviets to do us the favor of attacking in fair weather."

Laughter in the audience.

"Not so!" Weinberger huffed, sorting his papers. "On the day of the test, it was rainy and stormy in Hawaii. In fact, ash from a recent eruption at Mauna Loa hung heavily in the sky."

Several days later, Bob Seraphin, a taciturn top staffer at the subcommittee, called my office. Seraphin was famous for his sour disposition. Behind his back, the military guys sarcastically referred to him as Mr. Warmth. In this case, he was chortling and laughing so hard he could barely contain himself. He crowed that he had something that would blow my mind. I had him rush right over.

"Look at this, sir," Seraphin said, thrusting a transcript of Weinberger's testimony at me.

Weinberger had edited his response to read, "On further review, the weather was clear on the day of the Hawaii test. No volcanic action was reported."

Astounding! The nation's secretary of defense had told a bald-faced lie in public. Now, with television cameras long gone and Americans duly misinformed, he was trying to use the written record to scoop his poop from the stall.

I seized a pen and inserted a comment immediately following his confession:

"In the future, the committee and I would ask the secretary to tell the truth."

Turning to Seraphin, I snapped, "When the record is printed, send the rat bastard a copy of this." I didn't expect Weinberger to respond. He didn't. But the exchange stands in the permanent record to this day.

I was relaxing with Sue and the kids at our Porter Street home in northwest Washington, DC, when Reagan had first gone on national television to unveil SDI as a "nuclear umbrella." It would protect the United States, he said, "rendering . . . nuclear weapons impotent and obsolete." He showed a chart featuring an orb, Earth. Above it hung a red arc. Animated missiles bonked off the umbrella to "prove" SDI would shield America from danger. It looked like a Saturday cartoon show.

I nearly spilled my drink. Missile defense is exceedingly complex and technical. To reduce it to a virtual crayon drawing was ludicrous.

Star Wars exposed Reagan's inability to grasp how, at a minimum, SDI would likely provoke the enemy to ramp up its arsenal of MIRV-mounted missiles to overwhelm it.[6] With ICBM technology, the counter cost to the Soviets would be a fraction of SDI's trillion-dollar price tag.[7] A new arms race would ensue, dooming Reagan's professed desire for sharp reductions in nuclear arsenals.

There were other, more deadly problems. SDI would best be used as a key component of an offensive attack, and the Soviets knew it. ICBMs could be launched in a first-strike attack while the SDI defense held in reserve to mop up the other side's missiles in any feeble retaliatory strike.[8] Such a development would likely lead the Soviets to preemptively attack us while SDI was being staged. The superpowers would become those scorpions in a bottle—the last thing I came to Congress to allow.

At the request of my Congressman John P. Murtha of Pennsylvania, my subcommittee chairman, I led a House Defense Appropriations Subcommittee investigation into SDI in the late eighties. Congressman Robert Livingston, a Louisiana Republican, was assigned to join me.

In a discussion with Lieutenant General James Abrahamson, the first director of the Strategic Defense Initiative, I asserted that the Soviets had no choice but to consider SDI as a first-strike threat to their homeland.[9]

"You can't be serious!" Abrahamson replied.

"I'm as serious as the chairman of the US Joint Chiefs of Staff," I replied.

The chairman, General John Vessey, had said in a hearing that no military commander could afford to speculate on the intentions of his adversary. Rather, he had to assess what his foe was *capable* of doing, and plan accordingly.

"So, Jim," I said to Abrahamson, "if the Soviet Supreme Commander knows America's SDI could help a first-strike attack but gambles his country's survival on our good intentions, how long would he keep his job?"

Awkward silence. I switched arguments. "Let's talk about probability theory."[10]

"Fine." General Abrahamson held degrees in aeronautical engineering from MIT and the University of Oklahoma. As he leaned into the table for the discussion, the stars on his shoulders gleamed brighter than his blue eyes.

"Any attack on us would involve more than one warhead," I submitted. "Agree?"

"Yes," Abrahamson said. "For success, an enemy would want redundancy."

I suggested a scenario in which the North Koreans attacked with ten ICBMs. "Now," I said, "let's assign our missile defense a highly inflated single-shot success rate of, say, 80 percent."

"You're feeling generous tonight," Abrahamson smiled. "Those odds would be prohibitive to Pyongyang. They'd never shoot. I rest my case."

"Wait, we're not through," I replied. "SDI's 80 percent intercept rate has to be applied to the whole attack," I said. "Ten missiles, not one."

Bob Sherman and I had run the probability theory exercise against such an attack at least a thousand times.

I continued. "With two attacking and two defending missiles, you have to multiply 80 percent by 80 percent. That leaves 64 percent defense effectiveness. Multiply each subsequent degradation by 80 percent over ten missiles and, in the end, the defense has only an 11 percent chance of stopping the entire attack. Put the other way, the enemy has a 90 percent chance of killing us with at least one thermonuclear warhead. The odds are nine to one that the city you're trying to defend is now a cinder. How can that be a defense?"

Abrahamson had no answer.

I actually enjoyed serious discussions of this kind with intelligent military officers, of which we had many. Secretary Weinberger, though, was another matter. Our discussions went something like this:

Me: "Missile defense works best as part of an aggressive offense."

Weinberger: "You don't understand. We mean it as a defense!"

Me: "What you mean doesn't matter. What matters is how it functions."

Weinberger: "Yes, and we mean it to function as a defense!"

Eventually I gave up going around in that circle. Bob Sherman once quipped that trying to discuss deterrence theory with Weinberger was like trying to discuss relativity theory with a chimpanzee.

My report to the Appropriations Subcommittee recommended a major cut in SDI's budget. I argued that the dubious program had long odds of success. Its massive budget would cannibalize critically needed funds for military readiness and conventional arms. With a committee dominated by hawks, this argument was the only viable one I thought I could use. Livingston, my colleague, disagreed strongly, but the committee, led by Congressman John Murtha, a former marine, went along with a number of my suggestions.

In contrast to the Reagan buildup, the Nuclear Freeze was in equal parts a grassroots political movement and a serious arms-control proposal at the height of the Cold War. No other arms-control proposal has come remotely close to its intrinsic genius to this very day. In its key arms-control feature, it banned ballistic-missile flight tests—thus preventing improvement of first-strike accuracy. US and Soviet surveillance satellites would easily observe even a single such test, making compliance of a mutual freeze easy to verify. Moreover, the absence of flight testing would degrade the reliability of existing weapons. That was the point: if an aggressor can't be certain his weapons will destroy their targets, it would be suicidal to initiate use of them. He'd have telegraphed his aggressive intention and either missed his target or experienced a malfunction, either of which would be calamitous.

This logic escaped Reagan. First, he questioned the patriotism of congressional Freeze leaders.[11] Although we weren't named, everyone knew who we were: Ed Markey of Massachusetts, Tom Downey of New York, Pat Schroeder of Colorado, Ron Dellums of California, and me. Ironically, Reagan's smear also splattered on the presiding officer of his first inauguration, Republican senator Mark Hatfield, who had introduced a Freeze resolution in the Senate with Ted Kennedy.

Despite the passage of the Freeze resolution by the House and the endorsement of a number of cities and states, it failed to pass the Senate. For all of that, the Nuclear Freeze movement did move the administration 180 degrees from Weinberger's blather about prevailing in a nuclear war to Reagan's well-put conclusion, "A nuclear war cannot be won and must never be fought."[12] A remarkable achievement.

Yet the president held to the concept of SDI. He seemed oblivious to the war-provoking implications of his nuclear policy. The technically advanced system he envisioned included laser battle stations on Earth and in orbit that would blast enemy warheads out of the sky. With this shield, he repeated, he would render nuclear weapons obsolete. Easy to draw on a TV chart; impossible to do.

In contrast, the Freeze added no arms and didn't cost a dime. Of course, the Freeze would have resulted in the loss of hundreds of billions of dollars in contracts, which likely was one reason conservatives and their congressional allies attacked the Freeze proposal with everything they had.

In 1989, White House vote counters discovered that an amendment by my friend Bob Mrazek of New York, cutting hundreds of millions of SDI funds, would likely pass. The White House called Mrazek and a dozen other House skeptics and me to meet the president for some heavy lobbying.

Reagan strode into the Cabinet Room followed by Vice President George H. W. Bush, Defense Secretary Weinberger, and Secretary of State George Shultz. It was the A-Team. They were there to give us a full-court press.

As soon as greetings were out of the way, the president took a seat across the table from us and gave us a genial smile. He offered no jelly beans, his trademark greeting gesture. Still, this was as up close and personal as one could hope to get to the leader of the free world. At length, he began the meeting, reading from a pack of index cards to the dozen of us sitting five feet on the other side of the table. *He's surely not doing this,* I thought. But he was. He repeated his dream of rendering nuclear weapons obsolete with the SDI shield.

Mrazek decided the best way to reach Reagan was to bring up a movie.

"Mr. President," he said, "You must remember George C. Scott in the film *Patton.*"

Reagan nodded.

"Remember the part where Patton's Third Army is racing through France, but Karl Malden [General Omar Bradley] sends the limited gasoline supplies to General Montgomery, leaving none for Patton's advance?"

The president was still listening. He liked movies.

"Patton objects, saying if he had the fuel, he could drive his Third Army all the way to Berlin. Bradley disagrees, pointing out the heavily fortified Nazi defenses in Patton's way in the German border town of Metz."

Reagan nodded.

"Well, here's the point, Mr. President. Patton scoffs, saying no fixed defense made by man can block the ingenuity of another man determined to get around it. The Germans demonstrated that with the Maginot Line. And that's the problem with SDI, sir: it's a fixed defense, just as Patton was talking about."

Silence in the room.

Reagan blinked his pale blue eyes.

Then he picked up his index cards again. "SDI will shield future Americans . . ."

When we left the White House, no one seemed comfortable discussing what we had just seen. Senility, I thought. I was not surprised to learn after his death in 2004 that he had suffered from Alzheimer's Disease.

SDI was fortunately never deployed, in part because leading engineers and physicists concluded it was not technically feasible. Congress also lost its ardor for the undertaking. In 1988, it went so far as to enact my amendment to ban testing of anti-satellite weapons—the first time that any form of arms control was legislated by statute. In relatively quick succession, the United States and the Soviet Union entered into a thaw in the Cold War, stretching into the first Bush presidency—a golden era of mutual and verifiable arms-control agreements, moving the world back from the edge of a nuclear abyss.

It is impossible to identify every factor that created the U-turn away from the arms race. Some things are clear, however. It seems self-evident that without Mikhail Gorbachev's rise to power in the Soviet Union in 1985, it would not have happened. So was the response to him by British Prime Minister Margaret Thatcher, who had been a Cold War hawk. After conferring with Gorbachev in London, she enthused that we (the West) "can work with this man." The endorsement from the "Iron Lady" at Number Ten Downing Street was not lost on her friend and ideological soulmate, Ronald Reagan. Then, too, there was the popularity of the Nuclear Freeze movement, which had cut a large swath through grassroots America, eclipsing nonsense about "prevailing" in a nuclear war.

Finally, there was Reagan, himself, despite his many grave faults. It is a rare president who, especially toward the end of a second term, ignores an opportunity to leave a mark on world history. Reagan was no exception. At a Washington summit in 1987, Reagan and Gorbachev agreed to eliminate an entire class of nuclear arms—intermediate-range missiles designed for theater conflicts, particularly in Europe. That agreement, the INF Treaty, was precisely what Congressmen Dicks, Downey, and I urged on a senior Gorbachev aide, Georgi Arbatov, in a private meeting in Kiev, Ukraine, one year earlier. Reagan was followed by George H. W. Bush, Bill Clinton, and Barack Obama, who each saw further arms-control agreements, capped by the New START Treaty, which cut deeply into each side's arsenal of ICBMs as well as nuclear warheads. Under that agreement, the number of deployed and stockpiled warheads was slashed from 10,000 on each side in the 1970s to 1,500 by 2011.

But the progress was not to last. By the middle of his first term, Donald Trump, inarguably the most the ill-prepared and ill-informed president in American history, walked out of the INF and New START Treaties. In response, Russian President Vladimir Putin busied himself by building up his ICBM missile forces.[13] Trump has expressed little concern for the dangers of a new arms race or of militarizing space. He has called for a "Space Force," an entirely new branch of the military, and a space-based antimissile missile program to go with it. In 2019, Trump let the New START Treaty expire. Putin, no friend of arms control, seemed all too happy to follow suit. The demise of INF and New START leaves the United States with no strategy for a strategic arms discussion with either Russia or China. And it leaves the world stripped of treaties to prevent a nuclear arms race.

No less an authority than former defense secretary William Perry wrote in 2016 that the world's nuclear powers are closer to a nuclear catastrophe than at any time in history.[14]

It's time for another grassroots Nuclear Freeze Movement.

16
Corn for Porn

I hold that compromise, like the one I struck with Admiral Yost of the Coast Guard, is one of life's high arts. Too many Americans don't understand its importance. Once, a prominent businessman who should have known better leaned over to me during a Portland dinner party and betrayed his naivete.

"Les," he asked, "why is it that we send folks with great promise to Congress, but when they get there, they always stoop to compromise?"

Uh, because we work in a democracy, not a dictatorship?

It may surprise the uninitiated public or right-wing firebrands who enjoy shutting down the government to get their way, but the US Constitution is the product of compromise.

The Founders almost ran aground over a dispute between heavily populated states and lightly populated ones. Delegates from populous areas demanded a Congress represented on the basis of population. Thinly settled provinces, worried they'd be treated like a doormat, insisted on equal representation regardless of population.

Tempers flared. Nerves frayed. But after a month of give-and-take, a committee hammered out the Great Connecticut Compromise. Each state would have equal representation in the upper body: two senators. The number of representatives in the House would be based on a state's population.

Presto! No one got 100 percent of what they wanted, but to paraphrase the Rolling Stones two centuries later, everyone got what they needed.

It was one of the great compromises in history.

I love that story.

In Congress, I enjoyed studying where disputants were coming from and figuring out how to give them enough of what they needed to reach agreement on a bill that could pass.

Solutions require active listening and connecting the dots until a pattern comes into view to show a way out of the dilemma.

This is how I designed the great "Corn-for-Porn Compromise."

In 1991, subcommittees of the House and Senate were stymied as they tried to iron out differences between their separate versions of a spending bill for the Department of Interior and related agencies. The impasse rested on two issues. House members demanded long-overdue increases in fees paid by ranchers who grazed their cattle on the government's western range. Committee senators insisted on an amendment by Senator Jesse Helms that was an anathema to those of us on the House committee: a ban on the National Endowment for the Arts from funding art that depicted sexual activities or organs in a patently offensive way.[1]

Most of the senators were western-state conservatives who supported Helms's amendment. Few politicians wanted to be in favor of "lewd" art. It didn't seem to matter that with no definition of terms, the measure might have applied to Michelangelo's statue of David.

The senators also were hopping angry over any thought of higher grazing fees. House members had tried for years to bring public-land grazing fees closer to market levels. For our part, led by Congressman Sidney Yates of Illinois, Helms's trademark demagoguery was a nonstarter.

The standoff continued for four days. Members on both sides were tired and irritable. I began to think the deliberations would never end.

Then, taking stock of all I had heard from the other side of the table, I studied the faces of the senators scowling at us. Most of the men were rural westerners. I could almost smell cow dung on their boots. I began to connect the dots.

I smiled to myself. They didn't give a real damn about the NEA, but they would bleed for their ranchers. Without consulting Yates or anyone else, I spoke.

"Mr. Chairman," I said, "I move that the House defer to the Senate on grazing fees and that the Senate defer to the House and drop the Helms Amendment."

Long pause.

Then Republican James McClure of Idaho, the Senate chairman, broke the silence and the impasse.

"Every man has a price," he said. "Congressman AuCoin, you've just met mine."

His colleagues readily agreed. I had landed a big fish.

When I walked into the corridor, the compromise was already being called "Corn for Porn." Arts advocates and agriculture lobbyists were laughing in celebration.

You might wonder what the adage *strange political bedfellows* means. When you do, think of Michelangelo and a herd of Herefords.

17
Don't Short People

SHORT | *noun* | *Definition: On Wall Street, betting that a security will not perform*

In the mid-1970s, I took time out to coach ten tykes on my son's city parks and recreation basketball team. A lot of learning occurred as I worked with my motley group of Washington, DC, fifth graders. I would never have supposed, though, that those boys would teach me as much about myself and human potential as anything I learned elsewhere in the most credentialed zip code in the country.

My ragtag basketball team included noodle-thin introverts, wide-eyed naïfs, at least one half-pint with Coke-bottle thick glasses, and a lad named Charley who could barely dribble the ball. I loved them, but luckily I had a couple of players of genuine talent and a few others of more than passable competence.

The rules deemed that each boy should play equal minutes per game. No benchwarmers. In this league, experience trumped winning. I understood the point and admired its virtue.

Yet I was a political animal. I liked to win.

Given that, I came to our first game with a plan. I would play my starters for the first half of each quarter and then insert the scrubs for the last four minutes of the period. The idea was to let the first string run up a lead that wouldn't entirely evaporate when the second unit hit the floor. Equal playing time distributed in a way that maximized the odds of reeling in a win.

Brilliant, I thought.

By the game-ending buzzer, I wanted to put a bag over my head.

At the four-minute mark of the first quarter, I had called time out and told the scrubs to check into the game, together. Their expressions devastated me. As they trudged to the floor, they seemed to know they were chattel, used solely to eat up time until the stars returned.

We got trounced.

Worse, I had unwittingly reinforced several boys' inherent lack of self-esteem. My stomach turned.

From then on, I mixed the scrubs with first-string players in every quarter of every game. And each talented player would be judged by more than his own stats. He'd also be responsible for helping his teammates. Mentoring, really.

We started winning a few games, then a lot more.

By the championship game, my collection of misfits and cast-offs went nose-to-nose with a well-uniformed team from Chevy Chase, a posh DC suburb. The bench boys I embarrassed in Game One contributed timely buckets. In the last seconds, one of my big forwards rebounded a Chevy Chase miss and threw the ball three-quarters of the court's length to little Charley, the lad who had come to me to learn to dribble. Charley caught the ball over his shoulder, dribbled five steps, and went up for a perfectly executed game-winning layup.

Amid the celebration, a parent came up to thank me for bringing his son "out of his shell."

What those knobby-kneed boys showed me—a fairly new thirty-something congressman trying to pull a legislative staff of strangers into a team on Capitol Hill—was that you can't know the extent of one's talent until you give him or her, and their teammates, a chance to work in tandem. Hasty judgment shortchanges them and the greater whole.

Sometimes I wish I'd stayed on the Hill long enough to give an internship to my motley group of hoopsters.

* * *

I'm proud that so many of my interns and aides parlayed their experience in my office into careers of achievement and distinction. At work, I expanded the practice of matching people of latent talent with high achievers, letting the ensuing alchemy raise the level of each other's game. Esprit de corps in my Capitol Hill office was palpable. Turnover in my staff was one of the lowest in the US House. I didn't make them who they are, of course. But I helped them find out who they are. Each of them went on to become exemplary professionals. Some built highly visible careers. To cite some examples:

Adam Silver, a college intern cum legislative assistant, is commissioner of the National Basketball Association. Robert Taylor is a London-based international banker. When Robert started with me, he was an Oregon field representative and my aide-de-camp during travels throughout my district.

My lifelong friend Bob Crane, the award-winning reporter I stole from the New York *Daily News*, went on to be chief of staff for three other members of Congress. A staff director of my Oregon office, Bernie Bottomly, is the third-ranking executive at TriMet, the Portland region's nationally celebrated transportation agency. Like Robert, Bernie started out as my Oregon trip driver.

Legislative Director Michelle Giguerre founded one of the premiere lobbying firms in Oregon. She came to me as an eighteen-year-old summer intern straight out of Linfield College.

My Washington office manager, Deborah Kafoury, is the second-term chair of Multnomah County, the most populous county in Oregon. Before that, she served as majority leader in the Oregon House of Representatives.

Three senior aides—Chief of Staff Gary Conkling, Press Secretary Dave Fiskum, and Oregon Staff Director Pat McCormick—founded one of the largest public relations and government affairs companies in Oregon.

Kevin Lynch, my Appropriations Committee aide for natural resources, is the managing director for external affairs for one of the largest renewable-energy generators in the United States. Bob Sherman, my aide on the Defense Appropriations Subcommittee, negotiated on a European land-mine agreement for the US Arms Control Agency and ran the US Department of Energy's program for terrorist-proofing American strategic weapons.

Another press secretary, Rachel Gorlin, owns her own Washington-based political consulting firm. John Atkins, also an AuCoin press secretary, became city manager of two municipalities in greater Portland.

Sue Kirchhoff, a former intern, got a master's degree in journalism and became an award-winning reporter for the *Congressional Quarterly*. In Sue's career, she also reported from Washington, DC, for *USA Today*, the *Boston Globe*, and Reuters News Service.

Having started with me as a caseworker in my Portland office and a legislative correspondent on Capitol Hill, Betsy Cody became a senior researcher in the Natural Resources Division of the Congressional Research Service, a component of the Library of Congress. Sue Van Brocklin was an assistant press secretary in my Washington office. Today, she is director of public relations for a major advertising and public information firm in Portland.

Kevin Smith was once one of my district representatives and before that my district driver. He rose through the ranks to become my legislative director in Washington and capped his government career as chief of staff for Oregon governor Barbara Roberts.

There are so many other stories of this kind that they could fill another volume of this book. I hope those I haven't named will understand the space limitation and accept my regrets. Because I'm proud of my alumni. Every single one of them.

18
My Son Filled the Vice President's Shoes

Basketball has more virtues than I can count.

At Redmond Union High, it helped build my self-confidence and the will to not just win, but to do what's necessary to be able to win. It also taught me that without defeat, there is no victory; that if you're afraid to shoot, you'll never score.

For relaxation, I kept playing hoops in my congressional years. On free weekends, I would put aside thoughts of ICBM missiles and Reaganomics and coach my son, Kelly, in the House Members' gym. He was a high school varsity forward. Our workouts honed his game. It also helped build a lifelong bond between us.

On one of our Saturday outings in the eighties, we saw George Herbert Walker Bush throw the mother of all tantrums on one of the gym's paddle-ball courts. The sight of the Vice President of the United States having a meltdown during a pickup game is something one is unlikely to forget. Kelly hasn't; neither have I.

Arriving early, Kelly announced that he had forgotten his sneakers. *Teenagers.*

Luckily, two things that made the gym distinct came immediately into play. First, former congressmen, of which Bush was one, have lifetime access to the gym if their dues are up-to-date. They can even keep their original lockers. Second, the code of the gym dictates that if someone needs to borrow an item—in this situation, a pair of shoes—the borrower can do so from any locker so long as the borrowed item is returned. The practice went back decades. Lockers were not secured because everyone—Democrats and Republicans—trusted each other (then).

Amid the rows of empty lockers, I took Kelly around to find court shoes that fit. Following repeated disappointments, we arrived at a locker stenciled, "Geo. H. W. Bush." *What the hell,* I thought; *everyone's equal here, and the big man, a former congressman, knows the rules.* I reached in and pulled out a pair of white high-tops, size ten and a half to eleven. A perfect fit.

As Kelly laced up, I flirted with the idea that I might have learned a physical fact the KGB didn't know about the man one heartbeat away from the presidency. Kelly interrupted this thought, waving me to the court, and there we spent the next two hours in a spirited workout. Afterward, we broke down what had happened on the court as Kelly showered and dressed and I prepared for a steam bath. Then–*crash!*–double doors at the front and rear entrances to the gym flew open and six men in dark suits and earpieces fanned out across the gym, poking into nooks, crannies, even the sauna.

"You don't want to miss what's coming," I told Kelly. Within minutes, the Veep and three of his former congressional colleagues strode into the locker room.

I had one foot in the steam room when I heard the putative future leader of the free world cry out in a nasal twang, "My shoes are *warm!*" I cut my steam bath short and a few minutes later spotted Kelly in a green chair at courtside, watching the Veep in warm shoes playing a doubles match of paddleball. I dressed quickly to get within range of Kelly in case trouble erupted. It did.

One of Bush's volleys landed so close to the out-of-bounds line that a furious argument ensued. My sixteen-year-old son watched the fireworks, sitting directly behind the line.

"In!" Bush roared.

"Out!" shouted Representative Sonny Montgomery, a Mississippi Dixiecrat. The argument escalated until the vice president of the United States spun around to glare at Kelly.

"Kid!" Bush howled. "In or out?"

Kelly didn't hesitate. "Out," he said. He was so matter-of-fact, he could have been hanging out at our neighborhood park.

The vice president of the United States jumped up until his knees almost struck the chin of his carmine-red face. With clenched fists, he let out a blood-curdling "Noooooooooooo!" He wasn't kidding. His pals doubled up with laughter.

That day taught me several things about Bush. About Kelly too.

Bush was mercurial.

Kelly isn't easily intimidated.

And he can more than fill big shoes.

19
Timber, Wilderness, and the Owl

By the 1980s, forest wilderness had long since become the Gordian Knot of Oregon politics. The state's verdant federal forests were an Eden of natural wonders that Oregonians worshiped. Yet the vast, predominately Douglas fir stands produced high-quality wood faster than almost any trees in the world—which was why wilderness preserves were an anathema to the Northwest timber industry, one of the state's top employers. Oregon logging companies and sawmills had profited from Doug-fir harvests from federal timber sales for decades. Every environmental proposal for wilderness protection was a red flag for mill owners and their workers, who saw such proposals as a diminution of their timber base, even though federal lands belonged to everyone.

The hostility between wilderness and logging advocates reminded me of the lyric from an old song, "When an irresistible force . . . meets an immovable object . . . something's gotta give."

For the longest time, nothing did.

Then came the 1982 Reagan recession.

It kicked the bottom out of the housing market, leaving most Northwest timber firms holding commercial contracts for federal timber purchased at high prerecession prices. Harvesting the timber for pennies on the dollar threatened a wave of bankruptcies in the industry and the loss of thousands of jobs.

In the 1982 lame-duck session of the Congress, my colleagues and I in the Oregon delegation tried to head off the economic calamity. We proposed to let the companies return to the government unlogged trees for which they held contracts. In shorthand, it was called "timber contract relief." Firms would to pay a penalty to get out from under ruinous costs and survive for another day.

A visiting mill owner from my district put it to me this way: "Contract relief," he exclaimed, "is a hundred times more important than our old fights over wilderness."

With his words, an idea struck. If I could get Congress to attach an Oregon wilderness bill to the industry's must-pass bill for timber-contract relief, we could save the industry, but only if it would accept pristine old-growth forest reserves at the same time. For logging companies, ancient groves of huge trees represent immense stores of fine wood grain and, thus, spectacular economic potential. For wilderness advocates, virgin stands are cherished for their primordial web of life, which protects a forest's genetic diversity and provides habitat for wildlife that rely on an untouched forest's symbiosis of birth, death, and decay.

Those contrasting values had been at war with each other for decades in the Pacific Northwest. But here was a chance to strike a bargain that would save both the industry and environmentally important ancient forest groves. The opportunity was not likely to come again.

First, though, I had to bury the hatchet with my Democratic colleague Jim Weaver, a member of the House committee with jurisdiction over wilderness. A firebrand from Oregon's Fourth Congressional District, Weaver often made me uncomfortable with his antics. He had routinely thrown red meat to Oregon's most vocal environmental activists, often at my expense, and, looking back on it, not completely without cause. I had been slow to recognize the importance of wilderness. Also, there was the matter of temperament. We were fire and ice. Weaver valued populism and ostentation; I, discretion and decorum. We were not predestined to be best friends.

In 1982, however, our desire for new wilderness set-asides turned us into legislative partners. We worked out a strategy over several dinners at the Palm restaurant in downtown Washington. Our meetings were the first time Weaver and I had had a one-on-one conversation of any length. I discovered that he was far cleverer than I had thought. In turn, Jim might have learned that I had a forest conservation conscience he had not previously detected. At any rate, he seized on my wilderness idea.

The announcement of our proposal shocked the industry and the environmental community alike. No one had considered linking wilderness to an economic lifeline for mill owners and loggers. Nor did anyone expect such a blockbuster in a short lame-duck session. But there Weaver and I were, proposing to give mortal enemies what each craved most if they would respect the legitimate needs of the other. As an exercise in civics, it was a thing of beauty.

In the Senate, Mark Hatfield responded coolly to our bolt-out-of-the-blue proposal. We hadn't clued him in, and he was sore, probably remembering when the House delegation, led then by veteran Democrats Al Ullman and Bob Duncan, had stonewalled his 1979 wilderness bill.

Weaver and I moved ahead anyway. He got our million-acre wilderness bill out of his committee on a party-line vote. Steve Forrester, reporting for the Eugene *Register-Guard*, noted that in the committee room I stood near Weaver as a signal to keep wavering Democrats in line. It was an implicit reminder, Forrester noted, that as an Appropriations Committee member, I had purse-strings power to reward or punish colleagues.[1] On the House floor, our bill won a majority. However, faced with imminent adjournment, we had to resort to an expedited procedure that required a two-thirds vote for passage. We won a simple majority but fell short of the higher bar.

To make matters worse, Senator Howard Metzenbaum of Ohio, a liberal populist, effectively killed timber-contract relief in that session with a threatened filibuster against what he called the "big timber-company bailout."

Thus, when the gavel dropped to close the lame-duck session in late December, wilderness advocates and timber companies alike were left with nothing in their Christmas stockings.

However, Weaver, Hatfield, and I had crossed the Rubicon. Next year would see both contract relief and designation of new Oregon wilderness, issues that were either an anathema or manna from heaven, depending on which side you asked.

Timber Contract Relief: Hatfield, Metzenbaum, and Me

In the new Congress, Howard Metzenbaum resumed his objections to aid for federal timber purchasers whose "speculative bidding" put themselves in dire straits. Hatfield talked the Ohioan into a series of private meetings in his Appropriations Committee office. At Hatfield's invitation, I joined the talks. He wanted my presence to remind Metzenbaum that one of his fellow Democrats faced a rigorous reelection campaign and needed the bill.

As luck would have it, Metzenbaum's legislative assistant was the nephew of late Allard Lowenstein a congressman of New York, leader in the civil rights movement of the sixties and one of the masterminds of Senator Eugene McCarthy's antiwar presidential campaign in 1968. When the aide greeted me, I explained our mutual McCarthy connection. From then on, Metzenbaum seemed to regard me as a fellow crusader. It took a lot of hard bargaining, but Hatfield and I reached a compromise with him. The requirement for mills to pay a fine was a key concession to Metzenbaum and not entirely inappropriate, given that a contract is a solemn agreement that should not be lightly undone by legislation. The bill flew through Congress, giving Northwest sawmills a needed lifeline. In my mind's eye, I revisited a scene from my Redmond boyhood, where three mills provided several hundred jobs. When the factory whistle signaled the end of the day shift, I would watch workers in hardhats carry their empty lunch pails through the gate and jump into their pickups, heading for supper at home or maybe a cold beer at a local tavern. With the new bill, another generation of millworkers would return to that ritual with their economic hopes restored. They had teetered too long on the brink, having no hope at all.

Oregon Wilderness Act

Shortly after the contract-relief bill passed, Weaver and I introduced our 1,006,395-acre wilderness bill. The final version, passed 252–93 by the House, providing 930,400 acres of wilderness-designated lands and 156,900 acres for the Cascades Recreational Area.[2] We had picked up Ron Wyden, then a second-term congressman, as a cosponsor. In the Oregon delegation, the only no votes came from the usual suspects, Republican conservatives Bob Smith and Denny Smith.

The bill was not attached to timber-contract relief, which had already passed, but it was connected by implication. Once the Northwest delegation saved the region's mills, it was impossible for the industry to wage war against the wilderness legislation.

Now Oregon wilderness became a question for the Senate and, given his seniority, for Mark Hatfield. The senator and I had been meeting for weeks to discuss ideas for his bill and a strategy to pass it. He wanted no part of a time-consuming conference committee, given the demands of his chairmanship of the Senate Appropriations Committee. The alternative he chose was to persuade Speaker Tom Foley to hold any Senate-passed bill at the desk for an immediate House vote, which, if approved would go directly to the president to be signed into law. To win my support, the senator promised to move on no bill unless we mutually agreed with its terms.

Hatfield assured me that "my colleague" (his term for Oregon's junior senator, Bob Packwood) was on board.[3] For as long as I knew Hatfield, I never heard him refer to Packwood by name. It was always "my colleague." To deliver the sobriquet, Hatfield's voice always dropped an octave. The sarcasm was hard to miss. Maybe Hatfield's comment reflected the junior senator's reputation. A Capitol Hill joke held that the most dangerous spot in the Capitol was any place between Packwood and a television camera.

On June 6, the House took the Hatfield (and AuCoin-influenced) bill from the desk and passed it without amendment. The Act almost doubled the state's wilderness acreage. Some of the protected forests were home to trees as old as Jamestown, Virginia, the first English settlement in the Americas founded in 1607.[4] Rising out of the alchemy of decay and rebirth on the forest floor, western hemlocks and Douglas firs reached three hundred feet tall or higher. Experiencing a natural forest's continuum of death and rebirth comes as close to experiencing immortality as anything on earth. Such a forest's banks of genetic diversity, containing elements too numerous to count, work to ensure the health of the entire ecosystem. John Muir had this complexity in mind when he wrote, "The clearest way into the Universe is through a forest wilderness."[5]

Timber Harvest Controversy

Having settled the wilderness fight, I thought Northwest forest wars were largely over.

Wrong. They were just getting started.

Several grassroots environmental activists charged that Hatfield, Norm Dicks of Washington, and I had forced unsustainable levels of logging with the power of our respective seats on the Senate and House Appropriations Committees. They pointed to annual harvests in the national forests of Oregon and Washington of more than 4 billion board feet—well above historical averages of 2.6 to 3 billion board feet. Having just earned the Sierra Club's Distinguished Service Award for the Oregon Wilderness Act, I chafed at the characterization. By every official measure of sustainable harvests, the charge was false.

No less an authority than Randal O'Toole, a forest economist and environmentalist, wrote as much. O'Toole had mastered the Forest Service's

FORPLAN (Forest Plan) computer program, which allowed him to calculate the timber-harvest capacity for each forest in the region.[6]

Writing in the Northwest environmental newsletter *Forest Watch*, O'Toole pointed out that critics had inflated the harvest numbers. They had mistakenly counted timber that had previously been sold, often pre-thinned, returned to the government through the Timber Contract Relief Act, and sold again.[7] Excluding the buyback volume[8] from returned sales, O'Toole showed that net harvests[9] of new green timber were actually lower than average: 2.6 billion board feet (BBF) in 1986 and 1987, 2.3 BBF in 1988, and 1.9 BBF[10] in 1989. Never did Congress exceed what the Forest Service testified as being achievable within the context of the agency's multiple-use mission.[11]

It would have been helpful if O'Toole's article, meticulously researched, had dispelled the misrepresentation of congressional overcutting. It did not. Once a meme is repeated often enough, it becomes conventional wisdom. As a policy maker, you can't correct such treatment; you have to let it go or risk an ulcer. Years later, a high-level interdisciplinary team of scientists did show the Forest Service's allowable harvest estimates to be excessive.[12] But their findings were not available in the eighties and early nineties. In their absence, the only official estimates Hatfield, Dicks, and I could rely on were those delivered in testimony year after year by the chief of the Forest Service.

Comes the owl

When the Oregon Wilderness Act became law, Congress passed nineteen other state wilderness bills, more than in any other year since the enactment of the Wilderness Act of 1964.[13]

Passage of the Oregon act, along with one in neighboring Washington State, was a signal achievement, but by definition, neither act addressed thousands of acres of old-growth forest otherwise available for logging over time.

This fact led to the next flash point in Northwest forest politics.

In 1989, conservationists appealed the Forest Service's first Northwest master operating plan. Litigants charged that the agency's Environmental Impact Statement (EIS) failed to adequately assess the environmental consequences for the spotted owl. Failure to do so was a violation of the National Environmental Policy Act, which requires such impact statements to identify the environmental effects of proposed federal agency actions.

I gave passing notice to the court challenge. Some group was always bringing suit against the Forest Service. At my direction, however, Kevin Lynch, my appropriations aide, followed developments closely. The Dartmouth grad hailed from Connecticut, but he learned forest policy so thoroughly that most timber representatives and forest environmentalists respected him, as did Hatfield. Meanwhile, with wilderness behind me, I refocused on the legislative battle against the Reagan administration's military policies.

Then in 1989, a federal district judge ruled for the conservationists.

His remedy was a bombshell.

The judge enjoined all logging in the western national forests in Oregon and Washington until the Forest Service revised its EIS. Loggers, millwrights, homebuilders, and timber-dependent towns went into a frenzy. Angry protests erupted in communities throughout the Northwest. Tens of thousands of wood-products jobs were threatened. "Jobs, Not Owls" became a slogan of outrage in timber-dependent communities—a sentiment that lingers today. The political blowback was the most frenzied I had ever encountered in the Northwest. Logging communities demanded the repeal of the Endangered Species Act, although the lawsuit was brought not under the ESA but the Forest Management Act and the National Environmental Policy Act. Antienvironmental and antigovernment demagogues from other states moved in to exploit the tsunami of anger.

I couldn't decide which group's behavior offended me most—antienvironmentalists whose reductionist thinking suggested that their government cared more about some bird than about people, the Forest Service for its fumbling ineptitude, or those environmental activists who evinced no compassion for working-class people caught in an economic nightmare beyond their imagination or control. With all that as background, Northwest members of Congress caucused almost nonstop in search of a way to protect the owl while bringing relief to economically crippled communities.

By this time, the working relationship between Senator Hatfield and me had grown close. Meeting in Hatfield's office, we worried that pressure building in timber communities would erupt into violence. If only we knew the environmentalists' bottom line. It was evident that they wanted more than to ensure the recovery of the owl. Several leaders stated they wanted old-growth stands protected from logging even where no owls were known to exist. But how much old growth, and where?

"Why don't we hold a summit?" I asked.

"A summit?" Hatfield responded.

"Bring the whole Oregon delegation home and have the governor join us, invite two panels, one representing the industry, the other, the environmentalists. Tell the agencies to send expert representatives. For the first time, make everybody show their cards, instead of bashing each other."

Hatfield liked it. What could we lose?

On June 28, we convened the summit in Salem. It was the only time in memory that the governor and the entire Oregon delegation, House and Senate alike, Democrats and Republicans, gathered together in the state to address a single issue. It was also the first time environmental and timber industry leaders were required to air their differences in front of each other. For eight hours, the antagonists, occupying facing tables, stated their case and responded to each other. The governor and the delegation cross-examined both sides.

John Hampton, the Willamina Lumber owner, used a paper napkin to express the timber industry's frustration with the environmental movement. He tore the paper in half to illustrate various bills that over time had put logging off-limits in federal forests. Then he tore it again, demonstrating further set-asides. Plaintively, he asked, "When does it end, or does it? The industry wants an endgame and predictability." For their part, the environmentalists spoke of the spotted owl significance to forest health as well as its desire to prevent logging from fragmenting remaining ancient forest stands, holistic ecosystems.

At length, the delegation and Governor Goldschmidt recessed to a back room. We returned to propose a compromise hammered out during the break—a two-year cooling-off period in which each side would give something and gain something. To the industry, we offered annual harvests of less than it wanted but more than what was allowed under the injunction. For the environmentalists, we proposed to create legal protection of Oregon's old-growth forests in all stands of four hundred acres or more to protect both the owl and the ancient forests for their mutual ecological value. If accepted, our intent was to turn the appropriations rider into permanent law. In return, litigants would have to agree to ask the courts to drop the injunctions on sales and refrain from filing judicial and administrative appeals.

Timber industry representatives agreed on the spot.

Six days later, a deeply divided environmental community countered with a proposal against fragmentation of old-growth forests so stringent that the overall harvest level would be less than allowed by the court injunction. The delegation rejected it.

That left one alternative, something no one in the delegation was eager to undertake. We were forced to legislate a solution that should have been developed by the Forest Service and BLM. We expressed our ire at the agencies' failure in a stern note accompanying the amendment we ultimately passed:

> The extraordinary measures included in this section, particularly with regard to judicial processes, have been reluctantly agreed to because of the failure of the agencies to take steps on their own to resolve these matters in a manner which could have prevented the current situation.[14]

The vehicle for our amendment was the annual appropriations bill for the Forest Service and BLM. In the House-Senate conference report on this must-pass bill, we prescribed a temporary timber sales program and deemed it sufficient to meet the laws on which the injunction was based, effectively lifting the court's injunction. The amendment also ordered the Forest Service to complete its environmental study within one year, when the rider would expire.[15] Because it was an appropriations amendment, the legislative work had fallen to Hatfield in the Senate and Representative Norm Dicks of Washington and me in the House, the only Northwest members of the Appropriations Committees. Several environmental groups conferred with Senator Pat Leahy of Vermont to explore ways to block Hatfield's amendment in the Senate. When it was apparent that the amendment would pass in any event, representatives of the Sierra Club and Audubon Society worked with Hatfield to strengthen its environmental provisions. With their assistance, the proposal became Section 318 of the Interior Appropriations Conference Report for Fiscal 1990. In addition to providing an interim supply of timber, it broke significant new environmental ground long sought by many environmental advocates. In statutory language, we called for:

- Recognizing old-growth forests in law for the first time because of their ecological value.
- Ordering federal agencies to minimize fragmenting intact old-growth stands and creating citizens' review committees to review timber sales for maximum compliance with the order.
- Protecting known spotted-owl habitat areas for the first time. In Oregon, depending on the forest, the provision called for 1,250 to 2,500 acres per nesting pair.
- Directing that timber harvests be avoided in areas not known to be occupied by the spotted owl but which were suitable owl habitat.
- Requiring the Forest Service to adopt a scientifically adequate plan for the conservation of the spotted owl within one year.
- Mandating that each Forest Service and BLM district appoint a citizens' committee to make recommendations about which proposed timber sales, consistent with the amendment, should proceed and which should not.

None of this appeased several local environmentalists, who, in outrage, dubbed Section 318 "The Rider from Hell" and condemned Hatfield and me for our work on it. However, the entire Northwest delegation, including House Speaker Tom Foley, supported the amendment. The Sierra Club acknowledged Senator Hatfield for his work on Section 318 and its preservation and legal recognition of old-growth forests. The measure's legitimacy was upheld in a unanimous decision by the US Supreme Court.[16]

Here was a textbook distinction between governing values and advocacy values. Advocacy asserts whole-loaf positions and pushes decision makers to adopt them. Governing requires a consideration of multiple demands and weighing their consequences. Each set of values is vital in a free society. It is a mistake, however, to blur their differences.

In this case, the congressional delegation owed a duty to forest health and the owl but also to thousands of idled workers. Forest environmentalists had no dual duty. To the exclusion of other considerations, their job was to focus on one goal: preserving old-growth forests. Andy Kerr, head of the Oregon Natural Resources Council, epitomized the viewpoint. "Expecting the Oregon delegation to deal with [ancient forests issues]," he once said, "is just about like expecting the Mississippi delegation in 1960 to deal rationally with segregation."[17]

Section 318 was hardly perfect, but without it or some similar alternative, the result would have been no timber harvests whatsoever in the federal forests of western Oregon, Washington, and Northern California. I had heard many harvest figures bandied about over the years, but zero was not one of them—not even from the most hard-eyed activist. For this reason, I've always been disappointed with the vituperation Andy Kerr and some other environmentalists directed at those of us who wrote Section 318. What would they have had us say to workers who, without notice, would sink into an economic abyss that could not be justified on any environmental basis? Kerr's answer, quoted in Kathie Durbin's book *Tree Huggers,* was, "We aren't humanitarians, we're environmentalists."[18]

Most critics of Section 318 also neglected to mention the environmental features of the amendment. Some simply misrepresented the measure. For instance, Durbin, a beat reporter for the *Oregonian,* figuratively gasped that Section 318's "sufficiency" language would last "forever."[19] In truth, it lasted until the specific sales it insulated were harvested, a process that would have taken several years. Durbin also asserted that the rider mandated that the forest agencies "sell an additional 8 billion board feet of timber by October of 1990—about 90 percent of the volume sold over a recent two-year period, squeezed into a single year."[20] She failed to reveal that the measure covered both the harvest year in which it was enacted and that of the previous year, one in which the injunction prohibited harvesting. Therefore, the legislation's two-year program provided for 5.8 billion board feet in the owl national forests of Oregon and Washington. That worked out to the equivalent of 2.9 billion board feet a year, a level commensurate with the historical average. It also authorized 1.9 billion in the BLM's O&C Lands.

Then the plot thickened.

When Section 318 expired, the Forest Service revealed it still had no science-based plan for the spotted owl. In fairness, the agency had tried. It brought in a panel of outside scientific experts whose work might have met the test, but higher-ups in the Bush administration blocked its findings from being offered.

In response, Judge William L. Dwyer of the Ninth US Circuit Court of Appeals issued a blistering ruling in May 1991 along with another injunction. His sharp words did little to conceal his contempt for decision makers in Washington, DC:

The records of this case [and of the BLM case] show a remarkable series of violations of the environmental laws. . . . Had the
Forest Service done what Congress directed it to do—adopt a
lawful plan by last fall—this case would have ended some time
ago. More is involved here than a simple failure by an agency
to comply with its governing statute. The most recent violation
of NFMA [National Forest Management Act] exemplifies
a deliberate and systematic refusal by the Forest Service to
comply with the laws protecting wildlife. This is not the doing
of the scientists, foresters, rangers, and others at the working
level of these agencies. It reflects the decisions made by higher
authorities in the executive branch of government.[21]

If Judge Dwyer was contemptuous, I was furious. In writing Section 318,
Hatfield, Dicks, and I had the support of the entire regional delegation, but
we spent a lot of blood, sweat, and political capital to no avail.

The new injunction kept the region roiling long after I left the Congress and Bill Clinton had become the forty-second president of the United
States. Having promised, if elected, to hold a Northwest forest summit of
his own, Clinton did so in Portland on April 2, 1993, accompanied by Vice
President Al Gore and four cabinet secretaries.

Following the daylong conference, the president appointed a multi-
disciplinary scientific team to address the forest and wildlife issue compre-
hensively. It was led by wildlife biology scientist Dr. Jack Ward Thomas,
who went on to become chief of the Forest Service during Clinton's administration. The Forest Ecosystem Management Assessment Team (FEMAT)
developed a region-wide ecosystem approach to forests, which considered
the spotted owl and other key species. The new approach managed entire
ecosystems even if their natural habitat crossed the man-made boundaries
of individual national forests. It also put 80 percent of the Northwest's federal forests off-limits to logging.[22] In response, the court lifted the injunction against logging, ruling that this plan finally protected the viability of
the owl throughout its range.

While Clinton Administration plan offered a regional timber sales
goal of one billion board feet per year, that level was never reached.[23] In
2015, federal timber sales in the region—counting Forest Service and
BLM forests—totaled less than 600 million board feet, about 15 percent

of the pre-owl federal harvest. The plan's promised reemployment training program enrolled 586 displaced timber workers between 1992 and 1994. Another retraining program, to create ecosystem restoration specialists, served twenty people from 1994 to 1996.[24]

It's easy to understand how an economic jolt of this magnitude embittered men and women in timber country. I only wish that FEMAT's comprehensive science had been at hand long before I began work on the House subcommittee. It might have prevented the boom-bust. As it happened, in the absence of such science, disputants and policy makers were flying blind for years, responding to opinions based, at best, on educated guesses about what constituted forest health and, at worst, on economic greed and political advantage. In that atmosphere, lacking a viable scientific point of reference, we had the Forest Service's allowable-cut estimate as the only authoritative measure of responsible harvest volumes. It was a flawed measure, as the FEMAT study revealed. But no one knew it at the time, not even forest environmental activists.

More than two decades after leaving Congress, I have watched political battles continue over management of the federal forests in the Northwest. Drought and insect infestation have turned thousands of acres of woodlands into wildfire tinder. The conditions have prompted proposals to thin forests to reduce the risk of conflagrations. To no one's surprise, commercial interests—in the name of public safety and forest health—see an opportunity to increase the harvest of timber, including old-growth trees. The big trees have far more commercial value than small trees. But ironically, old-growth trees are more fire-resistant than younger, small ones.

This wrenching saga, played out over several decades, still simmers today in many communities in and around spotted-owl forests west of the Cascades while other communities have slowly recovered. A new resource management plan published by the BLM has provoked echoes of timber-versus-environment arguments of the eighties and nineties. Some counties, once dependent on federal timber sales for employment and municipal income, have cut or eliminated services—the easy ones first, such as libraries; the harder ones later, such as law enforcement. Local officials file lawsuits and rail at the loss of sawmill and manufacturing jobs from diminished federal timber sales. All the while, acres of decks of raw logs from privately owned timberlands lay ready to be loaded aboard cargo vessels in Coos Bay, bound for sawmills in Asia.

In Northwest forest politics, irony will never go extinct.

20
James Watt Didn't Like Me One Bit

When Ronald Reagan took office, he handed the keys to critical environmental agencies over to reactionary blunt instruments. They were people who had made careers not of protecting our air, land, and water but of commoditizing them. For the Environmental Protection Agency, he named Ann Gorsuch, a Colorado state representative and member of a right-wing group of zealots known around Denver as the "House of Crazies." A cattle rancher named Robert F. Buford was named to head the Bureau of Land Management. And Reagan chose Oregon's John B. Crowell, a lawyer with the Louisiana-Pacific timber company, as the top Department of Agriculture supervisor of the US Forest Service.

But the Gipper didn't stop there.

To run the agency most responsible for the health of our public lands, the Interior Department, he named James G. Watt, the former point man for the Mountain States Legal Foundation, a property rights organization that litigated against the application of laws deemed inconvenient to corporations. Watt had sued the government in opposition to affirmative action, in favor of limiting safety inspections of businesses, and against reduced utility rates for the elderly. After that, he moved on to lobby for the conservative, highly partisan US Chamber of Commerce, the largest lobbying group in the country.

If anyone gave Watt the benefit of the doubt when he arrived at Interior, he quickly disabused them. With pomp and merriment, he directed that the official seal of the Department of Interior, the bison, be reversed. Having faced left since its creation in 1849, he made the bison face right. The humor of the stunt was lost on most of the national political community, but not its significance. Almost overnight, Watt became the biggest lightning rod in the Reagan cabinet. That's something, considering that Caspar Weinberger, Edwin Meese, William Bennett, and Alexander Haig were cabinet secretaries.

Beyond his arrogance and hostility toward the environment, the boisterous Watt had a penchant for imbuing his policies with a theology reminiscent of the eighteenth century.[1] Like the early Puritan minister Cotton Mather, Watt believed man's divine duty was to subjugate the land. "My responsibility," Watt told the *Washington Post*, "is to follow the Scriptures, which call upon us to occupy the land until Jesus returns."[2] In the same manner, Mather had preached that it was man's God-ordained destiny to transform the dismal, hostile American wilderness into an earthly paradise, where the sober, frugal, hardworking faithful would convert it into fruitful farms and shining cities on hills. The Puritans were to subdue the "howling Wilderness,"[3] the vast domain of Satan. Among Lucifer's minions were diabolical flesh-eating animals and native "savages."

Watt took over the Department of Interior in 1981 at the same time I joined the House Appropriations subcommittee that handled his budget. Appearing before my panel for the first time, his long torso pitched him high in his witness chair. From that perch, he threw thunderbolts, informing us just how things were going to run now that he had arrived in Washington. "We're going back through a reassessment of our values," he intoned, shoving his thick lenses back to the bridge of his nose. "We're going back to the fundamentals—fundamental economics, fundamental social structures, fundamental religion, fundamental basic concepts."[4]

Swatting back at challenging questions, he paused to flash a toothy smile worthy of a piranha. "I never use the words *Democrats* and *Republicans*," he asserted. "It's *liberals* and *Americans*."[5]

Sitting across the table from him, I scribbled a note to myself:

"Warrior on a religious crusade."

In his first months, Watt imposed a moratorium on the creation of additional national parks. He proposed opening wilderness areas to further mining activity. He sought to bypass Congress on decisions to release wilderness study areas to other uses. He announced a lease program to allow commercial oil drilling in the Outer Continental Shelf off California, from Point Conception off Santa Barbara to the Oregon border, an area known for decades as being prone to earthquakes.

That offshore oil-drilling proposal—Lease Sale 53, in the argot of Watt's Minerals Management Service—sent anti-Watt feeling over the top and millions of Californians on the warpath. The prospect of an oil spill befouling some of California's most scenic coastlines was a political declaration of war. Ocean fishermen had nightmares of a seismic event and subsequent spill that would devastate fisheries. My staff's research showed that ocean currents from northern California ran north up the Oregon Coast. An oil spill would harm Oregon coastal fisheries as well as California's.

In the US Senate, Alan Cranston of California took the floor to call for Watt's resignation. Newspaper editorials condemned the drilling. Most of the California congressional delegation, including some Republicans (a few, in those days, were environmentally inclined) issued critical press releases and made scathing speeches on the House floor.

A few days before my Appropriations subcommittee scheduled a vote on the Department of Interior's budget, I sat in my office late in the afternoon, pondering how Watt might be stopped. As a cabinet secretary, Watt indisputably had the power to approve the drilling. Any ordinary bill to block him, assuming it could survive a Senate filibuster, would run into a certain Reagan veto.

Watt, then, held all the cards. Public opinion and congressional opposition did not faze him. Stopping him seemed impossible.

Unless . . .

I phoned Phil Burton with an idea. The liberal lion from California was a friend of mine, an environmental champion, and one of the legendary strategists in the House.

"Let me run an idea past you," I said. "What if I use the appropriations bill to cut Watt's funding for the offshore drilling? Every damned dime." As chair of the Democratic caucus, Burton knew every minefield in the House. I, on the other hand, had been an appropriator for only a few months; I needed to understand any unintended consequences.

I had nothing to worry about.

Burton boomed, "AuCoin, if you offer that amendment, two things will happen. One, I'll back you, every step of the way. Two, when you win—and you will—they'll carry you on their shoulders in San Francisco."

My amendment passed the Interior Appropriations Subcommittee on a straight party-line vote, 4–3. I won on the strength of animosity toward Watt and outrage over his exploitive environmental ideas. In the full committee, the rider sailed through with strong Democratic support. Even Silvio Conte of Massachusetts joined me. He was the committee's ranking Republican member and had gotten wind of Watt's designs for oil drilling off Georges Bank, a large elevated seabed running from Cape Cod to Nova

Scotia, my grandfather's fishery. The amendment sailed through the House and was accepted by the Senate without a challenge. Overall, the underlying bill was too important to veto. Reagan signed it.

In the ensuing years, members from other states legislated offshore drilling bans. As late as 2001, even then-governor Jeb Bush of Florida opposed drilling in waters off his state. (As a 2016 candidate for president, he flip-flopped on drilling.)

James Watt was a proud man with thin skin. My Republican friends told me my amendment wounded him. They said I started a legislative avalanche against him, creating a personal grudge he nursed. At the same time, Watt was a growing political liability for Reagan. When the secretary defended his decision to authorize the sale of more than a billion tons of coal from federal lands in Wyoming, he referred to his coal-advisory panel as consisting of "a black, a woman, two Jews, and a cripple."[6] That stirred the political pot so much that he resigned.

Watt went back to lobbying, and in 1995 was indicted on multiple counts of felony perjury and obstruction of justice in connection with a grand jury investigation of influence peddling at the Department of Housing and Urban Development. Watt pleaded guilty to a misdemeanor count of withholding documents from the grand jury. He was put on five years' probation, ordered to pay a $5,000 fine and perform five hundred hours of community service.[7]

More than a decade later, when Watt and I had long since returned to private life, my wife, Sue, and I visited our daughter, Stacy, in Jackson, Wyoming. We were enjoying an espresso downtown. Our granddaughter Morgan was in tow. Suddenly the shop's door opened and Watt and his wife walked in. *Oh, right,* I said to myself; *they retired here.*

As if in a western movie, Watt's gaze immediately locked on me. Stiffening, he dropped his smile. While he and his wife, Leilani, looked for a place to sit, I heard her hiss under her breath, "You don't have to talk to *him!*"

Likewise, for me, of course. I smiled at Sue and Stacy.

In politics, you love it when your work leaves a lasting impression.

21

Fascists Aren't Commies. Got That?

Two Democratic congressmen and two Republicans made up our fact-finding team to war-torn Central America in the spring of 1983. Why did I go? I thought the Reagan Administration was backing fascists and oligarchs because they were capitalists. We stopped first in Mexico City. In a small hotel room there, we met a Salvadoran refugee—a young woman seized and tortured by her government for leafleting at the University of El Salvador. This was a time when most of Central America was ablaze with revolution and repression. The Reagan administration was up to its neck in it, backing the wrong sides. It saw Castro and the KGB behind every mangrove tree. My friend Congressman George Miller of California and I accepted an invitation from the Unitarian Universalist Service Committee (UUSC) to investigate the armed violence and alleged human rights abuses. The UUSC, a nonsectarian organization that promotes human rights and social justice worldwide, funded small trips to the region by members of Congress. It had the advantage of access to both rebels and government officials.

Outspoken critics of Reagan policy, George and I relished the opportunity to talk to both sides engulfed in the conflict. Two conservative Republican colleagues traveled with us, which made the trip bipartisan.

John McAward, our UUSC guide and translator, set up the meeting with representatives of Mexico's Zapatista Army of National Liberation. The leftist group had been giving succor to the Salvadoran refugee sitting before us.

She told us the army had arrested her on a campus for handing out leaflets protesting the ruling Nationalist Republican Alliance (ARENA) party's repression. Salvadoran soldiers locked her in a pitch-dark vertical cell. Once a day, they slid a plate of food to her through a slot at the bottom of the door. She had just enough space to crouch down to reach it. The troops allowed no breaks, except when they brought her out to take turns raping her. When they finished, they threw her back. The woman told us the ordeal went on for months before she was saved during a raid by antigovernment insurgents, the Farabundo Martí National Liberation Front (FMLA). With their help, she hiked to safety in Mexico.

I recoiled at the Salvadoran government's depravity. In our hotel room, drawn drapes filtered the sun as we tried to absorb her dark story.

Republican congressman Don Ritter of Pennsylvania spoke first. "Are you a Communist?" he asked.

That seemed to be significant to him. His conservative mate, Republican congressman Jim Sensenbrenner of Wisconsin, harrumphed in agreement.[1]

A look of astonishment swept the woman's face. She recovered and hotly denied any Marxist loyalty.

I snapped, "Her problem would seem, Don, that she isn't sufficiently Fascist."

Ritter's grotesque question epitomized Reagan's policy in Central America: a right-wing government's atrocities against its people were to be regretted but were the price of thwarting international communism and its assault on capitalism. As such, the United States was aiding and abetting the military-led Salvadoran government in its civil war with the FMLA.

In next-door Guatemala, the evangelical Christian dictator, Efraín Ríos Montt, kept his boot on the throat of his people, also with military aid from America. Ríos Montt had ousted an elected president in a coup d'état in 1982. For Washington's neoconservative elite at the time, that not seem to matter. For them, democracy was a feeble alternative to hidebound opposition to Communism, which right-wing governments kept at bay from America.

For the Reagan administration, nothing in the region rose higher in importance than stopping the Cuba-leaning Sandinistas in Nicaragua, who had toppled the US ward, Anastasio Somoza DeBayle, a West Point graduate and heir to a dictatorial neo-Fascist dynasty. With Somoza's ouster by insurgents in 1979, the United States evacuated most of his National Guardsmen to Buenos Aires. There, the Argentine junta trained them in the art of guerrilla warfare. The fighters came to be known as the Contras, or counterrevolutionaries. Soon after the 1980 presidential election, Reagan escalated their mission. Led and financed by the CIA, the Contras waged a full-scale war against the Sandinista government. Although the former national guardsmen had enforced the Somoza dictatorship by means of murder, kidnapping and torture, Reagan called them "freedom fighters."

Throughout the 1980s, I joined a dozen or so other colleagues to crusade against US policy in Central America. One was House Intelligence Committee Chair Edward Boland[2] of Massachusetts, Tip O'Neill's closest friend and former Washington roommate and author of the amendment that finally banned the Reagan administration's covert financial support of the Contras.

On the floor of the House, I told my colleagues that, under Reagan, any dictator bright enough to say he was anti-Communist seemed to qualify him for Reagan's support. Of course, Hitler hadn't been a Communist, either, but that irony was lost to the Reagan neocons. Nor did they see that by cozying up to neo-Fascist tyrants, they were not blocking leftist insurgencies so much as spawning an anger that fostered them.

The examples were plentiful, global, and historical. Besides leftist Nicaragua, one can count the Islamic Republic of Iran, Argentina,[3] Communist Cuba, and the Socialist Republic of Vietnam, among others. That history put a lie to Ronald Reagan's conceit of America as a Shining City on the Hill "whose beacon light guides freedom-loving people everywhere."[4]

On my congressional group's last evening in Mexico City, we had an early dinner with the US ambassador, who gave us a cursory overview of the region.

America's chief envoy to Mexico is a critical position. He has, or should have, his hand on the pulse of Central America. Reagan, fixated as he was on the region's insurgencies, might have appointed for this post a Foreign Service officer who was schooled in the area's history and politics, grounded in geopolitics, and imbued with a desire to rub shoulders with the Mexican people. Instead, the president named his old Hollywood friend John Gavin, a former actor from the fifties known for his mannequin good looks and not much more. Gavin's dismal film career foretold his diplomatic skills. When our party met him at the chancery, the diplomat breezily explained that he commuted each week from his home Beverly Hills, where his wife, actress Constance Towers, stayed. He spent his weekends there before returning to the Mexican capital on Monday morning. With no foreign policy experience, Gavin made diplomatic life sound like one more excursion for someone on Hollywood's list of the rich and famous. He was the only US ambassador I ever met who thoroughly embarrassed me as an American, both as an elected official, and as a visitor representing my country.

Following dinner, our party returned to the hotel. We were about to turn in when the phone rang. A breathless Gavin told us to return to the embassy. At once.

It was a bit after ten o'clock.

The ambassador came right to the point. "The State Department says it's too dangerous for you in El Salvador." The military-supported ARENA party, alerted to our arrival, was railing against us. An article in a government newspaper denounced us by name, vowing that the sovereign nation would not welcome US congressmen who blasphemed it. This was serious news from a country that was committing 6,250 violent deaths annually until its twelve-year civil war ended.[5] A United Nations Truth Commission found that more than 85 percent of the killings, kidnappings, and torture had been the work of the government and its allies, including paramilitaries, death squads, and army units trained by the United States.

Gavin's report set off a heated back-and-forth, pitting Miller and me against the ambassador. For once, Ritter and Sensenbrenner held their tongues. They seemed to sense what George and I suspected: that this may have been a Washington ploy to ward off two liberal critics of the Salvadoran government. When Gavin's admonishments failed to move us, the ambassador announced that he had a cable from the "highest authority in the Department of State," George Shultz, the secretary, warning us off.

"Mr. Ambassador," I said, "Let me see the cable."

Gavin pulled it from his tailored blue mohair suit. Standing, I read it aloud. Mostly boilerplate. Then the telling paragraph. A known member of a death squad allied with Salvador's ruling party had been seen for several days in the San Francisco Bay Area, casing places frequented by George Miller. The incident had occurred a year earlier, after George's first visit to the country, in which several ARENA party leaders felt he had insulted their nation's honor.

Miller sat frozen in his chair. "George," I asked, "Did anyone tell you about this?"

"No," he replied, ashen-faced.

Turning to Gavin, I said, "Mr. Ambassador, will you explain why our government did not tell a United States congressman that he had been under surveillance by an assassin in the pay of a foreign government?"

Gavin professed no knowledge, which was probably correct. But when he tried to minimize the matter, Miller exploded with his booming voice, hurling words better suited to a merchant ship that an American embassy.

"Mr. Miller!" Gavin responded indignantly in a poor imitation of a British peer.

But George was just getting warmed up. "This goddamned administration! If I had been a Republican congressman . . ." More profanity followed as his decibel level rose. The choice of words began to refer to parts of the human anatomy and what George Shultz and "the whole Reagan mob" could do with them.

Gavin had enough. "Mr. Miller, if you don't stop, I'll call the marine guards to escort you out of the building!"

I could see the headlines back home: OUT-OF-CONTROL CONGRESSMAN EXPELLED FROM US EMBASSY IN MEXICO CITY.

Breaking in, I asked for calm. "Mr. Ambassador, I think we have to appreciate that George has just had the shock of his life. Let's not be hasty."

Both men cooled down. Catastrophe averted.

Back in our room, Miller thanked me. "You gave me a chance to climb back down," he said.

"You think I'd let them frog-walk you out of John-Boy's embassy?" I said. "You're already a hero in your district. Ousted by Gavin would have earned you a coronation and gone to your head." Our group decided not to tempt fate. We went on to our planned second stop, Guatemala, to observe the works of President Ríos Montt.

Observers said the Pentecostal Christian strongman ruled with a Bible in one hand and an automatic rifle in the other. He was known for his "guns and beans" domestic policy. There was a clearer way to say it: "If you're with us, we'll feed you; if not, we'll kill you."

Ríos Montt's stated piety pleased Reagan, who praised him as a man of great personal integrity.

Human rights workers on the ground told a different story. "Rural women suspected of guerrilla sympathies were raped before execution. Children were thrown into burning homes and tossed into the air and speared with bayonets. Repeatedly, we heard stories of children being picked up by the ankles and swung against poles, smashing their heads."[6]

Villagers confirmed these stories. The rebels often made their base in indigenous towns high in the Guatemalan mountains. Under Ríos Montt's scorched-earth policy, the army destroyed villages suspected of cooperating with the insurgents. Inhabitants were slaughtered.

In one village, we interviewed a woman who within days of our arrival had seen her husband disemboweled for denying he gave chickens to the rebels. Her face seemed waxen, her unfocused eyes as lifeless as a dead fish. The pall of sadism and death hung over the whole village, where the government had treated its people as wheat to the scythe.

From the banks of the Potomac River at Foggy Bottom, the view was quite different. The State Department's 1982 international human rights survey praised improvements in Guatemala's human rights situation. Reagan sent Ríos Montt $6 million in military equipment, including UH-1H helicopters and A-37 aircraft used in counterinsurgency operations.

Congressman Ritter—the man who had inquired about a gang-raped woman's political philosophy—wrote later that Reagan's military aid was a limited amount of spare parts for helicopters that were bought from American firms. He believed the military matériel gave the United States leverage with the dictatorship. He failed to mention that hovering army helicopters blew down houses in native Indian villages suspected of supporting guerrillas.

Miller and I returned to the partisan hothouse of Washington with fresh ammunition and pressed our fight with the administration. We debated the issue on the House floor, distributed articles demonstrating the human rights abuses of the Guatemalan and Salvadoran regimes to our colleagues, and spoke at teach-ins about the issue.

About one year later, we went on our own to El Salvador with Miller's legislative assistant, Cindy Arnson, who later became director of the Latin America Program at the Wilson Center in Washington, DC, a federally chartered foreign policy think tank.

At a buffet dinner there, hosted by US Army advisors, Miller and I seethed as Arnson pointed out one known government death squad member after another mixing easily with US officers and enjoying food and drink paid for by US taxpayers.

The scene would have shocked most of our colleagues. Unfortunately, few members—and even fewer Americans—had any real idea what was going on, in part because the US media was paying scant attention to the fraternal relationship between US military officers and their Salvadoran counterparts. The press also failed to report closely on a military school at Fort Benning near Columbus, Georgia, where many friendships of this sort were forged. It was the US government's School of the Americas,[7] a cold-war institution founded in 1946 to train military officers of allied South American nations.

Although it had attracted little attention in the public or the Congress, by the eighties, activists were calling it "The School of Assassins." They accused the school's alumni, general-grade officers, of massacres and torture against anti-Fascist insurgents when they returned to their home countries.[8]

By the beginning of Reagan's second term, the United States continued to ship weapons and munitions to the Contras—in violation of the Boland Amendment, which banned it unconditionally. To get around Congress, the Reagan strategists cut a covert deal with Iran, selling the fundamentalist Islamic regime Hawk and TOW missiles laundered through Israel in exchange for Iran's help in freeing hostages held by Hezbollah, Iran's radical proxy, in Lebanon. Proceeds from the illegal missile sales were used to arm the Nicaraguan Contras. In 1984 alone, Washington aid reached an astounding $24 million, an amount likely made expensive because, generally speaking, Nicaragua's body politic rejected the Contras for the sadistic, blood-thirsty killers they were.

The Contras were cited multiple times by two human rights organizations, Americas Watch and Witness for Peace, for mass killings, summary executions, torture, and kidnappings. Numerous Reagan officials were indicted for the illicit arms deal in what came to be known as the Iran-Contra scandal. After several Congressional investigations, Reagan ultimately owned up to the unlawful scheme in a nationally televised address. "Mistakes were made," he famously said—using the timeworn passive tense to avoid naming names. Charges against some of the conspirators were later downgraded when the administration refused to declassify certain documents. In the end, eleven of fourteen administration officials were convicted. Those whose convictions were not vacated on appeal were pardoned by President George H. W. Bush, former vice president under Reagan.[9]

Then the war came home to my district.

On April 28, 1987, twenty-seven-year-old Benjamin Linder of Portland, a University of Washington graduate and mechanical engineer, was killed in a Contra attack on the village of San José de Bocay, Nicaragua.

Linder had spent three and a half years in the hills, voluntarily building small hydroelectric plants to provide electricity to villagers for the first time. Across the United States and in Oregon, his death created a sensation. US Embassy officials in Nicaragua admitted that they not only did not investigate the incident but had no interest in doing so. White House press secretary Marlin Fitzwater attributed the killing to stray bullets in a battle between the Contras and government forces.

Back home I met with Ben's parents, David and Elizabeth Linder. They weren't buying the White House explanation. After listening to their description of Ben and reading some of his letters, I wasn't buying it either. The idea that Ben went to Nicaragua as a Sandinista mercenary was ludicrous. The young man I pictured was a peace lover who wanted to make a difference in the lives of the Nicaraguan poor. If he had been my son, he'd have inspired me.

Congressional right-wingers had a different opinion. They held tight to the Reagan narrative that the Contras were "freedom fighters." Anyone who felt otherwise was disloyal to the United States.

On May 14, 1987, the neoconservatives demonstrated their callousness at a subcommittee meeting of the House Foreign Affairs Subcommittee on Western Hemisphere Affairs. David and Elizabeth Linder had come to testify about their son's work and death.

When Elizabeth Linder, in a blue plaid cotton dress, concluded her remarks, Connie Mack, a Republican from Florida, pounced.

A grandson and namesake of baseball's longest-tenured manager who led the Philadelphia Athletics from 1901 to 1950, Mack looked daggers at the Linders. "I just don't understand how you can use your grief to politicize this situation," Mack told her. "You're caught here in a crossfire between two different beliefs. . . . I don't mean to be cruel, but I think by coming here today, you asked for it."

That son of a bitch! Who did he think he was? But at the dais as a guest of the panel, I had no standing to speak.

"Asked for it?" Elizabeth Linder replied. "That was about the cruelest thing you could have said."

"You came here to blame this government," Mack said.

"Yes," she affirmed.

". . . to blame the President," he continued.

"Yes," she repeated.

"It's not a question of blame," Mack asserted.

"Yes, it is," she insisted. She added that Ben chose his work out of compassion. She denied he went there seeking danger.

"Then I suggest to you," Mack responded, "that the responsibility lays on your son's shoulders, not the government."

"I disagree," she retorted.[10]

I could not restrain myself. "I suggest that you, Mr. Mack, are a cold-blooded ideologue and an embarrassment to this committee." The chairman had to gavel down audience's applause.

George Miller phoned me a few months later to propose another trip to the region, this time to Nicaragua. We would travel with our colleagues, Don Edwards of California and Mike Lowry of Washington, and with Edith Wilkie, the director of the House Arms Control and Foreign Policy Caucus. When Miller agreed to a side trip to San José de Bocay, the site of Ben Linder's killing, I was all in.

The villagers whom Ben Linder loved greeted us happily amid the ruckus of chickens, dogs, and children at play on San José de Bocay's dirt streets. Two American volunteers translated for us. We were the first American visitors they had seen since Ben's parents retrieved their son's body. Villagers described Benjamin Linder as fun loving and revered by adults and children alike. When Ben wasn't magically producing hydroelectric power, he often donned a clown's outfit and rode his unicycle through the village. The peasants' laughter drove away their fears of the jungle war. At least for a while.

The volunteers spoke at length about the day Ben died. There was no firefight. The Contras had attacked the unarmed village, destroyed the dam, and captured Ben.

"Then they shot him with a pistol, in the temple," one said.

"The trouble is, there's no reliable proof," I lamented. "The autopsy was done in Managua by a Sandinista doctor. No one in Washington will take it seriously."

"Hold it," a young woman said. She returned with a photograph of Linder in death, a bullet hole in the temple. A colleague had taken it and developed it in a lab in Managua.

"May I keep this?" I asked.

"Of course. If it would help."

"I know how to use it."

Linder was the first American killed in the war. By forces armed and trained by his own government. I was determined not to let the Contras get away with it.

Congressman Julian Dixon was a California liberal who eschewed flamboyance, a trait that would be helpful in dealing with the Washington, DC,

Police Department. His even-handedness had earned him the chair of the rules committee of the 1984 Democratic National Convention. Now we sat in the office of the House Appropriations Subcommittee on the District of Columbia, a panel he led. The photograph rested delicately on his fingertips while he studied it gingerly from various angles.

"Well, what do you say?" I asked. *Come on, Julian!* I had joined his subcommittee as a bonus assignment earlier in the year.

"Bring in local police forensics?"

"Yes," I exclaimed. "Nicaragua naturally isn't within our jurisdiction, so DC cops would have to volunteer. But if we can pull this off, we might get the only independent analysis that'll ever be done."

Dixon reached for the telephone. "Okay," he said, punching the number.

When the conversation ended, he turned to me. "An analyst will pick up the photo tomorrow."

Having taken a day to study the photo of Ben Linder's head wound, the director of the Washington PD Forensic Science Laboratory was emphatic.

"It bears all the signs of an execution. From the looks of it, I'd say it came from a nine millimeter sidearm. Standard US Army issue."

"Coup de grâce?" I asked.

"I'd bet on it. Look at the temple. Powder burns. Clearly visible even in a photograph."

Bound to protect the cop's identity, I couldn't call a press conference to expose the White House's fiction. But keeping the officer's name secret, I showed the photo privately to colleagues who had been timid about opposing to Reagan's "freedom fighters." The photo and its forensics analysis turned several votes, which coincided with the steady unraveling of Reagan's Central America policy.

In August 1987, Costa Rican president Óscar Arias negotiated a peace process signed by Central America's five presidents, in virtual defiance of the Reagan administration. For his effort, Arias won the 1987 Nobel Peace Prize. Known as *Esquipulas*, the talks promoted demilitarization, termination of assistance to irregular forces, and free elections. The end of both the Guatemalan and Salvadoran civil wars was rooted in this diplomatic breakthrough.

When Arias was still working the peace talks, I met with him in Washington with a small group of my colleagues. A small man with a soft voice, he spoke like someone who knew his mind. How had he appealed to the heads of his neighboring countries? "I believed I touched their hearts. I told them, we need to choose between life and death. The superpowers are providing the arms; we are providing the death."

Incredulously, the Reagan White House objected to Nicaragua's seat at the table because the Sandinistas had come to power in a coup d'état against Anastasio Somoza. It didn't matter that Somoza had seized power in his own military putsch. The International Court of Justice ruled for the Sandinistas, who were then treated as legitimate participants in the Esquipulas talks. Coupled with the administration's Iran-Contra scandal, the Reagan doctrine for Central America came to an ignoble end.

I trace much of the savagery of modern American politics to the bitter brawl over Reagan's policy in the region. And as a high priest of scorched-earth politics, no one comes close to former congressman Newt Gingrich, a reactionary who rose from backbencher to House Speaker on the strength of invective and defamation. To this day, I regard him as one of the most dangerous men in American politics. Purdue University political scientist Bert A. Rockman cited him as a principal instigator of the current ideological civil war that has paralyzed and polarized the national politics.[11]

In 1984, Gingrich and other House supporters of Reagan's Central America policy questioned the patriotism of those of us who opposed it. We believed the Central American conflicts were, at heart, civil wars waged against tyranny and repression, not proxy rebellions supported by the Soviet Union. Gingrich & Co. regarded all such thoughts as treasonous.

The Georgian insurgent took the House floor at ten o'clock on May 8, long after the day's regular business had concluded and most members had gone home for the night. While C-SPAN's cameras rolled, he smeared dozens of members by name—only Democrats—as being blind to Central American Communism in opposing Reagan's Contra "freedom fighters" and their effort to topple the Nicaraguan Sandinista regime.[12] In those years, the C-SPAN cameras were required to focus solely on the speaker—no camera pans of the empty chamber were allowed. Knowing this, the Georgian would cite a comment by one Democratic member after another, often out of context, as proof of his or her Marxist sympathies. Each time, he looked from side to side, suggesting to viewers that the chamber was full of members. Then he'd say, "If the gentleman or woman would care to defend himself or deny his words, I'd be happy to yield to him or her now." *Pause.* "No? In that case," he said, "Here's what another hate-America-first Democrat said on ..."

It was a tactic that wickedly and accurately echoed Joe McCarthy's witch hunts of the fifties. Today, the Gingrich touch has mutated into a destruction-derby politics that seems to know no bounds. Shutting down the government has become a permissible partisan tactic. So is yelling "Liar!" at a US president during a State of the Union address. Or a partisan congressional leader vowing that his top priority is to stop a newly inaugurated president in his tracks. Or deeming as an impeachable "high crime and misdemeanor" a presidential lie about extramarital sex. Or a congressional majority party's refusal to even meet with a president's nominee to the Supreme Court. Or Republican-controlled state legislatures passing laws to make voting even more difficult for those who have the least in the richest society in the world.[13] Or a president, the recidivist liar that he has shown himself to be, pardoning and endorsing a rogue sheriff convicted of criminal contempt for systematically violating the constitutional rights of Latino immigrants.

We can't go on this way.

I acknowledge that a sizable number of Americans—largely white, without college degrees, resentful of immigrants, stoked by right-wing media and feeling left behind—are responding to the politics of blame. But I hold hope that we will find a way to overcome this aberration in our nation's history. We've done it before.

The Washington Monument rises in the center of the Capitol Mall. It is the tallest structure in our nation's capital. Visitors notice that the stone is whiter on the bottom third than higher up. The reason is that the great obelisk stood unfinished for twenty-five years during the "Know Nothings" political era of the mid-1800s. Then, as now, it was a time of profound political disquiet, much of it at the expense of immigrants to our country. When the darkness finally receded, work began anew on the monument, but with stone from a different quarry. I want to believe that the damage being inflicted today will, like the monument, be repaired by genuine leaders, and that the work to form a more perfect union will somehow resume.

22
Tip O'Neill, Man of the House

Thomas P. "Tip" O'Neill, my favorite House Speaker, was the antithesis of Newt Gingrich. Whereas the right-wing revolutionary from Georgia did more than perhaps anyone else to destroy bipartisanship in Congress,[1] Tip's raison d'être was "country first, party second." He had friends on both sides of the aisle and loved people and their stories. He was a throwback to a simpler time, when Democrats served up meat and potatoes instead of quiche, and no one wondered whether the party favored the working class or Wall Street.

To Tip, America was about a worker making a living wage to feed the family, earning a decent retirement, maybe helping the kids off to college, and getting time off from the job to be with the family. For his entire life, Tip lived in Cambridge, Massachusetts, a few blocks from the house where he was born. After the sixties, neoliberalism dominated Democratic thought. But there was no "neo" in Tip's liberalism. Government existed to regulate capitalism so that all people reaped their share of its economic benefits. A Boston waterman could say O'Neill had a deep keel—he knew who he was, and no storm could blow him off course. Drawing from these reserves, Tip called early for Nixon's impeachment, stopped Ford's last-gasp effort to extend the Vietnam War, and led the loyal opposition to Reagan's dystopian budgets. When he retired from Washington in 1986, the *Almanac of American Politics* named him "the most effective and accomplished Speaker the nation has had for 40 years." A Harris poll showed him with a national favorability rating of 63 percent.[2]

Tip, however, was blissfully detached from popular culture. For his colleagues, that made him all the more loveable. Once, in Los Angeles, Tip was chatting at a fund-raiser with a handsome young man who seemed to think that Tip knew who he was. After the young man left, the Speaker asked a friend, "Who was that?"

The answer: "Warren Beatty."

Tip blinked. "The lion tamer's son?"[3]

Then there was the time when Barney Frank, a member of the Speaker's state delegation, gave O'Neill a head's up that he was going to announce his homosexuality. Tip, a devout Catholic, was concerned only about Barney's political well-being. Frank assured him that he would be OK. When Tip walked out to the House floor, the first person he saw was Pat Schroeder, the liberal Democrat from Colorado.

"Pat!" O'Neill exclaimed, "You won't believe this." Grabbing her arm, he said, "Barney's coming out of the room!"

No other Speaker I knew would regularly amble onto the floor, drop himself into a seat, and survey the scene for an hour or so. To an untrained eye, he seemed to be taking a break from office work. Actually, this is where much of his real work occurred. His political antennae caught the smallest signal in a face over here or body language over there, each act helping him connect the dots in House politics. Deducing what was happening on the floor—for whom, to whom, and why—kept him one step ahead of both friend and foe.

"What's the news?" he liked to ask. The more he knew about the denizens of the House—their problems, their plans, their contretemps—the better he could run this hothouse of ambition, self-regard, and good and bad intentions. When he took a seat in the chamber, it didn't take long for my colleagues to wander over. Soon he would be surrounded by five or six members, listening to his stories, giving him information.

I knew almost nothing about O'Neill when I arrived in Washington. But I came to love the man. Loved him for his savvy, his old-school ways, his unreconstructed liberalism, even his rough-hewn manner and malapropisms.

In turn, Tip loved my wife, Sue, or Suzie, as he called her. She hated to be called Suzie, but for Tip, she made an exception. *Suzie* actually sounded good coming from that lilting Boston-Irish brogue.

Tip once made her disappear.

The event was an orientation dinner for new freshman and spouses, the incoming class after ours. The program featured a panel of four current spouses, speaking about Washington life from their perspective. I was proud of Sue, who spoke simply, clearly, and from the heart with a smile that made her eyes dance. Afterward, as we headed for the door, a Boston-Irish voice boomed from behind us.

"Suzie, darlin'!" It was Tip, all six-foot-three and three hundred pounds of him. "Wonderful job, darlin'!" He gave her a hug. From behind, where I stood, my wife vanished. She was wholly engulfed in his embrace.

I often wished I was an ethnic American, like the Irish-Americans I knew with their clannish charm. (Actually, I was ethnic, an Acadian-French American. Without a father around to explain it, I arrived at manhood having not given that a thought.)

I was never more beguiled than early one morning when Tip and a couple of aides walked into the House members' dining room and spotted my children for the first time. My daughter, Stacy, and son, Kelly, were having breakfast with me. The garrulous House Speaker couldn't resist coming to our table.

"Tip," I said, "meet my son and daughter."

"I hope you kids are having a good mornin'," he smiled. He tussled Kelly's hair and said, "What's your name, son?"

"Kelly, sir; Kelly AuCoin." Kelly pronounced the last name in the "semi-French" way I had used for years—O'Coin.

By this time, Tip and I had worked together for more than six years. But at the sound of "Kelly," coupled with that O-apostrophe, the speaker forgot himself.

"Ah, a good lad from the Old Sod!" He stood, beaming at Kelly.

I hated to do it but knew he'd realize soon enough. "Tip," I said, "Remember, we're Acadian French. A-u-C-o-i-n."

"Oh, right," he said. "Well, Kelly and Stacy, you're so good lookin', you could pass as Irish." He was still grinning when he shambled away.

Tip O'Neill had allies of all sorts among congressional Democrats and even many Republicans. Those who were closest to him were Irish-Americans he had served and socialized with for years.

Several of these men would grab a table for Tip and themselves at the annual House Gymnasium Association's steak feed, a fund-raiser that helped finance the gym's operations. By prearrangement, the House would go into a parliamentary business session that precluded amendments for up to four hours, creating a respite from roll-call votes. When the feed started, members would walk to the cafeteria in the Longworth House Office basement, which for one night was transformed into a bistro with tablecloths and low lights. Few members wanted to miss this opportunity to enjoy choice beef, baked potatoes, greens and salad, and convivial conversation. In those days, it was the one time of year when you could chat at length with dozens of colleagues with nothing at all to distract you. Grudges were checked at the door.

It was a ritual for Speakers to invite the day's presiding officer of the House, the Speaker Pro Tempore, to join his table. I didn't know about this tradition when I presided over the foreign aid bill and the House parliamentarian whispered to me that Tip was waiting for me at the steak feed.

"Have a seat next to me!" Tip bellowed when I arrived. He had tucked a cloth napkin under his collar and held a knife and fork in each hand. It was an honor to be named Speaker Pro Tempore and a greater one to dine with the House Speaker and his pals. I heard political inside information I could not have come by any other way. In time, Tip put down his cutlery and plopped his napkin on the table. He was ready to swap stories and called on his old roommate, Eddie Boland.[4]

"Hey, Eddie. Tell that one about that guy in the Legislature from South Boston."

Boland started chuckling. "This old fellow had to be . . ."

"No!" Tip interrupted. "Not *him*, the other one!"

On it went for more than an hour, story after story in shorthand. I would not have believed it had I not witnessed it.

"How about that time we all went over to Susan [O'Neill's] house for dinner?" Joe Moakley, the Rules Committee chair, piped. Everyone doubled up with laughter.

Joe Early sputtered, "Then there was Fast Eddie O'Shannon at Fenway Park . . ." The hilarity was so raucous, Tip momentarily choked on his cigar smoke.

I was in awe. These friends had survived so many political battles for so many years and told their favorite stories so often, they had no need to finish them. Using just labels was a good way to fit in more stories.

But the point always arrived when, for a heartbeat, Tip, cigar in hand, would quietly disengage and gaze into middle space, listening to the lilt of the familiar Irish voices around him. In that moment, there was no arms race, no genocide in Central America, no warring partisanship. Just mirth, and old stories, and memories, and the company of men he loved.

I feel a deep loss when I look at Congress today. I mentioned this when recently I ran into to Jim Malloy, the House doorkeeper in Tip's era. Jim shook his head, then said something about having and losing. The rumpled, aging Irishman understood that nothing lasts forever. "But, congressman," he said, "we've gotta remember, we were here when it was what it was."

23
Other Characters I Knew

Tip O'Neill wasn't the only larger-than-life figure under the Capitol dome. In truth, the institution has always attracted a slew of them. I discovered a veritable menagerie—saints and statesmen, yes, but also miscreants, ogres, petty thieves, knaves, fools, and weirdos.

Consider Dan Flood of Wilkes-Barre, Pennsylvania. Here was a former Shakespearean actor who wore a pointed waxed moustache and a black cape with a red silk lining. Chair of the powerful Labor, Health, and Human Services Appropriations Subcommittee, he once rushed back to his district when rising waters threatened a flood. He strode on the bank of the raging Susquehanna River, raised both arms and shouted, "Halt!" Locals still talk about how the water crested safely.

Otto Passman of Louisiana despised foreign aid, but as chair of the Foreign Affairs Appropriations Subcommittee, he had to floor-manage the aid bill every year. Passman had a remarkable tic, if you could call it that. While speaking on the floor, he would suddenly fling an arm into the air as if it had a mind of its own. A leg would follow, sometimes kicking backward like an untamed bronc. We used to say Otto wore out his suits from the inside.

Tom Steed, an old bull Democrat from Oklahoma, came up to me one day to complain about the length of a weekly caucus meeting. The caucus had gone into overtime, delaying the start of House business. "Les," Steed drawled, "do ya know the difference between a caucus and a cactus?"

I turned to him and smiled. "Why, no, Tom, tell me."

"With your cactus, all the pricks are on the outside."

I'll also always remember two rogues. One had an altruistic streak. The other, so far as I could tell, did not. The former was "Good-Time Charlie" Wilson of Texas. The Hollywood movie *Charlie Wilson's War* is based on his life. The latter was John "Blackjack" Murphy of Staten Island, chair of the Merchant Marine and Fisheries Committee.

Wilson became interested in politics when his dog was killed in 1946. A neighbor, a local elected official, was upset that Wilson's dog had soiled his garden. He killed the dog by putting fine bits of glass into its food. Wilson, in an act of revenge, doused his neighbor's yard in gasoline and set it on fire. Then he borrowed his family's car to drive voters to the polls. Along the way, he said that while it wasn't his place to tell folks how to vote, they might like to know that the politician had killed Wilson's dog. The man not only lost the election but had to suffer through Wilson's post-election lecture on why he should never again harm a dog.

In Congress, Wilson was the wildest sumbitch ever to serve in the modern era. Yet the oddly lovable, womanizing, Scotch-swilling swashbuckler from Lufkin, Texas, got Congress to give the Mujahideen modern weapons that drove the Russians out of Afghanistan in 1989, thus helping bring down the Soviet empire.

Wilson sat two chairs up from me on the House Defense Appropriations Subcommittee for more than a decade. From that perch, I saw and (to an extent) helped him engineer what became the largest covert program in US history—$1 billion—despite the initial timidity of the CIA and the odd diffidence of the Reagan White House. And it was done entirely within the clandestine budget, with no publicly recorded vote ever taken.

I quickly came to know and like the complex Charlie Wilson—the private and public man—who was at once more disturbing and charming than either his movie incarnation or the figure described in the book of the same title that inspired the film.[1] He was a long-legged, ramrod-straight Naval Academy graduate with a square jaw, wicked wit, and booming *basso profundo* laugh. In his Arlington, Virginia, condo overlooking the Iwo Jima Memorial, the Potomac River, and the Capitol Mall beyond, Wilson entertained elegantly, soirees that I suspected were funded by his friends in the defense lobby.

That he had so many such friends, and carried their mail so brazenly, was one of Wilson's many deep flaws. I recall him in committee losing a debate on a dubious weapons system that even Defense Secretary Caspar Weinberger didn't want (and *that's* saying something). Wilson held up the vote long enough to duck into the telephone booth and emerge with fresh talking points from the arms maker. I don't remember if on his second try he won or lost; the point is that Wilson was butt-naked complicit with the defense lobby and didn't give a damn. You'd think a man like that would be irredeemable. But I admired Wilson for defying his Bible-thumping conservative district and its history of racial bigotry. He was a strong supporter of civil rights, minimum-wage increases, Medicaid, and anti-poverty programs.

On women's issues, Wilson was a dependable yes vote. He supported abortion rights, parental leave, and the Equal Rights Amendment. Yet the hedonist in him collected women like a boy might collect marbles. His office staff was exclusively female, drop-dead beautiful, and full bosomed. Everybody called them "Charlie's Angels."

In the movie, a visiting constituent glances at those aides and asks Tom Hanks (Wilson) why all the women he hired were gorgeous. Hanks's reply is one I heard Wilson use in real life more than once: "You can always teach 'em to type, but you can't teach 'em to grow tits."

Aside from constituent service and stellar votes on social and economic issues, Wilson's individual legislative efforts were unremarkable for many years. However, in the late 1970s he engaged in an act of foreign policy hubris that, seen now, foretold his Afghanistan adventure.

Ever the Annapolis man, Wilson admired the Nicaraguan strongman, Anastasio Somoza, a West Point graduate, and threatened to wreck the Carter Administration's Panama Canal treaty if Carter didn't resume support for the dictator. Wilson arranged a meeting between Somoza and a high-ranking CIA official in a bid to save the tyrant. But when Somoza fondled Tina Simons, Wilson's girlfriend at the time, Wilson dropped him like a dead armadillo. (Fascism was one thing; a man's *woman* was another!)

I've always believed that Wilson's single-minded support for the subjugated Afghans came in equal measure from a zest for danger, revulsion at Communism, and empathy for a people who told him of daughters raped, children mutilated, sons and fathers decapitated, and pregnant women bayoneted in the stomach. He said they would fight the Russians with stones if necessary.

They didn't have to.

Wilson forced the United States to ship surface-to-air infantry missiles, commonly known as "Stingers," to the Mujahideen. The rebels' skill with the advanced weapon virtually drove Soviet helicopter warships and fixed-wing aircraft from the skies, the beginning of the end for the Soviet occupation and the first military defeat for their armed forces.

Wilson traveled frequently to the region as modern arms began to arrive. Inevitably, he would bring along a personal cache of booze and a beautiful woman on his arm. Sex, war, and alcohol were the trifecta in the hierarchy of Wilson's tastes.

Wilson stormed home from one such trip with blood in his eye. A US Air Force colonel had banned his female companion from flying out of Pakistan with him on a government plane. Wilson and the officer almost came to blows before Wilson placed one call to the presidential palace in Islamabad. Soon, General Mohammad Zia-ul-Haq's personal jet arrived, picked up Wilson and his date, and roared off, leaving the American colonel slack-jawed on the tarmac.

Wilson would get his revenge in the Defense Appropriations Subcommittee. He passed an amendment (over my objection) to remove the officer's plane. And just to make sure the colonel and his superiors got the message, Wilson's measure reassigned the jet to the Texas Air National Guard.

In a larger sense, the Afghan issue brought out brilliant legislative skills few knew Wilson possessed. There's a scene in the movie—true to life—in which he promises Midwest congressmen, in return for their support, to deliver the Congressional Black Caucus votes for the Farm Bill, a political act as unnatural as the physical act Wilson told the air force colonel to perform on himself.

Wilson retired from Congress in 1996. Three years later, he married Barbara Alberstadt, a former ballerina, and returned home to Lufkin, Texas. He died there on February 10, 2010, at the age of seventy-six. He was buried two weeks later at Arlington National Cemetery with full military honors.

In life, Wilson disturbed me with his antics and cracked me up with his wit. I can't decide if he was a good bad guy or a bad good guy. However, he never hurt anyone who was in need. And he was my friend.

Then there was the John "Blackjack" Murphy of Staten Island, a toxic guy with elegant edges who drew people to him. Affable. Articulate. Urbane. Self-confident in a way that suggested his West Point pedigree with a Patton flair. I never asked anyone how he got his nickname. Maybe I didn't want to know. When people speak of black Irish, a term with ambiguous roots, they usually have in mind someone who looked like Jack Murphy—walnut hair, ebony eyes, and a complexion with an olive undertone. Murphy turned the head of more than one tourist when he strode from his office across the Capitol grounds to the House floor. There, you could tell who was influential by the reduction of background chatter when members spoke. When Jack Murphy spoke, the House chamber grew quiet.

Murphy was chair of my House Merchant Marine and Fisheries Committee during four of my first six years in the Congress. When Murphy ascended to the chairmanship, he made it seem like predestination. Then he turned what had been a sleepy, obscure committee into a panel that had its say on the Panama Canal Treaty, US maritime law, and vast wildlife refuges in Alaska's outback.

Soon after he took the chair, heavy hors d'oeuvres began to show up in the staff room for the enjoyment of members. No one asked who picked up the tab. New committee staff aides arrived, wearing sleek clothes and professionally coiffed hair, a far different look than their pedestrian predecessors. The new aides responded quickly to Murphy's needs but seemed somewhat distant when committee members made requests.

In 1976, I was up for my first reelection. It would be tough because a lot of Republicans considered the district's first Democrat a prime target.[2] Enlisting the fund-raising assistance of House leaders would be important to stave off the Republican onslaught.

Right away, Murphy agreed to help.

About a week later, while House members milled noisily on the floor during a fifteen-minute roll-call vote, Murphy approached me with his million-dollar smile and thrust out his hand. When I shook it, I felt a wad in my palm. I knew it was cash, which was illegal as hell, but I was too stunned to move. Murphy winked and went on. I bumbled to a quiet corner of the Speaker's Lobby and sat down. At first, I couldn't open my fist. When I did, $4,000 lay in my palm—eight crisp five-hundred-dollar bills. Only an idiot would believe it came from anywhere but a special interest. If I had lodged a complaint in those days, it wasn't clear how—or if—the Ethics Committee would respond. If I merely winged Murphy, he could launch the mother of all retaliations. A gift to charity flashed across my mind. No. I'd still be culpable and, worse, drawn into Murphy's orbit. I had to return the money. When the next roll-call vote came around, I found Murphy sitting alone in the back of the chamber.

I offered a handshake of my own. "Jack," I said. "Sorry, but there's no way I can take this." With the wad gone, a huge weight had been lifted.

As I walked away, Murphy called out, "Back home, we call it 'walking around money.'" *Walking around money!* The stash equaled the entire budget of my first race for the Oregon legislature. Such criminal gifts must have happened with some regularity, which shocked me. So did the devil-may-care manner in which Murphy offered it. Where other men, such as Tip O'Neill, harbored foibles amid altruism, in Murphy I found a moral abyss. From then on, I stayed as far away from him as possible. In 1980, I moved to the Appropriations Committee.

Soon, Murphy also demonstrated a taste for dictators.

His roommate at West Point had been the right-wing Nicaraguan strongman, Anastasio Somoza. Somoza's rule was so ruthless, his plundering of the Nicaraguan treasury so catastrophic, that in the late seventies, President Jimmy Carter sent a high-level delegation to Managua at the height of the country's civil war to tell the besieged despot that the United States had withdrawn its aid and support.

When the president's diplomats were escorted into Somoza's palace, they saw a stunning sight: John "Blackjack" Murphy sitting at Somoza's side. The congressman's loyalty to his old roommate didn't stop history, though. Somoza was ousted and later assassinated by the Sandinista rebels. To no one's surprise, the Sandinista government loathed the United States for its decades of support for right-wing dictators.

In Murphy's 1978 reelection race, the *Village Voice* revealed more of his ethically challenged behavior.[3] He served on the corporate board of a front company for the Shah of Iran. The US Justice Department investigated him for playing middleman between the Shah and two oil companies that were willing to finance a Manhattan office in exchange for Iranian oil. He accepted an illegal campaign contribution from Tongsun Park of South Korea, a major figure in the 1976 scandal the media called "Koreagate." Working with Park, South Korea's Central Intelligence Agency allegedly funneled bribes and favors to ten congressmen, hoping to reverse President Richard Nixon's decision to withdraw troops from South Korea. No connection was ever made between Park's political contribution and favors performed by Murphy. (The House reprimanded three other congressmen; a fourth was unanimously cleared by the House Ethics Committee; and the statute of limitations expired for three others. One went to trial and was acquitted. One other, California Democrat Richard T. Hanna, pleaded guilty to conspiring to commit bribery and served one year of a six- to thirty-month federal prison sentence.[4])

Three years later, however, Murphy's high-flying act imploded. As a highly decorated platoon leader in the Korean War, a man of power and prestige in Washington, he had it all. But in 1980, the ABSCAM[5] scandal rocked the capital. The FBI videotaped Murphy and six other congressmen on separate occasions pocketing $50,000 bribes and illegal gratuities from undercover agents posing as Arab businessmen seeking legislative favors. The sting operation resulted in convictions of every bribe taker. Murphy served sixteen months in federal prison. When released, he lived out of the public eye until his death in 2015 at the age of eighty-eight.

On any given day, 435 life stories are unfolding under the dome of the US Capitol. Most, I still believe, are altruistic; some are vile. All are human.

Despite a swarm of highly compensated, grasping lobbyists seeking to affect the outcome of votes, our leaders are supposed to be exemplars of virtue. We forget that Congress is a pot of stew that intermixes almost every conceivable personal background and human trait. Its men and women are chosen from vastly different corners of the nation on the basis of the voters' hopes, anger, biases, good will, hatreds, or whims at a given moment called Election Day. As Winston Churchill observed, "Indeed, it has been said that democracy is the worst form of government except for all the other forms that have been tried from time to time."[6]

Power magnifies temptation even in the best of leaders. In Washington, streams of temptations come in guises from subtle to blunt. Some in power succumb. Sycophants are like flies drawn to honey, befriending and fawning over leaders not because of *who* they are but *what* they are and expecting consideration in return. I've seen them turn men and women into moral pretzels. This may explain Blackjack Murphy. He could have suffered what some psychologists call "criminal superoptimism," [7] wherein people of unusual ability reach a tipping point and come to believe they are infallible, that the rules don't apply to them, that the risk of being caught is the next best test of their superiority. Others are simply evil.

Whatever the case, we elect them, saints and scoundrels alike. If we make a mistake, we can throw them out. If election rules are skewed, we must fight to change them. Otherwise, we're culpable. Because Cassius was right: "The fault, dear Brutus, is not in our stars, but in ourselves."

24
Alaska Beckons the Father's Son

I arrived in Alaska almost exactly forty years after my father escaped there from my family. It was my first visit. More remarkable, at forty-five, I was nearly my dad's age when he died, broken and alone in Los Angeles. My father had eyed Alaska as a place to be part of the federal government's frenetic development of the territory in 1947. My purpose in 1987 was just the opposite—to prevent development in the pristine coastal plain of the Arctic National Wildlife Refuge (ANWR).

Covering nineteen million acres of Alaska's north coast, ANWR is the largest protected refuge in the United States. It is also home to thirty-seven species of land mammals, eight species of marine mammals, forty-two fish species, and more than two hundred migratory bird species. Established in 1960 to protect its extraordinary wildlife, the Arctic Refuge is a place where natural processes have, until recently, remained essentially uninfluenced by humans.[1]

In the eighties, the Reagan administration asked Congress to open 1.5 million acres of the biologically diverse coastal plain to oil production. The move triggered an epic battle between pro–oil industry conservatives and conservationists determined to protect the calving grounds of North America's largest herd of migratory caribou, as well as large populations of polar and grizzly bears, musk oxen, wolves, arctic foxes, and millions of migratory birds.

To block Reagan and the oil industry, Congressman Morris Udall of Arizona introduced a bill to designate the area as federally protected wilderness. Wilderness status affords the highest level of land protection under US law, prescribing its landscapes as a place "where man himself is a visitor who does not remain."[2] No roads, structures, or motorized or mechanized vehicles are permitted in a wilderness.

Alaska's lone US congressman, Don Young, a tobacco-chewing fur trapper, simultaneously pushed a bill to permit oil exploration and development in the region. According to independent estimates, exploitation of ANWR as envisioned by Young would generate an amount of crude oil equal to the country's total petroleum consumption for more than a year, at an estimated value of $251 billion. The figure did not include secondary economic benefits to Alaska and nearby states, including Oregon, where Portland's struggling shipyards stood to gain substantial ship-repair work. Port officials had made this more than clear to me.

In politics, this situation is known as being in a tight-assed spot. For years, I was the go-to man in the Oregon delegation for Portland's shipyards. On the other hand, I had helped write the Alaska National Interest Lands Conservation Act in 1980, which created ANWR. Although my heart was with the Udall bill, I owed it to my state to see the refuge before deciding how to vote. British Petroleum paid half the cost of my trip, and the Sierra Club paid the other. Kevin Lynch, my natural-resources aide, came with me.

The Arctic Refuge is the nave of a vast natural cathedral and the wide blue sky its ceiling. Having arrived in early October, before autumn's first snow, we helicoptered over the refuge, over undulating herds of caribou under the *chop, chop, chop* of our copter. Wildflowers had sprung up with lichen on the rocky expanse. The beauty of the place was at once harsh and vulnerable. Flying over miles of tundra, tracks from a World War II jeep were visible below us, untouched for more than forty years. If the land had not recovered from a single pass of a two-thousand-pound army jeep, how could it endure the heavy machinery and vehicles involved in drilling and pumping a hundred thousand barrels of oil a day?[3]

We spent many hours in briefings by the Bureau of Land Management and British Petroleum, listening to how oil could be safely extracted from what could be the largest field in North America.

When the tour was over, Kevin and I clambered aboard our plane for our return to Anchorage. It was a Markair 737 reconfigured to carry cargo but for a few dozen passenger seats. When we buckled in, the flight attendant asked us if we wanted drinks. Kevin asked for Tanqueray gin and tonic. "Two," I chimed. "Make them doubles." The sun was setting as our plane prepared to depart Deadhorse, Alaska, for the state capital. When we had lifted off, I asked Kevin for his opinion about the oil and gas proposal. It was my practice to ask my aides to think through decisions I faced. It helped them grow. Kevin gave me a mischievous look and threw the question back to me, "What do *you* think?"

I parried. "I asked you first."

He hesitated, figuring, he said years later, that I was testing him.

"Nah," he answered, with a broad Irish grin. I would have been disappointed with any other response.

I tossed my head back in laughter. "Nah," I agreed. Then I took a hearty quaff of my drink. No cocktail tasted better.

I would disclose my decision about ANWR to Bob Woodell first. Woodell was the Port of Portland's new executive director, a brilliant member of the original executive team at Nike. He had thrown himself into the stern task of making the Port of Portland a winning competitor against other Pacific Coast ports. It was no easy challenge; Portland's harbor and shipyards lay upriver on the Willamette near its confluence with the Columbia, about a hundred miles from the sea. Ship-repair work from ANWR's development looked to be a never-to-be-repeated opportunity to offset that geographical disadvantage. I admired Woodell. His zeal and keen mind mirrored his courage in not letting a spinal cord injury bar him from success, despite his confinement to a wheelchair. "I am what I am, and what the world has made me," he had said shortly after he fractured his spine in the sixties. "I may never walk again, but I have a loving family, and I can focus on what's important. I will live with that."

You hate to disappoint a man of that caliber. But I had to.

"Bob," I began, "I'm breaking this to you first, privately, because I respect you and what you're doing at the port." I explained that carving out time for the four-day trip was a measure of how seriously I took the issue. That said, having seen the refuge and having all my questions answered by British Petroleum, the Bureau of Land Management, and environmental experts, I was convinced the region's ecological values far outweighed arguments for development. I went on to describe the flora and fauna, the fragility of the ecosystem, the more than forty-year-old tracks on the tundra.

When I finished, Woodell looked up at me with a smile that lit his eyes. He replied, "You've done your homework, congressman. We can't expect or ask for more." It was remarkable. The man might have had a broken body, but his integrity was strong as an oak.

I wish I could say that all my constituents were as tolerant of disagreement as Bob Woodell. They weren't. Yet in those days, I had noticed a political paradox. If I told it like it was—if I said to constituents, "This is what I believe; these are the reasons I believe it; we may disagree, but I have too much respect for you to blow smoke"—I won almost as much regard from voters who disagreed with me as those who concurred.

It was similar to physics, if that's imaginable. Opposite magnetic poles attract. Physics does not, of course, govern human behavior, but you'd be surprised how often disagreement, if honestly and respectfully stated, may appeal to a voter on the other side of an issue.

Since my day, of course, shout radio, *Fox News*, and tidal waves of negative campaign spending have pushed most Americans into the trenches of an ideological civil war. Politicians risk fury from their base if they deviate from the accepted script. Yet something tells me that more than a few of us still respect a leader who, out of principle, sails into the wind. A leader, that is, who says, "If my stance makes you want to vote against me, then do it. This seat is yours, not mine; I'm just holding it in trust. If you at least appreciate the thought I've given to the issue, though, I hope you'll consider that I'm doing the job I was elected to do."

It's harder, today. But not impossible.

25

It Wasn't Misogyny, but It Wasn't Good

My compass pointed to respect for women, and Peter Reilly knew it.

The young congressional staffer had seen something he didn't like but kept it to himself until he knew I was alone in my office. Then he cracked open the door.

"Boss, could I see you for a minute? It's important."

Reilly wore his trademark sunny smile, but something seemed awry. "Sure, Pete," I said. "Take a seat." I was fond of this upbeat Princeton grad who, from his first day, had been a popular member of my staff. I motioned to my informal sitting area.

"I'm afraid this is sensitive," Peter said. "No one saw me come in."

I rang Bob Crane, my chief of staff, whose desk was just off the back door to my office. "Bob, no interruptions for a while, OK?" Crane didn't need an explanation.

Turning to Reilly, I was concerned. "You alright, Pete?"

"It's not me," he replied, starting to redden. "It's about the women in the back office."

I doubted this was going to be about anything good.

Reilly reached his hand toward me, as if to keep me seated. "I love working here, Les. We're doing great stuff."

"But the women, Pete?" My trepidation was growing.

Reilly's face flushed. "I really don't want to get anyone in trouble. This has been eating at me for a while. I hope . . . all these people are friends . . . I don't want to hurt . . . like to keep this private . . . I felt I could talk to you."

"Of course," I said. Knowing Reilly, this had to be important. "What is it?"

"It started with the *Sports Illustrated* swimsuit edition," he began, referring to an annual issue that almost rivaled *Playboy* and *Penthouse* for the exposure of female flesh. The magazine was one of several dozen delivered unsolicited in every Congressional office. It arrived with all others in the mail that landed on the interns' shared desk each morning for sorting.

"Every year it sets off a commotion. Guys play keep-away with it and stuff. Then they go on and on, saying crude and vivid things about the models' body parts. Now sexual banter has become routine. It's just out of character for this office."

"What do the women say?"

"They try to keep their heads down. If they object, the guys are like, 'Hey, can't you take a joke?' Or, 'I'll bet you could compete.' Les, the women haven't complained to me. But I know they're uncomfortable. I'm no prude, but this is wrong. It took me awhile, but I had to come to you."

Reilly couldn't tell, but I was furious. "I admire that, Pete. It can't have been easy for you to come in. You can go. I'll take care of this."

I sat alone, fuming, for several minutes. Sexist behavior was common in many Capitol Hill offices and still is. But I had not encountered it in my shop.

Goddammit! Who did they think ... !?! In this *office?!*

My male legislative aides were good men. As I thought back on it, though, I had detected an occasional bit of machismo. Still, I was surprised any were capable of pulling such crass stunts in front of their female colleagues.

I let work continue in the office for four or five hours. I wanted to put distance between Reilly's meeting and my response. At five o'clock, I told Crane I wanted every male on the staff to come to my office immediately. No exceptions.

Within minutes, eight of them filed in, looking quizzical. Reilly and Crane came too. This was one time when even Crane, my right arm, was in the dark. I knew only a few were culpable, and I had a good idea who the lotharios were without Reilly having to name them. By summoning them all, the perpetrators could save face. It also would make it difficult to identify the informer.

I swiveled my chair around from my desk and moved out a few feet to close the distance between us. There, I waited with a stone face and my chin resting on steepled fingers until everyone was present. No one uttered a word. They knew something was up.

"Gentlemen," I said. "Take a seat."

I looked each of them in the eye. Then dropped the hammer.

"I am a feminist," I began. "I despise sexism. My mom was a single parent in the forties and fifties. In those days, a divorcee often was seen as a loose woman. When Mom waited tables, men sometimes would shame her with sexual innuendoes. I have a daughter. And a wife. I have sworn that I'll never let them suffer what my mom did. Mom didn't have someone to spare her from sexist humiliation. But the women on this staff do. *Me*. Some of you are making sexist comments within earshot of the women of this office. They don't object anymore, because you shamed them for 'not taking a joke,' didn't you? Don't blame them, by the way. They haven't talked to me. They have no idea what I'm telling you. So let me put this as bluntly as I can:

"I. Am. Outraged.

"This isn't the boys' gym. It's a place where wrongs are corrected, not created. This stuff stops *now*. If it happens again, I'm throwing the guy who does it out the door. I don't care what position he has, what his value may be to the organization, or how long he has worked here—if he does it, I'll fire him on the spot."

I paused and panned the room.

Silence. They were looking at the floor.

"Do I make myself clear?"

They just nodded, even the oldest of them.

"Then get back to work."

They filed out the door like pups.

Twenty-five years later, Peter Reilly sent me a letter. By then he was a husband and father. This is what he wrote:

> I remember thinking how perfect your response was. The problem ended immediately, and you gave us a strong and powerful message. But you did it in a way that everyone had more respect for you after the incident was over, rather than some kind of anger or festering resentment toward you. To me, that was leadership. That back office was very quiet for a few hours afterward. But the problem never came up again.

Another observer might think I overreacted. After all, no real harm was intended. But almost thirty years later, the columnist Charles M. Blow of the *New York Times* put into words what drove me that day. He wrote in response to the dreadful behavior of Bill Cosby, Bill O'Reilly, Harvey Weinstein, and too many other American males:

> I must follow the advice on sexism that I proffer on racism: If you are not actively working to dismantle it, you are supporting it. It is not sufficient to simply not be a sexist yourself if you are a man. You must also recognize that you benefit from the system of sexism in ways to which you may not even be aware.
>
> Every man must become a feminist. Every man must work as hard as every woman to elevate gender equality and to eliminate gendered violence.[1]

It's a code to live by.

26
Abortion Rights

I have no idea when life begins.

At the moment of conception? Birth? Or as my friend, a rabbi's wife, said, only when the kid finishes college and moves out of the house?

The serious answer, of course, is found in a moral code.

But whose code?

Not mine, I say. Or any other politician's.

It must be the one held by the woman who faces an abortion choice. The government has no business intruding in this. For years, though, Congress has done just that, imposing its patriarchal will on women who are poor and depend on government-funded Medicaid. For the longest time, however, lawmakers avoided the wrath of the wives and daughters of middle-income families who enjoy nonsubsidized health care and vote regularly.

"No taxpayer-funded abortions!" was the continuing demand of the antiabortion movement. Yet federal workers, including the military, were free to make abortion choices in private clinics with their taxpayer-provided salaries. It was an inconsistency the antichoice lobby and its congressional allies chose to ignore. Better to use high office to pick on the poor and weak. They can't fight back. That, at least, was the state of play in my time—the late eighties and nineties, and into the 2000s.

Then Donald Trump won an Electoral College victory, and the anti-abortion movement instantly became more dangerous.

With two appointments in his first term, Trump gave the Supreme Court a conservative majority for the first time in fifty years. Emboldened by a presumed antiabortion court majority, the antiabortion movement now seeks an outright ban on legalized abortion, be it taxpayer funded or paid for privately. It intends to use the high court to accomplish this. Potential cases are working their way up through the judicial system now. In Ohio, the movement helped pass a law that would outlaw abortion at the first sign of a fetal heartbeat. That can be as early as five or six weeks into a pregnancy, before many women know they're pregnant.[1] The statute makes no exception in cases of rape or incest. Prison penalties await physicians who would ignore the law. Similar action is occurring in other states and with the same aim: to get the Supreme Court to roll back nearly fifty years of precedent and overturn *Roe v. Wade*, the landmark decision protecting a woman's right to choose.

In my day, I seethed when I listened to self-styled paladins of probity justify such an ideology, one that traumatizes millions of women.

In Congress, bullying those who favor abortion rights had been going on since 1976, when it outlawed Medicaid funds to end a pregnancy unless the life of the mother was at risk. By the time I got involved, every attempt to repeal the harsh measure had failed badly. Yet no amount of peer pressure could silence the advocates of a woman's right to make her own choices.

One day on the House floor, I sat through a debate on one of these amendments for the umpteenth time. Abortion rights congresswomen implored their colleagues to understand the agony a woman endures when she considers ending her pregnancy or physically goes through the procedure and is often haunted by the necessity of her decision. The urgency and dignity of their entreaties stirred something inside me. In contrast, the antiabortion leaders—mostly men— seemed smug about their power. I could almost hear them saying they knew what was best for the women of their country.

Before I knew it, I was speaking on the floor.

I recited an article about a prochoice woman who had discussed politics over lunch with her friend, a priest. The priest urged her to be "more understanding" of antiabortion activists. The woman was appalled.

"*Understand*, padre?" she said. "I understand that a middle-income woman can afford a safe abortion, and a poor woman cannot. I understand that a wealthy woman can be confident her personal choices remain private, and a poor woman cannot. I understand that one of us can get up from this table and give abortion not another second's thought. And one of us can never do it at all."[2]

I concluded: "It sickens me to watch this virtually all-male body making private choices for helpless women. I refuse to take it anymore without joining the fight."

Geraldine Ferraro, then the Democratic congresswoman from New York, came up to say she'd never heard a more empathetic speech from a man. Her compliment was the beginning of a wonderful friendship.

In July 1989, the world turned. The US Supreme Court upheld a Missouri law that "a government's decision to favor childbirth over abortion through the allocation of public funds does not violate *Roe v. Wade*."[3] It was the so-called *Webster* decision. It removed all doubt: opponents were free to make abortion a legislative football in cases where the woman received government-assisted medical care. (In *Roe v. Wade*, the court had been silent about cases involving government funds.[4])

Webster was a bombshell for the pro-choice community. It narrowed *Roe v. Wade* and shattered the assumption that the court would shield from politics a woman who wanted to control her body.

If it hadn't been clear, it was now; if poor women were to have a privacy shield, only legislators could provide it. Female government employees might be vulnerable too. It was clear that abortion rights advocates had to become more political than ever. The strength of antiabortion forces lay in the fact that their base tended to be single-issue voters. In response, pro-choice advocates moved to make abortion rights a litmus test, too.

The stage was set for a collision.

It came quickly.

A month after *Webster*, one of the most conservative members of the House tripped the wire.

Robert Dornan of California tried to amend the District of Columbia Appropriations Bill. He proposed to bar the city's government from using public funds—federal or local—for abortions involving victims of rape or incest. *Webster* was the wind beneath his wings.

The abortion rights forces, however, had become a formidable and organized bipartisan bloc. As the only member of the group who served on the Appropriations Committee, I led the House floor debate, staffed by my aide, the able Rachel Gorlin.

The *Webster* decision, I argued, reshaped the political landscape, "leading those of us who defend a woman's freedom of choice to draw a line in the sand, a line of decency, a line of fair play, and a line of serious politics."

As the House chamber grew still, I pressed on. "This is going to be a war fought in every precinct, in every district, in every state of this Union. It is a war that revolves around one question: Who decides? Who decides

160

the most personal, most private, most torturous decision a woman could be called on to make perhaps in a lifetime?"

A year earlier, I had asked one of Dornan's antichoice colleagues what his attitude would be if, God forbid, his daughter had been impregnated by a rapist. Congressman Chris Smith of New Jersey replied that he and his wife would want their daughter to produce the child.

I argued that, unlike Congressman Smith, if that nightmare were to happen in my family, I would not want my daughter's fate to be decided by him or any of the other 434 members of the House. It should be up to her—"her conscience, her judgment, her sense of morality, and her good sense. I do not think Mr. Dornan or anyone else in the House has the right to tell her what she must do."

I told my colleagues, "That line in the sand? If you cross it today—if you support this amendment—you will be held accountable in ways you have never dreamed possible at ballot boxes all over this country. The prochoice movement is mobilized. And from this day forward, it is going to take names and kick . . . ankles."

Hours later, the House rejected the 1989 Dornan proposal, 219–210. It was the first time in ten years that an antiabortion amendment had been defeated in the House. In October of that year, we defeated another antichoice amendment 216–206, this one on the Labor, Health, and Human Services Appropriations Bill.

President George H. W. Bush vetoed both bills because of our abortion rights language. But the prochoice bloc had demonstrated political muscle that changed the political equation. No longer could abortion rights legislators be regarded as pests who squandered the Congress's time.

When Bill Clinton replaced Bush in the White House, the full abortion ban was nearly defeated. But Henry Hyde, a Republican from Illinois, scraped up enough votes on both sides of the aisle to institute a modified ban, exempting not just mothers whose health was endangered, but, for the first time, victims of rape and incest, two groups he had previously refused to exempt.

The vicissitudes of politics produced conservative congressional majorities in 2010. They continue in the Senate today, and abortion restrictions have returned for poor women. They are attached to appropriations bills that must be renewed each year.

For sheer wackiness, nothing surpasses the oratory engendered by the abortion issue in the eighties. It captured the thinking of some of the most feverish anti-abortion zealots.

William Dannemeyer, a reactionary Republican from Southern California, told the House it couldn't make an informed decision on abortion without considering fiscal policy.

"If we are going to pay off (the national) debt," he declared, "somebody has got to be born to pay the taxes to pay it off. Now, since 1973, the decline in the birth rate per fertile female has reached the point where, as a civilization, we run the serious risk of disappearing from the face of this planet. . . . In the last few years, the rate of reproduction per fertile female is 1.8. Demographers tell us we need 2.1 to sustain a civilization."[5]

The House seemed stunned. Even Dannemeyer's archconservative colleagues appeared unable to believe what they heard.

Barbara Mikulski, the Maryland liberal, pinned Dannemeyer's ears back. "I am shocked," she said, "to hear that American women are meant to be breeder reactors to sustain civilization and pay off the deficit."[6]

Today, the seething debate is about to reach its apogee. The high court and the nation at large will likely face an existential issue: are women private individuals, able to control their bodies, their destiny? Or are they human incubators?

Roe v. Wade. If that decision is overturned, all women will suddenly lose their legal right to choose. Then what?

Will desperate women be forced back to an era when they can find relief only by breaking the law? Will abortion providers be subject to criminal penalties?

More fundamentally, will voters draw a line in the sand first? A line of decency, fair play, and serious politics? Will they rise in indignation against the hypocrisy of "prolife" politicians who oppose programs like child nutrition, infant health care, and early childhood education? I hope so. Because former congressman Barney Frank of Massachusetts was right when he said, "Pro-lifers who oppose abortion while voting against infant-nutrition programs seem to believe life begins at conception and ends at birth."[7]

27
Lady 'Rasslers

My commitment to women's rights was sorely tested at an early age when I was an army private at Fort Campbell.

In basic training, I had to crawl on my belly under barbed wire while machine gun fire screamed inches above my head. But nothing there began to prepare me for a professional wrestling ring facing someone I would never have expected to confront.

You may wonder how a nice boy like me could have gotten into a pro wrestling ring.

At the time, I had the same thought.

I had parlayed my journalism experience into a job as a columnist at the base's weekly newspaper. One of my articles was a profile about an offbeat sergeant who soldiered by day and, by night, promoted pro wrestling throughout Tennessee and Kentucky. The guy loved my write-up so much he proposed a deal. At twenty-five bucks a pop, he would pay me to write an article in local papers to promote an upcoming card and follow it with a blow-by-blow account of the action.

Two stories a week. *Sweet.* Eager to grow up fast, I was not inclined to turn down an offbeat experience. Certainly not when it meant earning some extra scratch.

Trouble arrived at my first outing.

As I pulled up to the night's venue, the old armory in Hopkinsville, Kentucky, I noticed a banner announcing that the main event featured "'rasslin' ladies." News to me. I walked into the armory and saw that the idea of screaming, hair-pulling female wrestlers had drawn a boisterous crowd— bib overalls, summer smocks, flattops, and pigtails.

In the locker room, Sarge paced like a caged puma. "Ring announcer didn't show," he snarled. "Ya'll have to do it." He looked straight at me.

Do what, I wanted to know. Introduce the wrestlers from a written script. Okay. Ring the bell to end the rounds. No-brainer. This was it? Grounds for a good bonus.

I should state here that I was nineteen but looked like a fifteen-year-old with the body of a dry noodle. Off-duty, I wore slacks and thin sixties-era neckties to look mature. In the South, however, I came off as a Yankee Sassypants.

When it was time to man up, I stood at midring and introduced bout after bout without a hitch, except for what could have been mild snickering in the audience. With authority, I rang the bell at ringside at the end of each round. Soon I was enjoying the work in a lowbrow way.

Then came the night's finale, pitting two "ladies" against each other. They played their parts beautifully. Both climbed through the ropes and pranced around the ring. The blonde in white tights and shoes lofted her arms to deafening cheers. She didn't need to wear a white hat to cue the crowd that she was the heroine. Her foe for the evening was a brunette dressed appropriately in all black. The crowd jeered. She scowled, threw them a one-finger salute, and drove them into hysterical boos.

As I introduced the women and turned the show over to the referee, I looked out at the audience. Tonight, they were being served up a full combination plate.

The ensuing morality play between Snow White and the Black Baroness ebbed and flowed through three rounds, which I signaled with the bell at courtside, sitting smartly on a stool next to the ring. Virtue and Evil entered the last round locked in a tie with one pin apiece. With the match hanging in the balance, the she-devil forced the crowd's darling to within a whisker of a pin.

Then, in what may have been an act of our Lord and Savior, Snow White let loose a surge of power, flipped her foe to the floor, and fell on top of her for the win. The victor left the ring on a wave of cheers while her victim protested vehemently to the referee. The ref at last threw up his arms and climbed through the ropes for the locker room. He left the sweat-soaked loser pulling the ropes and swearing at the crowd.

The paper cups, spit wads, programs and other debris rained down on the woman, but it seemed to enrage her further. Fifteen minutes passed. The Black Menace was now standing on the bottom rung of the ring, shrieking, swinging her fists, and threatening the crowd.

It dawned on me that, perched on my little ringside stool, I was the only official in an auditorium verging on mob violence. What to do seemed obvious: To make the ersatz performance seem real, I had to step up into the ring.

I climbed through the ropes and straightened my tie. Then I made a beeline to the Black Baroness.

"This fight is over," I shouted, pointing to the locker room. "Get to the shower!"

For a moment, bloodshot orbs held me in their gaze. Then the image of a bossy young Yankee came into focus, and she went into a fury. *Now, there's a real performer*, I thought. Just then, with a primordial shriek, she started after me, a fact that struck me as more than the script required.

I backpedaled quickly. The sweating hulk lunged. I jumped through the ropes. She vaulted over them. The playacting seemed over. Did she really want my blood? It appeared so when she hurled folding chairs at me as I ran and ducked. Zigging and zagging, I made it to the locker room and bolted the door behind me.

Sarge laughed along with the male wrestlers who, bitter enemies an hour earlier, were throwing playful punches at each other, enjoying the recreation I provided.

"I was trying to keep up the act for the audience!" I protested. "But your woman just tried to kill me!"

Sarge spit a plug of tobacco into a paper cup.

"Son," he drawled, "she was givin' our customers an hour of escape. What right do you have, messin' with an artist?"

Thus ended my first lesson in Kabuki acting. It was better than a lot of performance art I would come to observe in Congress.

"OK, officer, now you can have your plane!" As a member of the defense committee, I reassigned a fleet of F-16s to the Oregon Air Guard. To commemorate the transfer, I rode one of the fighters to Portland from Salt Lake City. Along the way, my pilot suggested doing a barrel roll. I said, "Maybe another time." Photo: AuCoin collection

[*Above*] The Darrar
family and friends. My
grandfather, Walter,
stands at the far left and
my grandmother, Hilda,
two to his left. My aunt
Jeanne, two to the left of
my grandmother, holds
her infant, Sonny. A few days
later, my grandparents and
my aunt's baby died in a
car wreck in Polk County.
Photo: AuCoin collection

[*Left*] With Congress
adjourned, Sue and I took
Stacy (*left*) and Kelly
(*right*) skating on the
Capitol Mall. Interregnums
between congresses offered
a two-month breather every
two years to focus on being
a family. Photo: AuCoin
collection

Having obtained funds for the Fort Clatsop Visitors' Center, I keynoted the celebration. Our Senate contest was more than a year away, but Bob Packwood invited himself to attend. The park ranger, Cynthia Orlando, sat between Packwood and me. She seemed eager for the event to end. Photo: AuCoin collection

In the late eighties, I fought for Medicaid funding for abortion in cases of rape or incest. In this photo, Sue, Stacy, and I, along with several congressional colleagues, helped lead a pro-choice march. Left to right: Sue, Les, Stacy, Ted Weiss, Barbara Boxer (CA), George Miller (D-CA), Tom Downey (D-NY), Howard Wolpe (D-MI), Anthony Beilenson (D-CA). Photo: AuCoin collection

Victory night, November 1974. At the age of thirty-two, I became the youngest congressman in Oregon history. I also was the first Democrat to ever win in the First Congressional District. Sue and I made sure Stacy and Kelly were with us for the moment. Photo: *Oregonian*

[*Top*] One month after the US and the PRC established diplomatic relations, I was the first congressman to lead a trade delegation to China. Four Oregon businessmen, their spouses, and Sue and I arrived in February 1979. Here I'm conferring with a vice chairman of the Standing Committee of the National People's Congress in Beijing. In 1978, I had brought to the floor of the US House the first bill to propose normal relations between the two countries. Photo: AuCoin collection

[*Left*] I gave my friend, Chinese ambassador Han Xu, a tour of the MAX light rail line when he visited Portland. After the slaughter in Tiananmen Square in 1989, I had a confrontation with the diplomat. I never saw him again. Photo: AuCoin collection

[*Right*] Sue and I were members of Speaker Jim Wright's 1986 mission to Moscow. At the Kremlin, I talked briefly to Mikhail Gorbachev about a bill I helped pass that banned flight tests on anti-satellite weapons. It was the first form of arms control ever conceived in and passed by Congress. Sue stands behind me. Photo: US House

Early in my career, I made the cross-country trip to Portland almost every Thursday, flying the red-eye back to Washington on Sunday. Airline staff would let me sleep for an hour in Chicago between flights. Once in Washington, I headed to the House gym for an 8 a.m. sauna and shower, slipped into fresh clothes, and worked until the House adjourned. Photo: AuCoin collection

Being outdoors was one of my great escapes from the cacophony of politics. Here I'm with friends, rafting the spring runoff on the Clackamas River. Photo: Bruce Forster

Congressman George Miller (D-CA) and I discuss our itinerary in Managua, Nicaragua. With us are Congressman Mike Lowry (D-WA) and Cindy Arenes, a Miller aide. George and I made multiple fact-finding trips to Central America in the 1980s to inspect human rights abuses of US-backed oligarchs in regional civil wars. Photo: AuCoin collection

My daughter Stacy and I finally rescued the Chernobelsky family, Soviet Refuseniks, from the Soviet Union in 1986, after I spent two years trying. As Jewish Refuseniks, Soviet authorities barred them from leaving the "Workers' Paradise." Left to right: daughter Elana (5), Mark, (12), mother Dina, and father, Naum. Photo: *Oregonian*

Grand Ronde tribal chair Mark Mercier answers skeptics in a tense hearing on my bill to restore the tribe's reservation. On Mercier's right is vice chair Kathryn Harrison. The hearing dispelled many scare-stories about the bill. Today the Grand Ronde is one of the most prosperous tribes in Oregon. Photo: AuCoin collection

During the spotted owl crisis in Oregon, congressional delegates and the governor met with timber company executives and environmentalists to find consensus on a plan to protect the owl and old-growth timber stands and lift a court injunction that had frozen all logging in the Northwest. Left to right: Les; Representative Denny Smith; Senator Mark Hatfield; Governor Neil Goldschmidt, Congressman Ron Wyden (behind Goldschmidt); and Congressman Peter DeFazio, forefront. Photo: Bob Warren

[*Right*] I converted my Volkswagen bus into an "office" during my first campaign for the Oregon House in 1970. Here, I pose for a news photo in downtown Hillsboro, while a volunteer works inside. In the end, I won a larger percentage of votes in my district than any other state, local, or national candidate. Photo: West Hills Photography

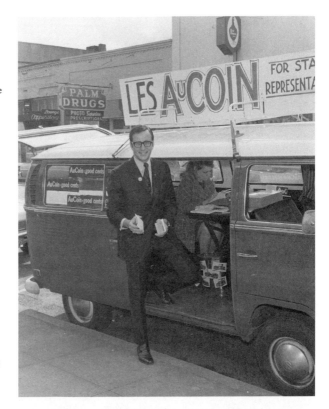

[*Below*] Sue and I arrive at the White House for the 1975 Christmas Ball. Entering the compound, our old VW bus sounded like a sputtering lawn mower. We had bought the rig ten years earlier and couldn't afford something new. Photo: US House

I scheduled regular town hall meetings across my district. It gave constituents a chance to ask questions and tell me what was on their minds. Today, many members of Congress conduct telephone "call-in" conferences by invitation and their aides screen out voters who might make the legislator uncomfortable. Photo: AuCoin collection

I am speaking to campaign volunteers on a casual weekend on the northern coast during my 1992 US Senate race. Building a statewide grassroots organization, group by group, was important to offset my campaign's fundraising disadvantage. Bob Packwood would outspend us 4 to 1. Photo: AuCoin collection

Fish in hand! On the Deschutes River north of Madras, on a perfect October day, a steelhead trout makes itself a gift to me. It was the first time I had hooked one of these iconic seagoing creatures. A keepsake memory. Photo: AuCoin collection

28
When I Kissed Off the NRA

One of the most rueful moments in my public life was my tactically peaceful coexistence with the gun lobby. By not standing up to the National Rifle Association and its allies from the beginning, I snarled my line but good. Courage had called for a cast both straight and true.

Historically, the Oregon congressional delegation's position on gun control was one of opposition as far back as anyone could remember. Even Oregon's Tiger of the Senate, Wayne Morse, opposed restrictions on guns.[1] For my part, though, I came to be ashamed of my stance. I am relieved that I atoned for it when I reached the peak of my influence in Washington.

I had always been uncomfortable with the National Rifle Association's extreme rhetoric and methods. On substance, though, I agreed that gun control wasn't crime control—a determined criminal could find a way to get a gun. Thus, I reasoned, why poke a political hornets' nest and provoke a fight that would dominate my time and energy in place of the issues I went to Washington to champion? I would discover that this was the same stance dozens of other western liberals adopted. Better not to antagonize the NRA. I never sought, wanted, or got the gun lobby's donations or endorsement. Their neutrality was enough.

At the time, the NRA had, and has now, a strong presence across my home state. In my district, there was a landmark I'll never forget, a gun store named Toys for Big Boys. When I did split with the NRA, it had sixty-two thousand members in Oregon, and there were perhaps 150 gun clubs in the state.

But split I did.

All this came down long before the gun mayhem of today.

Before the massacre at the Jewish synagogue in Pittsburgh.

Or the slaughter in Parkland, Florida.

Or Oregon's Umpqua Community College.

Or Sandy Hook Elementary School before that.

Or Columbine High School before that.

Or any of the multitude of tragic events in the ongoing series of mass shootings we see all too often on TV news.

For me, the tipping point came in 1991 with a US House vote on the Brady Handgun Violence Prevention Act or, as it came to be known, the Brady Bill. The bill by any measure was timid. It called for a simple seven-day waiting period while a background check could be run on firearms purchasers. But there were lots of exceptions. The waiting period, no major inconvenience for a normal buyer, would be phased out once a National Instant Criminal Background Check System could be set up. During the waiting period, authorities could identify and deny a purchase to the mentally disturbed, fugitives from justice, persons with a record of domestic abuse, or felons. This was no more a violation of the right to bear arms than the prohibition against yelling "Fire!" in a crowded theater violated the guarantee of free speech. More than 80 percent of the US public supported such commonsense restrictions.

But the public didn't have a political action committee.

The NRA did.

With its muscle, the NRA and its allies waged a relentless campaign against the bill. Through a barrage of phone calls to Capitol Hill offices and bolstered by television, radio, and newspaper ads; mailings; and in-person meetings, NRA lobbyists made sure every congressperson knew that on this vote, it was *Are you for or are you against the Second Amendment?*

To hear the NRA tell it, the bill was one step away from gun confiscation. The hyperbole angered me, but that was the least of it. I recoiled at the swagger of a lobby that rarely lost and seemed smugly certain that it had Congress's number.

In the previous year, I voted against the same bill, almost by rote. As soon as it was tallied, I felt like a moral pigmy. I had been wrong but couldn't take my vote back. But 1991 bought me a chance for redemption.

I decided that to come out for the Brady Bill, I wanted to inflict maximum political damage on the NRA and its allies. I went to work with Rachel Gorlin, my savvy press secretary and a superb editor. On March 18, as the roll-call vote drew ever nearer, I heralded my support for the bill in an op-ed published in the *Washington Post*.[2] By sailing into the wind, I wanted to kick up a gale that would give cover to House colleagues the gun lobby hoped to intimidate.

According to author Osha Gray Davidson, my op-ed hit Washington like a "tidal wave,"[3] which was what I'd hoped for. In rapid order, the NRA's previously impregnable dam sprang leaks everywhere. Three days after my essay appeared, a tearful father, Edward Prince, testified before a House committee while banks of TV cameras rolled. His son Christian, a nineteen-year-old Yale student, had been shot and killed in a robbery just a week earlier. Davidson described the hearing:

> When it was suggested the Brady Bill would violate the Second
> Amendment, the elder Prince, tears streaming down his face,
> demanded: "Was that a well-regulated militia that killed my
> son? There is only one infringement in this instance—namely,
> the infringement of Christian Prince's right to life, liberty, and
> property."[4]

From one of the deadliest neighborhoods in New York City, twelve busloads of residents arrived at about this time to lobby for the waiting period, gaining dramatic media coverage. They wore hats that read, "Seven Days Can Save a Life."

A few days before the showdown vote, I appeared on CNN's evening talk show, *Crossfire*, hosted by Michael Kinsley on the left and Pat Buchanan on the right. Their other guest, via satellite hookup from Los Angeles, was the outspoken gun-control opponent[5] and actor Charlton Heston, who had made dozens of movies, several on a Biblical theme.

With his rich baritone and broad shoulders, Heston magisterially took up the attack early, spurred on by the archconservative Buchanan. Heston intoned, "No one with a lick of sense thinks a waiting period is going to stop a criminal."

I replied, "I hate to disagree with Moses," gesturing to a bristling Heston on the monitor. "But he knows—or should know—that the state of New Jersey's waiting period has stopped thousands of felons. So let's drop the political blasphemy and let a good bill pass."

"The name's *Heston*," the actor snapped. He had lost his cool. For him, the show went downhill from there.

Now the NRA was losing ground fast. Jim Baker, one of its chief lobbyists, tried to pooh-pooh my gun reversal by saying I was never a big NRA supporter in the first place. This didn't surprise me, nor did it do much to reverse the tsunami surging against his organization and its allies.

For my part, I decided to adopt a political version of a Muhammad Ali rope-a-dope tactic: let your foe flail at you until pooped, then nail 'em with a right hook. Thus, I conducted a town hall meeting in Beaverton in which every constituent who had written me an anti–gun control letter got an invitation to attend. The ranters, as I anticipated, screamed their opposition while the TV cameras rolled. They had taken the bait. In return, for effect, I used a calm, patient voice to shoot down their hyperbolic arguments, one after another, also on camera. Thousands of Oregonians watched on television as the gun lobby supporters came off as a snarling mob. *Game, set, match.*

On March 19, 1991, a man stepped forward for the bill whom the NRA could not dismiss. In a speech at George Washington University, ex-president Ronald Reagan endorsed the Brady Bill, saying its waiting period "just makes common sense." That March marked the tenth anniversary of John Hinckley Jr.'s abortive assassination that wounded Reagan and permanently disabled his press secretary, James S. Brady, for whom the Brady Bill was named.

On May 8, 1991, with Reagan's crucial support, the bill passed the House, 239–186.[6]

It was one of the first gun-control measures to win House approval. More important, it reflected a tectonic shift in gun politics. Just three years earlier, the House had killed the same bill with forty-six votes to spare. The defeat of the invincible NRA was astounding.

The NRA did counter with a successful filibuster in the Senate, but it was a Pyrrhic victory. Two years later, the bill passed both the House and Senate and was signed into law by President Bill Clinton.

What good has it done? From November 30, 1998, through December 31, 2017, the Brady law has blocked nearly 1.5 million gun purchases, according to data from the National Instant Criminal Background Check System.[7]

That works out to just over 215 illegal gun purchases blocked every day. Over 975,000 of those attempted purchases were by felons or fugitives from justice, and more than 138,000 denials were to persons convicted of domestic violence.

Although I was no longer in office when Brady became law, I feel some ownership of its results. Observers said my change of mind in 1991 helped break the dike. I showed the NRA's vulnerability. Since then, Republican gun-lobby acolytes have controlled the Congress on the strength of unlimited dark money. They've protected themselves by gerrymandering their seats into safe districts. Just so, the NRA has become stronger than ever. In Donald Trump, they have a president who apes their talking points. He also wants to arm teachers. Me? I think what we should do with teachers is pay them.

It is risky to foretell the future. But a new politic might well have been released in the nation after the Parkland, Florida, school massacre and others that followed. Millennials are standing up, speaking up, and taking political action. For their generation, ending gun violence may be as politically consequential as ending the Vietnam War was to mine.

That scares the hell out of the NRA and its stable of politicians.

29
Housing, Woodsheds, and Bomb Shelters

For our work on housing legislation in November 1982, Jerry Patterson and I were summoned to the woodshed by Democratic leaders of the US House.

The tunnel from the Rayburn House Office Building seemed a lot longer than usual as Patterson and I trudged toward the fate awaiting us in the Capitol. The California Democrat and I were expecting an old-fashioned whupping.

The Speaker's messenger hadn't said what the House Democratic leaders wanted to discuss. He didn't have to. Patterson and I knew when you threaten to upset control of the House, you're playing with fire.

That wasn't our intention. Heck, I was one of Speaker Tip O'Neill's floor whips, a leadership position. But in the middle of the 1982 recession, the Democratic-led Rules Committee had inexplicably blocked floor consideration of the AuCoin-Patterson housing stimulus amendment while sending weaker anti-recessionary measures to the House.

"Reaganomics" had caused new construction starts to drop to the lowest level since the end of World War II. Our amendment would return tens of thousands of workers to their jobs, including many of the nearly 13 percent of Oregon's workers who had been idled.

In the House, strict rules of procedure apply. One of them prohibits enacting new laws within appropriations (funding) bills. Patterson and I had asked the Rules Committee to waive that proscription for our bill, knowing that the Rules Committee often did it to expedite friendly legislation.

We wanted to attach our bill as an amendment to the housing section of the Emergency Supplemental Appropriation, arguing that it addressed an economic crisis.

The Rules Committee's rejection was engineered by its chair, Richard Bolling of Missouri, a fifty-year House veteran with a huge store of self-regard and his own ideas about how the House should be run. His two failed bids for majority leader had done nothing to humble him.

When Patterson and I reached the elevator door in the Capitol's basement, I reflected, not for the first time, that if I'd picked anyone else as my cosponsor, I wouldn't be in this predicament. At first, Patterson had seemed perfect. He sat on the House Banking Committee's Housing Subcommittee, which had original jurisdiction over our bill. Normally, the subcommittee would send a bill like this rocketing to the floor, no rules waiver required. But I had overlooked something. A year earlier, Patterson tried and failed to defeat Henry B. Gonzales of Texas as chair of the subcommittee. The prickly founder of the Congressional Hispanic Caucus may have had his virtues, but forgiveness wasn't one of them. Gonzales refused to pass a single bill bearing Patterson's name.

Which left the Rules Committee as our option of last resort. It had the power to attach our bill to a funding bill. Rules Committee members seemed to receive us well at a hearing in which Patterson and I asked them to permit our bill as a floor amendment to the Emergency Supplemental Appropriation.

A few days later, the Rules Committee's rejection came down.

I got the word in my bed at Walter Reed Army Hospital, where doctors had sent me to treat a sudden flare-up of my kidney condition. The autoimmune disorder was not degenerative, but it had a habit of acting up at the most inopportune time.

The call came from a flabbergasted Bob Bannister. A Capitol Hill veteran, Bannister was senior staff vice president of government affairs with the National Association of Homebuilders. Our bill was his organization's top priority.

Propping my head up on my pillow, I thought I was hallucinating when Bannister gave me the news. Why would the Democratic-controlled Rules Committee thwart a bill by two senior Democrats aimed at attacking Reagan's recession? Soon I heard myself saying, "We've got to go get enough votes to defeat the rule."

To a layperson, such a maneuver might sound arcane. In the special world of the House, it was equivalent to the Great San Francisco earthquake of 1906. If we actually defeated the rule, Patterson and I would seize control of the floor from both the Rules Committee and House leaders. Once in charge, we could offer our amendment—or any other—and manage debate on both it and the underlying bill. House leaders would be rendered virtu-ally powerless.

In modern politics, I knew of the maneuver being pulled off only once, when Republicans sprang it on the Democrats to enact Ronald Reagan's revolutionary first budget plan. The wounds from that bitter brawl have not healed to this day.

Which explains why, on his end of the phone, my hubris left Bannister in a bit of shock.

"Really?" he asked.

A nurse was taking my blood pressure. I'd lay odds the reading was off the chart.

"Yes, really," I said.

"Look, find Patterson and you guys ask Tom Evans to round up Repub-lican votes." Evans, a Delaware Republican, was a housing enthusiast. I was betting he could get GOP votes if only to deal the Democratic leadership a defeat. But, hey, one favorable vote was as good as another. "The Home-builders should send a letter to every House member tonight," I said. "Call it the most important vote of the year. Ask Jerry to draft a 'Dear Colleague' letter signed by both of us to all Democrats. Tom can cover the Republicans. We've got to move fast."

Our success surprised even us. In record time, we got pledges from a House majority with votes to spare. We owned the votes to defeat Bolling and his rule and offer our own.

Patterson and I had no intention doing this. We just wanted enough votes to do so. Then, our party leaders would have to listen to us.

As we approached the double doors of the Speaker's room, we won-dered how angry our reception would be. They can control committee as-signments, expedite or delay one's amendments, share or withhold inside information, and generally help or hinder congressional careers.

The room looked like a star chamber. I almost wished I were back at Walter Reed.

The top three leaders, Speaker O'Neill, Majority Leader Jim Wright, and Majority Whip Tom Foley, sat beside each other at the far end. Two empty chairs awaited us at the other. Eddie Boland of Massachusetts, chairman of the Housing Appropriations Subcommittee whose legislation we threatened to shanghai, flanked us to our right. On our left sat Rules

Chairman Dick Bolling, who wore the lurid face of a man on the verge of either murder or a cerebral hemorrhage.

The majority leader asked us to explain ourselves. We did, making it clear why, with the economy in the tank, we had no other resort than to work against the Bolling committee when it denied us a reasonable chance to push our bill to put our constituents back to work.

Chairman Bolling broke in. "But it's just not proper *procedure*."

I couldn't hold back. "Dick," I said, "I've got unemployment in double digits. Half of the members of the Oregon District Council of Carpenters are out of work.[1] Frankly, their families can't eat 'proper procedure.'" For the longest moment, no one said anything.

The crisis was not limited to my congressional district, or even to Oregon or the West Coast. It was becoming a national calamity. Across the country, sales of existing homes had fallen by half over the previous three years, as had sales of new homes and building permits. Unemployment among construction workers had jumped to more than 22 percent in what was then one of America's six deepest recessions.[2]

Jim Wright rose and spoke. The majority leader hadn't tried to lay a glove on Patterson or me. Focusing on the imperious Bolling, he spoke in his best down-home Texas patois. "Now, Dick," he said softly, pausing for effect. "It looks to me like Les and Jerry, here ... (a gesture in our direction). .. have got the votes. And they surely do have a back-home problem." He ran a finger across his lips. His trademark eyebrows bounced up and down like birds about to take flight.

"It looks to me like we could do one of two things. We could . . . let them defeat the rule, but then where would we be?"

A swallow, suggesting deep thought.

"Or, Dick, you could take that rule there back to committee and . . . bring out another to make this housing thing in order . . . and our whole problem would go away. Now then, it's your call, Dick. A lot of our Democrats want to go home and tell folks they voted for that housing bill. But, like I said, it's entirely up to you."

A House veteran like Bolling knew what it meant when a majority leader spoke in those terms. He also had to have noticed that Tip O'Neill and Tom Foley remained mum, a message of its own. I marveled at Wright. By letting a proud man decide for himself, Bolling saved face. Bolling rose and grumbled that he'd do it. He was still mumbling as he left the room.

Within days, the appropriation cleared the House by a wide margin, and the Senate followed suit with an amendment identical to ours, introduced by Senator Richard Lugar, a highly respected Republican from Indiana. Next stop: the president's desk.

And a veto.

Such a big one to slip away.

President Reagan's accompanying message asserted, "We will not promote a housing recovery by going even deeper in debt. More red-ink spending will only make the housing recession worse."

I marveled at the president's hypocrisy. On ideas he opposed, he railed against red ink. But his tax cut for the wealthy and his military buildup, history's largest, had tripled the Gross Federal Debt from $900 billion to $2.8[3] trillion and it didn't bother him a bit. His budget also slashed domestic programs, including housing.[4] The administration's remedy for the arms race was to promote bomb shelters.

I wanted to ask Reagan, if we couldn't afford places to live in, how could we afford places to hide in? Would he have even understood the question? Thinking back to our White House meeting and remembering those vacant blues eyes, I answered my own question: probably not.

In Congress, such disappointments are more frequent than victories. One can work for hours, weeks, or months on strategies and maneuvers. When unforeseen obstacles pop up, you can pull off dazzling broken-field running. You can charge forward with everything you've got. But, despite your best effort, when you think you've got the Holy Grail, you sometimes lose. Victory is never final until the ink dries on a presidential signature. Folks who can't handle such disappointment don't last in Congress. To succeed, you have to release your disappointments and move on. In my case, even when I lost, I loved the chase, an intellectual exercise like no other in my experience. But I liked winning even better.

30
Rescue from the Soviet Union

I learned about Soviet persecution of a Ukrainian Jewish family, the Chernobelskys, from their Portland relatives and the broader Oregon Jewish community, which took up their plight as a cause. It was the late eighties, the Cold War had yet to thaw, and, inspired to save the four souls, I pushed myself into intrigue at the highest level of East-West relations. The effort would tax my imagination and require immense courage by each member of the extended Chernobelsky family. These included Raisa Premsyler, a physician who lives in Portland, her brother, Naum Chernobelsky, a Ukrainian husband and father, and Raisa and Naum's parents.

Raisa and the senior Chernobelskys had immigrated to Portland without incident in 1979. Other than another random act of bigotry against Jews, no one knows why Communist authorities barred Naum and his family from joining them. But they did. The Chernobelskys' escape to America was a daunting, arduous struggle—and the strangest, most vexing, and exhilarating experience of my eighteen years in Congress.

When I came into their world, Naum Chernobelsky and his wife, Dina, lived in Vinnytsya, an industrial city located 124 miles southwest of Kiev, with their two children, Mark, ten, and Elana, three. They were "refuseniks," four persecuted souls among many thousands of Soviet residents, mostly Jews, whose request to emigrate had been refused by anti-Semitic authorities. For trying to leave, Naum was fired from his career as a refrigeration engineer and imprisoned, typical treatment for refuseniks who wished to leave the "Worker's Paradise."

The story of Naum and his family, and how I leveraged my seat on the US House Defense Appropriations Subcommittee to spring the family free, is a story of perseverance and hope. Today, Naum and his family are naturalized American citizens who have resided in the metropolitan Portland area for the last twenty-eight years.

A Change of Committee

I had traded several years of House seniority for a junior seat on the Defense Subcommittee in January 1981, a decision that stunned some colleagues. One approached me while I lunched at the snack bar in the Democratic cloakroom. "Les," he said, "do you have a military post in your district?"

"Not one," I smiled, "except for small bases for the National Guard and Coast Guard." I knew where this was going.

"And military contractors," my colleague pressed, "Oregon has almost none?"

"Right."

"Then why on earth are you moving to the Defense Subcommittee?"

"Because," I replied, "the committee needs one member, at least, who sees the defense budget as a national-security blueprint, not a jobs bill." My colleague suddenly declared he had some business elsewhere and left. My decision to change committees also stemmed from America's disastrous involvement in the Vietnam War, which had made me a skeptic of military hubris.

Characterizing the insular Defense Subcommittee as a pork-barreling clique would be to put it charitably. The panel had long been a power center for congressional hawks representing districts dominated by defense contractors, military retirees, and active-duty military installations. Using my membership on the subcommittee, I could deny its members the luxury of rubber-stamping multi-billion-dollar weapons of mass destruction behind closed doors, some of which the Pentagon did not even want. Now the panel would have to debate and defend its actions. If I were beaten there, I could continue the fight on the House floor, where I would enjoy the same privileged standing they did.[1]

At about this time, the Reagan administration proposed developing and deploying several hundred "Peacekeeper" missiles, also known as the MX missile, a new first-strike, rail mounted intercontinental ballistic rocket with up to ten independently-targetable warheads, each capable of delivering a three-hundred-kiloton nuclear device. (By comparison, the yield of the atomic bomb dropped on Hiroshima in 1945 was fifteen kilotons.) A scarier, more destabilizing threat to the balance of terror between the United States and the Soviet Union could hardly be imagined. It all but guaranteed that a new, hideous chapter in the arms race was about to be touched off. I worked to help the House and Senate cap the number of MX missiles at fifty. It wasn't an outright kill, but no more MX missiles were ever deployed. All have since been decommissioned.

These battles and others drew media attention. On PBS's *MacNeil-Lehrer Report*, I went toe-to-toe with Richard Perle, an assistant secretary of defense, prominent neocon, and front man for the nuclear arms industry. Soon I got several invitations to speak about Reagan's military buildup, congressional efforts to restrain it, and events I had encountered on congressional visits to the Soviet Union.

Raisa Premsyler

At a meeting hosted by the Mittleman Jewish Community Center in Portland, I described the time my wife and I took a midnight ride on the floorboard of a US embassy car through the empty, snow-swept streets of Moscow. We and two other congressional couples had laid on top of each other and out of sight because we dared not attract attention on our way to a meeting with a group of refuseniks. Our drivers, two US Foreign Service officers, took us to a four-room apartment. There, thirty Jews of various ages had gathered to tell us their stories of state-sponsored repression. Despite their plight, they greeted us with beaming smiles and eager hugs. The aroma of turnips, potatoes, mutton, and tarragon drew our attention to a table filled with cooking and bottles of Russian vodka. Their warmth and generosity overwhelmed me; at the time, foodstuffs were difficult to come by in Moscow.

As our Foreign Service officers translated, we listened to stories of senseless repression. The anger burned inside me in the same way it had so many years earlier in the Nashville riots.

"I am no parasite, what they call," said one woman in functional English. She was a jobless physicist who was fired when she applied to emigrate to Israel. Parents told of school-aged children denied entrance to top Soviet universities despite a strong aptitude for math and science. "The authorities, they do not want Jews working in mathematics and science especially," a mother said. "They are 'too important' for Jews." One Soviet mathematician had distributed a study about such systematic exclusion of Jews at the élite Moscow State University. For this, he was sentenced to five years in internal exile.[2] On and on the stories flowed until someone glanced down from the apartment's the fifth-floor window. Plainclothes police had tailed us. Fortunately, inexplicably, they did not disrupt the meeting. When we

departed, they had vanished. The US Embassy later reported no recrimina-
tions against our hosts. Still, the rendezvous had been highly risky for the
refuseniks, and their fearlessness amazed me.

In my Mittleman Center audience, a dark-haired woman nodded
knowingly again and again. Giving her name as Raisa Premsyler, she rose
to say that as a Russian immigrant, she could attest that the Soviet system
prevailed through the use of fear and terror and that her family was one
of its victims. She described the plight of Naum's family and the arbitrary
decision of Soviet authorities to ban them from emigrating. Raisa was a
medical school graduate in residency at the Oregon Health Sciences University Hospital. She trembled as she described the Soviet system of gu-
lags, the KGB's surprise searches, anti-Semitic repression, and the jailing
of innocent Jews for "hooliganism," a catchall charge without definition in
law that meant anything or nothing. We spoke for several minutes after the
meeting broke up. She described her efforts to free her brother. I offered
to help. She said she was involved in several actions but, if needed, she
would reach out to me. I could not have known then the saga that would
soon unfold.

Naum Is Jailed

On February 4, 1986, a letter from Raisa landed on my desk in Washington.
The authorities had imprisoned Naum for hooliganism, bribery, and misconduct in the workplace. For his "crimes," he was sentenced to five years at
hard labor. I phoned Raisa immediately.

"Is urgent," Raisa said. "Until now, Dina and I thought we could work
quietly to get Naum free without making him controversial. But the situation is dangerous now. Will you help us?"

Of course I would. I already knew about the barbaric Soviet penal
system. The book *Prison Conditions in the Soviet Union*[3] describes detainees
wasting away for years in small, hot or cold airless cells with double and
triple bunks and a toilet consuming most of the floor space, leaving practically no room to move around. In such confines, inmates often sat or lay for
up to twenty-three hours a day. I could not imagine Naum's agony.

Dina and the children lived on a share of her parents' pension benefits
and an occasional remittance the Premsylers, now in Oregon, transferred
through a cousin in Israel to a friend in Soviet Georgia who delivered it
covertly to the Chernobelskys in Vinnytsya.

On the phone with Raisa, I said, "I don't know if I can pull this off. But if I fail, it won't be for a lack of trying." My words seemed to relieve her. Privately, I asked myself a question. Where do I start?

One of my young aides had an answer. She was Elana Stampfer, daughter of my friend Joshua Stampfer, a prominent Portland rabbi. She alerted me to Moscow-bound letters on behalf of Soviet Jewry that other House members were preparing. It was relatively easy to add the Chernobelsky family's name to every one of them.

If by some stroke of luck, the Soviets, in a calculated goodwill gesture, were to release families of interest to American politicians, I wanted Naum and his kin on the master list. With that goal in mind, I got thirty-five House colleagues to co-sign my letter to Soviet emigration authorities on Naum's behalf and wrote to Gorbachev and his foreign minister, Eduard Shevardnadze.

After four desultory months of writing letters, however, I needed to do more. Absent a miracle, a letter to a Soviet leader or an apparatchik seemed as useful as, say, a modern-day tweet into cyberspace. But I knew that an angler has to keep a fly in the water, where fish live, to have any hope of success. I had to close the distance of five thousand miles and seven time zones that separated me from Soviet authorities who would decide Naum's fate.

But who the hell did I know in Moscow?

Georgi Arbatov

Actually, I knew one man. Not well. We had met briefly in Moscow the previous year. That occasion, however, was a catastrophe thanks to several insulting anti-Soviet congressmen in my delegation. The official was Georgi Arbatov, a member of the Supreme Soviet and founder of Moscow's Institute for US and Canadian Studies (ISKRAN), an organization with significant political influence at the highest levels of the Kremlin. Given our distasteful encounter, I had almost expunged the meeting, and him, from my mind.

Arbatov was a tough Kremlin insider and survivor who advised Gorbachev on American policy as he had done for four previous Soviet leaders. Famous for his acerbic personality, he was the US media's go-to guy on the Soviet Union, appearing frequently on Ted Koppel's *Nightline* and the Sunday morning talk shows.

In our disastrous meeting, Tom Lantos, a California Democrat, Benjamin Gilman, a Republican from New York, and the other Americans attacked the Soviet Union so rudely that the meeting degenerated into a shouting match. In one odious volley, one of Arbatov's aides hurled the timeworn canard that America purposely delayed the allied invasion of France in World War II in order to bleed the heroic Soviet army. I slammed my hand on the table so hard that heads snapped around. "Everyone here is acting like an adolescent," I bellowed. I pointed at children's finger paintings on Arbatov's wall. "The future of those children—and ours—is what I thought we came to discuss instead of playing cheap word games. I'm ashamed of everything that's been said here and feel this meeting has been a total waste of time." With my outburst, the meeting ended in shambles, but to my good fortune, Arbatov would remember me.

Vitaly Churkin[4]

In the summer of 1986, I asked my military aide, Bob Sherman, to arrange a meeting with Vitaly Churkin, a diplomat from the Soviet Embassy. His official title was second first secretary of the legation, a rank that obscured a quick wit, agile mind, and an extraordinary knowledge of the arcane details of strategic weapons. (Neither Churkin nor I knew then that he would end up one of Moscow's top international envoys and its ambassador to the United Nations.)

Aware of Churkin's arms-control credentials, Sherman had been urging on him the idea of the Soviets unilaterally dismantling their primitive anti-satellite system. Sherman's point was that my ASAT flight-test ban would be easier to protect if the antiquated and unreliable Soviet SS-9 ASAT system—untested for four years—were dismantled. Churkin responded that the idea would have a lot more force if it came directly from a member of Congress. On this basis, I set up the meeting, mindful that, for him, a one-on-one relationship with a US congressman could be beneficial. The reverse was also true. I wondered where this would go.

After opening pleasantries, I went to work. "Look," I said, "your system is junk. We both know this. Its technology is roughly equivalent to the ASAT the United States deployed in the 1960s but abandoned because of its limitations."

I went on to say something like this: "You haven't flight-tested your weapon for years, and that's good because now I've put an American flight-test ban into law so long as you keep your de facto ban. Neither of us needs a new arms race in anti-satellite weapons and counter-ASAT weapons. Instability would be escalated, putting each of our early warning satellites at risk. My ASAT amendment was adopted as a rider on a one-year spending bill. It has to be renewed each year, and I can't be confident that I can renew it forever. So why don't you guys simply dismantle your defective system, as we did ours in the 1970s? It would stun American neoconservatives and possibly promote other arms-control measures."

I probably overestimated the influence of a second-level officer in the Soviet's Washington embassy. On the other hand, Churkin may have helped convince the Soviets to refrain from ASAT testing, a policy that remained in effect until after I left Congress.[5]

In the months to come, Churkin, Sherman, and I met four or five other times, a fact I was careful to make known to the State Department and the CIA.

By the end of 1986, Churkin and I had established a working relationship, good enough that I decided to make a run at him on the plight of the Chernobelsky family. What could I lose—that he would ignore me, as had countless Soviet immigration officials who probably had tossed my letters into a wastebasket?

Churkin listened intently to my summary of Naum's case. He said Naum had no chance to emigrate so long as he was imprisoned. However, after delivering that dose of reality, he said as he left, "Keep me posted."

I relayed Churkin's dire news to Raisa by phone.

She listened stoically but vowed nevertheless to keep faith.

I told her I would try other steps. I didn't tell her that I had no idea what they might be. Then I lost Churkin.

In January, he came to my office to announce that Moscow had called him home. He didn't disclose the nature of his new duties, so I didn't ask. However, I used the opportunity to brief him on Naum's latest status. Churkin's expression was impassive. If we had been playing poker, he could have held either two deuces or a royal flush. He promised to keep working on the case when he returned home. Sure. He said practically the same thing months earlier but had not provided a shred of news. But my job would now be immeasurably harder with no Soviet official in Washington to consult.

I spent the next two months writing more unanswered letters to high-level officials in Moscow and Kiev. I was spinning my wheels. But doing something—however small—beat doing nothing.

House Speaker Jim Wright goes to the USSR

In March 1987, three months after the retirement of Tip O'Neill and the ascension of Jim Wright of Texas as the forty-eighth Speaker of the US House of Representatives, Wright asked to meet with Mikhail Gorbachev and his top officials in Moscow. The Kremlin's acceptance elated Wright, who entered office with an outsized ambition and an expansive vision of the speakership. Maybe, Wright thought, he could do something to move the needle in the stalemated US-USSR Strategic Arms Reduction Talks in Geneva. He assembled the highest-ranking congressional delegation ever to visit the Soviet Union. The group included, among others, Wright's top two Democratic floor leaders, the second-ranking House Republican (then-congressman Dick Cheney), three committee chairmen, the chairman of the House's Helsinki Watch Commission, and four official congressional observers to the strategic missile talks in Geneva, of which I was one. Beyond the prospect of discussing geopolitics with the newly installed and intriguing Gorbachev, the trip would put me within shoulder-rubbing distance of the highest-ranking leaders in the USSR, a remarkable opportunity to discuss Naum's case. My hopes soared.

Wonderful news awaited me in Moscow. Raisa sent word that Naum had just been released from the labor camp and transferred to a type of community work-release program. The synchronicity was too perfect to be ignored. I couldn't believe that Naum's pardon and the Wright delegation's arrival was coincidental. Was this Churkin's work? There was no way to know anything except that Naum and his family were one step closer to emigrating. I decided to press his case to any Soviet official who could be remotely helpful.

Georgi Arbatov in Kiev

Before the US delegation arrived in Moscow, we detoured to Kiev, the capital of Ukraine, to avert a scheduling conflict with Secretary of State George Shultz, who appeared on a quick trip to Moscow the very day we planned to arrive. The layover in Kiev proved fortuitous.

Greeting us on the tarmac of Kyiv International Airport was Georgi Arbatov with a large welcoming party. A dozen grade-school girls bestowed bouquets of red carnations for each woman in our party.

Arbatov spotted my friend Congressman Norm Dicks of Washington State, a fellow member of the House Defense Appropriations Subcommittee.

"Norm!" Arbatov belted out. "You want to see Chernobyl? Is set!"

Dicks and I had forwarded a request for the tour because the design of the defunct nuclear power plant in Chernobyl that had melted down, exploded and poisoned hundreds of square miles with radioactive fallout was similar to the five Washington Public Power Supply System plants (acronym: WPPSS, pronounced "whoops") that were under construction in that state. They were already a hot issue in Pacific Northwest politics due to delays and cost overruns, and soon became ground zero for a monumental financial collapse and public bond default, the second-greatest in US history.

As everyone walked to the waiting buses, Norm tried to introduce Arbatov to me. "Oh, I know Mr. AuCoin very well!" the Russian smiled. This trip to Reagan's "Evil Empire" was already different than my first with Lantos and Gilman. I was glad I had spoken out in that previous meeting with Arbatov.

Local officials hosted a sumptuous banquet for us that evening at Catherine the Great's Mariyinsky Palace. When we returned to the hotel after midnight, Tom Downey of New York grabbed Norm Dicks and me to say that Arbatov wanted to meet privately with us in his room on the top floor. As congressional observers to the Geneva talks, we knew Arbatov had something big on his mind.

Arbatov's quarters were sumptuous. Just off the sitting room, a table strained under the weight of lox and caviar sandwiches, wines, and vodkas that went down smoother than water.

Our host wanted us to know that his new boss was a rare breed of Kremlin leader, one willing to negotiate although one who gravely doubted that Reagan wanted to stop the arms race. The conversation covered intermediate and long-range missile defenses, and intermediate-range missiles, and Reagan's "Star Wars" initiative. It lasted until three-thirty in the morning, through several sandwiches, much caviar, and no small amount of premium vodka.

Downey, Dicks, and I were careful not to reveal classified information. For any secret listeners, we made doubly sure to lean into the issue of Soviet Jewry. Downey remarked that the Soviets had to understand that Jewish emigration was not a cudgel that anti-Kremlin elements in the United States were using against the Soviets; it was, instead, a bedrock condition for far-reaching agreements on military, diplomatic, and economic issues in the eyes of most Americans.

The room turned cold.

Arbatov snapped, "The trouble is, once we release some of these people, they ask for more relatives, then more relatives, then still more. When does it end?" It doesn't, Downey said, reminding him that Moscow had signed the Helsinki Agreement on Human Rights, which guarantees free emigration. Arbatov went silent for several seconds. I don't know if he was considering the merit of the argument or repulsed by it.

Mikhail Gorbachev

When we finally arrived in Moscow, the first order of business was to meet the charismatic Gorbachev, the antithesis of the troglodytes who preceded him. The new leader greeted us in an opulent room in an upper floor of the Kremlin. He sat on one side of a long blond oak table, directly across from Speaker Wright. Flanking the Speaker: twenty other members of Congress. Flanking Gorbachev: two men, and two men alone. One was Anatoly Dobrynin, the storied former ambassador to the United States from 1962 to 1986; the other, an interpreter. Within reach of our beaming host was a single glass of water. No paper, no notes, no pen.

In a search for common ground, we discussed everything from Perestroika, Glasnost, nuclear weapons, Europe, human rights, Soviet Jewry, the Middle East, China, NATO and the Warsaw Pact. When we got to the issue of global energy supplies, one of the Americans mentioned Alaska's oil reserves. Gorbachev understood without the help of his interpreter. Laughing, he said he knew all about Alaska—a vast, untapped source of oil that had outsized economic implications in the global petroleum market. He put a finger to his temple and pulled a trigger to waves of laughter on both sides. Gorbachev so enjoyed himself that he kept us going well past the opening of the Bolshoi Ballet, where my wife, Sue, and other American spouses were waiting for us in box seats.

Georgi Arbatov in Moscow

On the next morning in the Kremlin, everyone got quickly to work. I attended the working group on arms control. A harried Georgi Arbatov arrived forty-five minutes late with an armload of files and papers. He tried without success to slip inconspicuously into the first chair from the door, just as the rest of the Soviet team unloaded on us. They listed America's military "provocations":

- Reagan had antagonistically continued nuclear testing in the face of the Kremlin's unilateral eighteen-month moratorium, an olive branch.
- Reagan unilaterally violated the terms of the Carter-Brezhnev Strategic Arms Limitation Treaty—unratified by the US Senate but adhered to by Moscow as another sign of goodwill.
- Worst of all, Reagan was obsessed with building his Strategic Defense Initiative (aka "Star Wars"), which, if deployed, would breach the 1972 Anti-Ballistic Missile Treaty that both sides had scrupulously followed for thirteen years.

These were actions of an aggressor, they charged, not actions of one who wanted peace. Reagan's policies made it difficult to refute the Soviets' claims. I urged patience, which provoked wild-eyed derision from Sergei Akhromeyev, marshal of the Soviet military's armed forces.

As the discussion moved down the table, I was able to whisper to Arbatov that I wanted his help on an immigration case of great importance. I scribbled Naum's name and address and the names of his family and slipped him the note. He accepted it with a thin smile, tucked it into his pocket and said, "I'll look into it."

The next morning, when our group reconvened, Arbatov surprised me by murmuring across the table that he needed more data about the Chernobelskys. Had he worked on this overnight? Could I be that fortunate?

"How can I get it to you?" I asked. It was the afternoon of our last day in Moscow.

"Will you be at the chili feed?" he asked.

The Speaker was throwing an authentic Texas chili feed at the American Embassy that evening. Of course, Sue and I would attend.

"Give it to me there," Arbatov said.

In our hotel room, I rushed to duplicate by hand the details from Naum's biography. Then Sue and I made sure to be among the first guests to arrive at the embassy; we were not going to miss Arbatov. As people trickled in, I searched the room. No Arbatov. I began to panic. Then he materialized off my right shoulder. He would have made a great spook.

"Georgi!" I beamed. "Here's the stuff you wanted. Please remember, this is important to me."

Slipping the documents into his coat pocket, he said, "I can't promise anything, but I'll do what I can." How many times had a Soviet official told me those same words?

Ambassador Yuri Dubinin in Moscow

During the arms-control discussions, I had noticed a pleasant-looking Soviet official sitting at the opposite end of the long table. He carried himself with dignity but had not uttered a word. He seemed to pay close attention each time I gave my reasons for unilateral Soviet arms restraint. When the session broke up, he came around the table and, saying nothing, shook my hand with both of his and smiled warmly. I had no chance to respond; everyone was moving to St. Catherine Hall for a lavish luncheon hosted by members of the Supreme Soviet.

As the meal and speeches ended, I made my way toward a door. Moving around the massive U-shaped table that had seated some two hundred people, I looked up to find before me the man who had watched me in working group. This time he spoke in perfect English. "I was impressed with your speech," he smiled. Thanking him, I pocketed his card and said I hoped that one day we might we might meet again. Then I rushed off to the bus to join the rest of the departing delegation.

In our room that night, I briefed Sue on the day's events. Describing the exchange with the dignified man, I retrieved his card in my suit jacket. It read, *Yuri Dubinin, Ambassador to the United States*. I had just experienced a meaningful encounter with one of the Soviet Union's top diplomats and acted as though he was part of the Kremlin wallpaper! I felt like a rube.

The next day gave me the opening to make amends. At the Foreign Ministry, I presented Minister Eduard Shevardnadze a "peace quilt" from Oregon made by students of Vose Elementary School in Beaverton. It depicted silhouettes of their hands reaching out to hands of Soviet children. The children designed the project when their teacher learned I would make this trip. Shevardnadze seemed touched as I explained the symbolism. "We should listen to our children," he said. Outside in the corridor, Ambassador Dubinin came up to say the quilt was a perfect gesture. I apologized for not having recognized him the previous day, feebly laying it off to travel fatigue. He shook it off in good humor. Maybe I had created a useful Washington-based relationship. As events played out, this would be true. But only after bitter disappointments.

Georgi Arbatov in Portland, Oregon

Three months after I returned from the Soviet Union, I learned that several high-ranking Russians were on their way to Portland and that Georgi Arbatov was be one of them. The occasion was a conference on US-Soviet relations hosted by Lewis and Clark College, a private school in my district with a reputation for high-level international exchanges. What were the odds of such an opportunity landing in my lap? I moved quickly, working with Jim Gardner, the college president, and Professor Joseph Ha to make arrangements for me to sit down with Arbatov. I asked for a private lunch at the Portland Downtown Hilton, in a small conference room with a private waiter and—this was important—not a word of it on any schedule. Gardner and Ha pulled it off with quiet aplomb, aided by my friend, Serge d'Rovencourt, the Hilton's inestimable general manager. I felt genuinely optimistic about freeing Naum and his family.

My euphoria was shattered when I stepped off my flight at Portland International. Bernie Bottomly, my district office manager, greeted me with grim news about the Lewis and Clark conference. Once a staff greenhorn, Bernie had become one of my top hands. He was a master of cool-headedness and political insight.

"Raisa damn near started World War Three tonight," he announced as gently as he could, knowing the news would crush my hopes. It was the last thing I needed to hear.

"What . . . ?" I exclaimed. "How . . . ?"

"The Lewis and Clark thing was a public meeting; she showed up," Bernie said. "She really got into it with Arbatov. It ended with Raisa shouting into his face: 'Why have you jailed my brother? Why won't you let him free?' The TV cameras caught it all. Arbatov was apoplectic. I thought he'd have a seizure. Then he hissed something to her in Russian and stormed off."

My heart sank. "You find out what he said?"

"I asked Raisa. She said his exact words were, 'Your brother is scum, a rotten criminal.'"

"Damn it!" I whispered. After so many months of effort, how quickly everything had gone south. My mind whirled. "And the lunch?"

"Still on. I can't imagine why."

I slammed my hand on the dashboard. Instead of cutting a deal, now I would have to scramble to control damage. What had Raisa been thinking? I chased all such thoughts out of my mind and concentrated on the job ahead.

At the Hilton the next day, Serge d' Rovencourt had outdone himself. Our room was designed for a conference of perhaps forty, but in the middle of it stood a single table set for two with sparkling glass and silver. I stepped inside to find Georgi Arkadyevich Arbatov at a window studying the view of Broadway four floors below. After exchanging pleasantries and making our menu choices, the waiter closed the door and the Russian and I got down to business.

"That woman has done grave damage to you and your request," Arbatov growled. "In front of my colleagues," he said, wagging his finger, "She used me to insult my government. Worse, for you, she brought undue attention to her brother." He leaned across the table. "How is it possible for me now to assist in the same case she used for this slander?"

He was still bristling. I could imagine how enraged he must have been at the college. Calmly, I apologized for Raisa and asked him to imagine the extreme stress she was under.

After a long silence, I said, "My friend, you're a man of standing in the world. Mrs. Premsyler is one woman living obscurely in Tigard, Oregon. Her words can't hurt you. They've angered you, of course, but they can't hurt you at home or anywhere else." On it went for the next two hours, with me mixing flattery, entreaties, and the argument that freeing this one refusenik family would buy a lot of congressional goodwill. In the end, Arbatov agreed to continue on the case. First, he said, time would have to pass. "It's impossible for us to act now. That woman's tactic cannot seem to be rewarded." He mentioned the anniversary of the Bolshevik Revolution in October. He made a vague reference to humanitarian gestures "involving several people" occurring on that occasion, implying that the Chernobel-skys might be released at that time. As part of a group of dozens, perhaps hundreds, Naum's case would not attract a lot of attention. It wasn't a hard-and-fast assurance that Naum and his family would be among them, but I pocketed it as if it were.

"I Trust You Completely"

Before returning to Washington, I phoned Raisa to describe the damage she had done. Gently, I made her realize that she had nearly demolished the most promising opportunity we had to free her brother and his family.

"I'm sorry," she said, "but the longer I listened to his bragging about his country, the less I could control myself."

"But I'd told you I was meeting him the next day to discuss Naum's release!"

"I shouldn't have done it. I couldn't help myself."

"We'll utterly fail to help Naum if you keep insulting the Soviet Union and raising his profile under these circumstances," I advised. "You have to decide to trust me or not."

"I trust you," Raisa whispered. "I trust you completely."

Hanging up the phone, I considered the poignancy of one stranger putting her full faith in another. The odds of success were incredibly long and would benefit only four people at best. Against these four lives, I weighed my obligations to hundreds of thousands of Oregonians who looked to me for representation. Then the shard of a half-forgotten rabbinical precept came to me: Whoever saves a single life saves the entire world.[6] Although I am a gentile, the universal imperative of that phrase had struck me long ago, when I heard it from a Jewish fellow GI in Germany. He had quoted it late one night during one of our philosophical conversations before lights out. Saving a living soul saves not only that person's life but also his progeny and every single contribution each one makes until the end of time. Fate had handed me a chance to make a difference beyond measure.

"I trust you," Raisa had whispered. "I trust you completely."

Ambassador Yuri Dubinin in Washington

It was August and time to open a new channel. I invited Yuri Dubinin, the Soviet ambassador, to lunch with me. His response came back with a twist. He wanted me to join him at the Soviet Embassy. It seemed like a courteous gesture from the debonair man who had been so complimentary in the Kremlin. On the other hand, anything we said on his home turf almost certainly would be recorded. I would not be able to speak as freely as I preferred, and he might not wish to speak at all about an issue involving Soviet Jewry. But I had no other option. I accepted the invitation.

The dour brick walls of the Soviet Embassy emanated coldness as I pulled up on Sixteenth Street Northwest. Atop a twelve-foot wrought-iron fence, a camera swerved in my direction. Its red eye zeroed in on me for several seconds before the gate squeaked open as if on its own. I parked in the cramped brick driveway and paused at the embassy's front door. No one emerged. I cracked the door ajar, observed a dimly lit vestibule, and stepped inside. There I waited, eying an interior security door with a one-way window. No sound of any kind. No greeting. No instructions. Finally, it swung open and a man of approximately my age, early forties, stepped forward to provide escort. He led me to the second floor, where a table had been set for four in the center of a ballroom. Off to the side, on an antique sofa, a man I didn't recognize sat limply and withheld his hand. A spook, I thought, or a party apparatchik, or both. Just then Dubinin, lean and suave, entered the room and greeted me warmly. Another civilian accompanied him. Again, no introductions.

Dubinin was a far cry from his predecessor, Anatoly Dobrynin, the storied dean of the Washington diplomatic corps who had watched out for Moscow's interests since before the Cuban Missile Crisis. In contrast, Dubinin was relatively obscure in Washington. Previously, he had served one year as the Soviet ambassador to the United Nations. The buzz in Washington was that, in pulling Dobrynin back to Moscow to become secretary of the Central Committee, Gorbachev wanted the old war horse's twenty-five years of America-watching at close hand, where he and Foreign Minister Eduard Shevardnadze would call the shots. If true, the Kremlin needed only a guy Friday in Washington to carry out instructions.

After an unproductive lunch, dominated by the ambassador's rant against working conditions in the embassy, Dubinin escorted me alone down some back stairs to ground level. My heart raced; within minutes, my opportunity would be gone. Could I raise Naum's case in a stairway? If I didn't, I couldn't raise it at all. I went for it. To the surprise of Dubinin, I blurted out the Chernobelsky story and explained why the ambassador's help could be pivotal. Awkwardly, I pushed the family's dossier into his hands. The diplomat stuffed the document in his pocket without comment.

The Interregnum

In last half of 1987, with a sense of futility and growing desperation, I renewed my foreign correspondence to high-ranking Soviet authorities and enlisted a hundred of my colleagues to send individual letters on Naum's behalf. I tried a series of international telephone calls to the various offices of OVIR, the Soviet immigration agency. The idea was fanciful, but it might produce results. I actually got through to an official in Kiev, near Naum's home.

My translator explained that she had an important American congressman on the line. Introducing myself, I said, "I'm calling about Naum

Chernobelsky of Vinnytsya, a Soviet Jew who wants to emigrate with his fam—"

"Hallo? Hallo?" came the official, whose phone apparently went on the fritz.

"I said—"

Click.

I marveled at the power of words to produce utter silence.

Then in September, stunning news arrived. Naum's wife, Dina, telephoned Raisa to report that the Soviet prosecutor had dropped all charges against her husband. Although that in itself didn't equate to free passage out of the USSR, it removed yet another obstacle to Naum's freedom.

Georgi Arbatov on the South Lawn of the White House

On December 8, 1987, Mikhail Gorbachev met Ronald Reagan at the White House to sign a treaty to eliminate the US and Soviet arsenals of intermediate-range nuclear missiles. White House workers had erected a stage immediately in front of the diplomatic entrance.

As we awaited Gorbachev's motorcade, a late arrival on the Soviet side limped with a cane onto the grounds. Arbatov! His left foot was laced into a high-topped boot. I had no idea that he would be there, nor did I know what ailed him.

As the program concluded, I spotted him hobbling alone along the White House colonnade to the East Wing exit.

"Georgi!" I called out.

He stopped, turned, and looked at me with an "Oh, shit!" expression.

In a weakened, raspy voice, he said he had broken his ankle, bandaged it tightly and stuffed it into the military boot. With that explanation, he started to leave, as if, with a magic slate, someone had erased our mutual history.

"Wait!" I called out. "I haven't heard from you in months. What can you tell me about the Chernobelskys, you know—the refusenik family you said you'd help?"

His rambling response was like nothing so much as a boxer bobbing, weaving, and ducking. His eyes darted furtively; he couldn't look me in the eye. Obviously, he'd done nothing for the family. Worse, his antics told me to get out of his face.

Another dead end.

I felt ill.

A Secret Letter

As the Christmas holiday drew near, I reflected on how none of my entreaties to the Soviets had borne fruit. Arbatov, in whom I had placed great hope, had deserted me. Ambassador Dubinin's attention began and ended with lust for his newly completed embassy, which was declared off-limits after Soviet bugs planted during construction of the new US Embassy in Moscow were discovered. Vitaly Churkin could not be reached in Moscow, despite some innovative efforts by my military aide, Bob Sherman.

My hopes could not have been lower. Then in mid-December came an invitation from Ambassador and Mrs. Yuri Dubinin to a special preview of a Soviet Life and Family exhibition at the State Department Auditorium. Given my state of mind, the ambassador could have invited Sue and me to a street cleaning and I would have accepted.

When I spotted the ambassador, he seemed to be struggling to put on a brave face amid a turnout that was embarrassingly sparse. He responded to our greeting with a thin smile and spoke through an interpreter, though he was fluent in English. He seemed determined to focus on a group of Georgian folk dancers. Our conversation was merely small talk between musical numbers. When Dubinin turned his attention back to the dancers, ignoring me again, my annoyance grew. I had my fill of Georgian folk dancing, Soviet propaganda, and studied indifference for one night. I whispered to Sue, "Let's get the hell out of here." But at that moment, an idea struck. I turned back to Dubinin's side.

"Before I leave, Mr. Ambassador," I said. "I want to mention that our daughter, Stacy, will be spending seventeen days in your country in January. She's a senior at Smith College in Massachusetts." It was a January mini-term abroad, and she would take in Moscow, Leningrad, and Tbilisi, the capital of Georgia.

Dubinin looked at me with eyes that shown. "Well, you must drop me a note about the dates of her visit," he beamed. English now. "I will tell our people in Moscow."

I had hit his button. Why, I'm not sure. Maybe a congressman's daughter's trip to his country was a pleasant contrast to the diplomatic bust he presided over that night.

You must drop me a note. Count on it, Mr. Ambassador.

I already knew what my next move would be for the Chernobelskys.

After talking it over with Sue at home, we had a lengthy discussion with Stacy. Would she carry a letter to Churkin in Moscow? The idea of enlisting Stacy's help was not far-fetched. She and her brother, Kelly, had served as summer pages in the US House and had accompanied Sue or me on the campaign trail. During their early teens, they had even teamed as surrogate speakers for me.

Stacy enthusiastically agreed to the assignment. At the time, she was considering graduate school in US-Soviet studies and had been my guest at congressional dinners on arms control and at a Harvard retreat on the subject. I mailed a letter to Dubinin with Stacy's itinerary.

"Mr. Ambassador," I wrote, "I would be pleased if you would do what you can to arrange for Stacy to meet Vitaly Churkin when she visits Moscow. My daughter is interested in Soviet economics, politics, and culture. She knows that Mr. Churkin and I enjoyed many mutually stimulating discussions of arms control when he was first secretary in your embassy in Washington. To meet a party official with whom her father worked so closely would mean the world to her. Thank you in advance for any courtesies you may extend her."

Next, I penned an emotional letter to Churkin, hoping against hope that Stacy would find a way to put it in his hand. My letter explained that now only he could help me win the release of the Chernobelskys. "If our friendship still holds any meaning," I added, "then I need your help now. Vitaly, after two years of hard work, I have no other resort."

Sue and I were satisfied that Stacy's mission posed no personal risks. US-Soviet relations had begun to thaw, and if something went awry for Stacy, it was beyond comprehension that any Soviet official in the Gorbachev era would punish the daughter of an American congressman for passing a personal message.

We briefed Stacy thoroughly—about the Chernobelskys, about Churkin (who would soon become a special advisor to the Soviet Foreign Minister), about how vital the passing of the letter might well be, and how no one in her group could know about her secret purpose.

Before embarking on the trip, Stacy placed my letter in an envelope, covered it with graffiti, and shoved it to the bottom of her stuffed purse. It would take a rabid investigator to find it, she reasoned. But if Churkin showed up, it would be within reach.

Stacy AuCoin's Covert Mission

Stacy's group was told no telephone service would be available to them. Halfway through Stacy's trip, I got a note from the ambassador. Without details, he said Stacy and Churkin had met briefly in Moscow. Sue and I restrained our excitement. Had the two merely said hello in a mass meeting? Had the encounter been too public to permit the passing of a letter, or, less likely, had Dubinin been in error? There was no knowing. If the mission failed, it wouldn't be the first time this roller coaster ran off the rails.

Then, on the night of January 28, 1989, Stacy phoned home after clearing US Customs in New Jersey. Sue and I got on extension phones to listen. Having established that she was healthy and had the experience of a lifetime, we posed the burning question: "Did you give the letter to Churkin?"

"Yes!" Stacy exclaimed. In Washington, Sue and I jumped up and down, shouting into our phones.

Stacy's rendezvous almost didn't happen.

On January 11, her last day in Moscow, she was exhausted from the sheer number of meetings. Some, she felt, were as numbing as a shot of Novocaine. Worse, Churkin had been nowhere to be seen. Maybe she would skip today's agenda. He was unlikely to show up, anyway. The bed was warm, comfortable. Then she remembered that the day's key meeting was to about Perestroika, Gorbachev's plan for the most radical liberalization of the Soviet economy in the history of the Bolshevik state. It was one of her favorite studies at Smith. She would attend.

The group convened in a nondescript building that wasn't a school but included several plain classrooms, each vacant. The Americans took seats as two twenty-something economists in boxy suits arrived and sat at a table in front. Behind them strode a well-tailored, prematurely white-haired man, perhaps in his early forties, exquisitely self-assured and smiling broadly. In every respect, the contrast with the other Russian speakers was striking.

"Where are each of you from?" he asked, in his perfect Oxford English accent. Same accent as Churkin, Stacy thought, her heart pounding.

The chaperone cut him off, "We're from several colleges in Massachusetts!" Before she could pose an economics question to the other speakers, he stepped in again. "When I lived in DC, the traffic often was a challenge," he said.

Now Stacy knew for sure he was fishing for her. She had to step in. "Yes, I live in DC," she blurted. "Nothing's worse than rush hour on the Fourteenth Street Bridge."

She beamed that stunning smile of hers.

Contact.

When the session broke up, Churkin came over to greet Stacy. He said he was sure of her identity because he remembered her framed photograph in my office. "How is your father?" he smiled.

"He's fine," she replied. "He sent me with a letter for you."

At this, Stacy reported, Churkin's eyes went wide, his smile dropped, and his once confident countenance lost its color.

Fear stabbed at Stacy. The letter. She'd left it in her coat, which hung in the cloakroom on the first floor! Her heart pounded as she worked to keep track of Churkin as everyone moved downstairs to the cloak racks.

Stacy thought Churkin still seemed rattled as he slipped on his overcoat. With the letter in hand, she approached him. "Here's my dad's letter," she said. Churkin palmed it and in one fluid motion, slipped into an inside pocket.

"He misses you," Stacy smiled.

Churkin laughed nervously at this, perhaps because of the audacity of the plan and its execution. Without another word, he slipped out the door.

Six months later, Soviet authorities approved the Chernobelsky family's application to emigrate to America. There was no explanation from the Soviets, no acknowledgment of my letter to Churkin, nor of Dina Chernobelsky's incessant pleading with OVIR authorities, nor of the many letters sent to the agency from across Oregon. I remembered how Churchill described the Soviet Union—a riddle wrapped in a mystery inside an enigma.

I never spoke again about these events with Churkin. The cumulative impact of all these efforts may never have been known, but to this day, I believe my entreaty to Churkin, and the extraordinary way it was delivered, was decisive. So do Raisa and Naum.

A New Life Begins

The news from the USSR set off waves of glee in the Oregon Jewish community, in my Washington and Portland offices, and within my family.

On October 28, 1988, Stacy and I joined Raisa and her family to greet Naum and his wife and children at Kennedy International Airport in New York.

It was a heart-gladdening moment when the Chernobelskys exited the jet bridge onto US soil. When the familial hugs and kisses were done, Naum, who had been well briefed on Stacy's role in his family's release, reached for Stacy.

"Anastasia! Anastasia!" he cried, hugging her hard between his stout arms and shoulders. His swarthy face glowed like polished bronze.

I had forgotten that "Stacy" derives from the famous Russian name, but Naum knew. A feeling swept over me that the whole odyssey was somehow preordained. Impossible, I know, but as I watched a family inhale its first breath of freedom, I believed it.

Stacy and I flew with the family to Portland International. As we began our descent, the pilot's voice came over the PA system. "Ladies and gentlemen, we in the cockpit and the service crew want you to know that when we land in a moment, a wonderful family of persecuted Soviet Jews will touch down in their new home in America, the land of the free and the brave." Applause thundered throughout the cabin.

Weeping relatives clutched and hugged Naum and his family when they emerged from the Jetway in Portland. Television cameras and news reporters crowded in to get the epic story.

Four years of mind-numbing analysis, dashed hopes, despair, crack-of-dawn phone calls, and furtively passed notes seemed almost dreamlike now. Stacy stood beside me watching the elation.

She squeezed my hand, but I found no words. I remembered the rabbinic saying: *Save one life . . .*

Stacy's smiling blue eyes gleamed up at me through her tears.

31
China Rediscovered

Long before China built the world's second-largest economy—forty-one years before Donald Trump punched it in the nose with a trade war—the Asian giant was an isolated, underdeveloped weakling shrouded in mystery. Still, I thought it might someday make a natural economic partner for Oregon and the United States.

Not that I thought about it a lot. I was a newly reelected thirty-six-year-old still trying not to get lost in the Capitol. Six years earlier, Richard Nixon had made a diplomatic opening to Beijing, producing a tantalizing but unenforceable joint communiqué stating that "normalization of relations is in the interest of all countries." In the years that followed, no further diplomacy occurred. Even if Congress had wanted to do something about that—and it didn't—it was institutionally ill-suited to the task. In its DNA, reaction has almost always trumped proaction. Back then, legislators' attention also remained roiled with the aftermath of impeachment, Nixon's resignation, and Gerald Ford's pathetic "Whip Inflation Now" buttons coupled with his relentless presidential vetoes.

This, then, was the way things stood in 1977, when I took a seat on the International Institutions Subcommittee of the House Banking Committee. The subcommittee assignment allowed me to play a part in the normalization of relations between the United States and China. But that would come later. At the outset, all I knew was that I had to beef up my legislative staff to handle my expanded portfolio.

I hired Gary Conkling, the news editor of the *Daily Astorian*, to assist me on all Banking Committee issues. He had impressed me with his knowledge of the Northwest economy and its history. No other journalist in my district, including reporters at the state's largest daily, the *Oregonian*, had shown a command of regional issues as deep or nuanced as Conkling had.

Before we could get started, though, my staff and I had to move into new quarters in the Cannon House Office Building, reorganize, and analyze the policy issues of the coming legislative year.

In the midst of setting up phones, unpacking boxes, and assigning work spaces, a young man named Joe Micallef showed up for work.

My staff was nonplussed. Who was Joe Micallef? Was this a hoax?

When I strode in from the House floor, I found a circle of human confusion in my reception area—Conkling, chief of staff Susan Geoghegan, press secretary Gene Maudlin, and twenty-year-old Joe Micallef. They stood gaping at each other.

"Congressman!" Micallef said when I stepped inside.

He had me at a loss.

"Remember?" he asked. "Professor Ha introduced us last winter at the American-Korean luncheon in Portland."

Ah, it came back to me.

Micallef was Professor Joseph Ha's prize student at Portland's Lewis and Clark College. I remembered him blushing in Portland when Ha raved that his brilliant undergrad would complete a four-year course of study in two years. I had remarked that I was always looking for bright young guys like him. For a brief time, he drove me around in my previous campaign. Now he was in my Capitol Hill office. I couldn't recall offering him a job, but I could always use a bright intern. And Joe needed no stipend. We just had to figure out what to do with him. To begin, I told him to analyze the jurisdiction of my new subcommittee. Did it offer a good policy foothold from which to work?

Yes, it did. Micallef found it quickly. It was breathtaking.

On its face, the panel's jurisdiction was pedestrian. It had exclusive jurisdiction over only one institution, the US Export-Import (EXIM) Bank, an agency that provided insurance and credits for US firms trading abroad. Micallef, however, noticed something odd. The bank was subject to the Jackson-Vanik Amendment's ban on assistance to US exporters doing business with nonmarket countries that discriminated against Jewish emigration. It was aimed at the Soviet Union, but for some reason, the amendment applied to China too.

Noting that China had no Jewish emigration problem, Micallef came up with an idea: Les could break new ground by removing the People's Republic of China from the bank charter's ban.

It was brilliant and daring—a subject on which I could almost literally feast. I told him to research any possible unintended problems and get the bill drafted. He did both in record time.

Just like that, a twenty-year-old prodigy on his way to graduate school identified an issue that would capture the attention of many American statesmen, US manufacturing leaders, and, not incidentally, high-ranking members of the Chinese Politburo in Beijing.

Conkling and I went right to work on strategy. Micallef moved on to MIT. From there, the young man and I would lose touch for the next forty years.[1]

In January 1978, I introduced the bill with cosponsors Henry Reuss of Wisconsin, chair of the Banking Committee, and Melvin Price of Illinois, chair of the House Armed Services Committee.

My life had taught me that dreaming big often produced big results.

Conkling was a dreamer, too, and his assistance in managing legislative tactics for the bill was as brilliant as Micallef's breakthrough discovery. For the bill's committee hearing, we recruited a standout group of outside witnesses. They included former CIA director George H. W. Bush, who later became the top envoy at the US Liaison Office in Beijing; former Senate Republican leader Hugh Scott of Pennsylvania; George Ball, former undersecretary of State in the Kennedy administration and a member of JFK's inner circle of Missile Crisis advisers; and Christopher Phillips, president of the National Council on US-China Trade.

Bush, however, disappointed me. As the years played out, it would not be the last time. A few days before the hearing, the future vice president's hurried, nasal voice on the phone made me imagine him standing in a booth with an impatient crowd queued up behind him. He spoke in his signature fragments: "Impossible to make the hearing. Last-minute trip to New Hampshire. Good luck. Hope you understand. Written testimony? No, sorry; can't do. Good bill, though. Bye."

My new star witness was George Ball, then a New York investment banker who gave my bill an endorsement startling in its vigor.

"The proposed legislation is designed to remove an anomaly in American law," he testified, "which, in my judgment, does not serve the interests of American private industry and—more important—the larger political and economic interests of the United States." Noting that even though full normalization of relations with China did not seem imminent, "Still, it seems foolish to maintain niggling discriminatory measures against the People's Republic of China, particularly when they work against the economic and commercial interests of Americans."[2]

When it was time to vote, Henry Hyde, a conservative Republican from Illinois, assaulted the idea of giving favors to "Red China." I countered that trade relations were not a gift, and if sixty other countries were trading with the PRC, banning EXIM Bank financial credits and insurance to American manufacturers punished only the US economy. The bill cleared the subcommittee and the Banking Committee and headed to the House floor.

On June 2, 1978, I opened floor debate with a statement drawing on George Ball's testimony to inoculate the bill from the looming attack by Hyde and allied red-baiters. On my side, Reuss, the Banking Committee chair, and Bill Stanton of Ohio, the committee's ranking Republican, weighed in with strong support. Everything was going exceptionally well.

Then the roof fell in.

Two veteran chairs of other committees stormed to the floor to attack the bill, each with foreign policy and international trade credentials. Clement Zablocki of the Foreign Relations Committee acted as though his office aides had roused him from a snooze to say, "Boss, a bunch of Banking Committee guys are trying to make China policy on the floor." Charles Vanik of the House Ways and Means Subcommittee on International Trade took umbrage at anyone who would touch the Jackson-Vanik Amendment, the law that had made him a national figure.

Vanik was having a particularly serious conniption. He hurled charges like a hyped-up machine gunner, spraying bullets in hopes some might hit a target.

He asserted that my bill was a run-around of the Jackson-Vanik Amendment, that it would be a tacit US endorsement of China's human rights behavior, that he wasn't sure what it did, and that the "Chinese haven't even asked for it."

My allies and I replied that none of his charges were on point. The bill didn't lay a glove on the Jackson-Vanik Amendment, written to apply to the USSR. Trade restrictions were an ineffective way to alter another country's domestic policies. Besides, the United States already had full-fledged trade agreements with four Communist countries that were not exemplars of human rights—Romania, Poland, Yugoslavia, and Hungary. Furthermore, why should China ask for the EXIM Bank assistance for US exporters? It had growing relations with other major trading partners, including our competitor, the European Common Market, which used an institution much like the US EXIM Bank.

My arguments did no good. Vanik's motion to defeat the bill carried, 179–138.

Losing a breakthrough foreign policy debate by forty-one votes was disappointing but not disheartening, especially for a second-term congressman who had given two House titans all they could handle in debate. I planned to resume the fight another day.

Later, when I reviewed what happened over the previous eighteen months, I realized something remarkable. The Carter administration had been virtually invisible. I had been too busy and too inexperienced to have noticed it. A State Department witness told my subcommittee that the legislation was unnecessary. With that single exception, the Carter administration had been missing in action. On a bill dealing with the People's Republic of China? I chalked it off to the Carter crowd's amateurism, a growing criticism among political watchers. Six months later, I would discover the real story when Washington and Beijing officially recognized each other as sovereign nations and restored normal relations.

The issues I raised during the debate, and the business coalition that supposed my proposal, drew a lot of national and international attention. Important officials in Beijing passed word through their contacts in the United States that they would be glad to invite me to visit China.[3] I was captivated. Conkling prepared a letter on my behalf to Han Xu, the head of China's Liaison Office in Washington. A few days later, Ambassador Han sent me an invitation to luncheon at his office on Northwest Connecticut Avenue and extended it to Conkling too.

The luncheon was sumptuous, and Han Xu's hospitality was as warm as the July day in which we met. With his butch haircut, gray-flecked hair, and generous smile, he looked every bit the man I'd seen in the news who, in Pakistan, had greeted then escorted Kissinger to Beijing in a secret meeting that led to Nixon's historic trip and diplomacy. I tried to keep my poise as I took a seat next to history personified.

Three of his colleagues at the round table shook hands but did not introduce themselves. They listened. And eyed me. I was sure the lunch's purpose was to size up the young congressman who had come out of nowhere.

I described Oregon as a neighbor on the Pacific Rim and stated my belief that mutual trade and normal relations would benefit our respective peoples. One anecdote seemed to resonate deeply with him. I described a flour mill in Astoria that sold most of its product to China before the revolution, and how the US decision to break off relations damaged the local economy. The mill had closed its Oregon operation and relocated to Vancouver, BC, where businesses enjoyed a more favorable trading relationship with China. "It's a good example," I said. "America needs to understand that a good relationship between our countries is better than a poor one both for China and the United States."

Han Xu beamed. "My government would like to invite you to visit China," he said brightly. "It would be happy to pay your way, and Mr. Conkling's."

I accepted the invitation with alacrity, but I politely declined the Chinese offer to pay. In appearance and fact, it was preferable for us to finance the trip.

"Could I bring a small group of Oregon businessmen and their wives?" I asked.

"Yes, of course."

Then I suggested making the trip in November, after the US off-year elections. "The Congress will be in recess," I said, "It would be an ideal time for me."

The ambassador smiled. "No, I believe it would be best for you to come soon after January." He explained that China had a serious shortage of hotel accommodations.

The real reason was a secret. US and Chinese negotiators were meeting covertly to hammer out a full and mutual diplomatic reconciliation. The nations would formally announce the agreement six months later in Beijing, on New Year's Day.

My party and I landed on Chinese soil February 12, 1979, the first American delegation to visit since relations had been normalization. I had assembled a delegation of Oregon businesspeople, trade officials, and spouses to travel with Conkling, my wife, Sue, and me.[4] Our twelve-day, five-city trip featured scenic tours, cultural events, and several high-level talks with government officials.

From the beginning, the China we experienced showed the effects of its decades-long isolation. As our airliner descended into the Shanghai-area airport, Sue and I looked down to see a man and a woman stop an oxen team in the middle of a field to gape as if our plane were a UFO. Our craft hit the runway in what Port of Portland director Lloyd Anderson called, "a modified crash landing." We clambered down open-air stairs to notice that ours was the only plane on the tarmac. Some fifty yards away, the terminal stood empty except for five uniformed soldiers watching with automatic rifles and caps with red stars. After a two-hour wait, we transferred to China Air for the trip to the capital. The cramped aircraft had two seats on each side of a single aisle. A huge white cloud of cold mist gushed into the cabin as we lifted off. One of our new local guides joked, "Chinese air conditioning!" Two flight attendants came through the cabin to hand out red rubber balls. Why rubber balls? I haven't the slightest idea.

Thirty-two years later, Sue and I would fly into Shanghai to a much different scene. Shanghai Pudong International sprawls across a 15.4-square-mile site with two cavernous passenger terminals (with multiple floors and connecting roadways), serving twenty million passengers a year. The terminals are flanked by four parallel runways, seventy-six gate positions, twenty-eight boarding bridges, thirteen baggage-transfer belts, shopping areas, restaurants, and banks.[5] Two subway lines and a sixteen-lane freeway connected the complex to the central city.

Shanghai's twenty-first-century airports symbolize China's spectacular economic rise. The primitive country we encountered on our first trip no longer exists. In three decades, the Chinese national economy eclipsed most Western expectations.[6] Gross domestic product (GDP) soared from $202.46 billion in 1980 to $6.988 trillion in 2011. The nation is the second-largest economic power in the world after the United States.[7] And it's not done. China is poised to become the world's leader in the next generation of 5G technology. This generation of wireless infrastructure is one hundred times faster than the world's current standard. China will use it to electronically connect billions of machines, automobiles, appliances, and data transmitters. If it configures its fifth-generation system in a Sino-proprietary way, it may offer high-tech manufacturers exclusive access to its system that discriminates against western manufacturers of high technology. The size of its market makes that prospect daunting.

Even in 1979, China's zeal for progress was evident almost everywhere. At the northern port city of Tianjin, longshoremen struggled to load and off-load cumbersome bulk cargo. Over green tea after our tour, port officials were eager to know how they could do better, an appetite for self-improvement we encountered at every stop. Lloyd Anderson, the president of the Port of Portland, and Ken Lewis, CEO of Lasco Shipping, explained the benefits of modern container shipping for swift loading and ease of transfer to rail. Today the Tianjin Port ranks tenth in the world in container traffic.[8]

In Guangzhou, two young girls followed Gary Conkling and me as we searched for an antique store. When we got lost, they tapped us on the shoulder and told us we'd taken a wrong turn. They said they had tailed us so they could listen to our English. Why? we asked. "It's our duty," they piped.[9]

In Guilin, where narrow mountain spires scrape the sky from a flat valley floor, I strolled alone through a neighborhood of squat, neatly kept houses. We were in southwest China, near the Vietnamese border. The tropical sun warmed my brow.

The deep voice came from behind me. "May I help you?"

Startled, I turned to find a young man in his thirties. I introduced myself and gave him my card, English on one side, Chinese on the other. He invited me into his parents' one-room house to critique his English. As we squatted on his dirt floor, he explained that he aimed to enroll at Beijing University. The school accepted two thousand students out of three million applications, but that didn't intimidate him. "With hard work, I will succeed," he smiled.

Here was a dirt-poor villager, living without plumbing or dependable electricity, craving to learn and confident of success. Books lined a shelf on his wall. The same work ethic, self-confidence and sense of direction were palpable in every factory, port, university, and commune we visited in our two-week trip. That night in bed, I felt I had seen a harbinger of Future China and contrasted it with America's diversions at the time—McDonald's "Happy Meals," nude streakers, the Sony Walkman, platform shoes, and pet rocks.

In a lecture that solidified my impressions, Gary Conking attended a briefing at the Brookings Institute in Washington. Noted sinologist Doak Barnett speculated that "market socialism" was in its infancy in China and could "shake the foundations of Communism and perhaps even capitalism."[10]

In spite of China's isolation and backwardness, the society was the beneficiary of thirty-five hundred years of history and invention. It didn't surprise me, then, that in some ways the civilization seemed to have left the West behind. In surgery, for instance, acupuncture was a common anesthetic because doctors considered it less risky than Western anesthesia.

At a Shanghai hospital, we watched, spellbound, from a catwalk as anesthesiologists used acupuncture in brain surgery.

The surgeon's drill that opened the patient's skull was anything but advanced, however. It could have come from a carpentry shop. Next came the saw, cutting a half-circle from the hole to a point above the patient's eyes. When the surgeon folded the scalp back, a nurse placed a white chipped porcelain pan within his reach. Soon, he held a tumor with forceps and plopped it into the pan. Nurses bound up the woman's head. Wheeling her out of the room, one of them pointed up toward us and spoke to the patient.

The patient smiled and waved at us.

In 1979, China's zeal for modernity did not extend to male-female behavior. The US State Department had warned us against any show of physical affection or familiarity with the then-culturally straitlaced Chinese.

I damn near broke the taboo at the Beijing Opera on our first night.

Despite our state of sleep starvation, our Beijing guide, Mrs. Chou, insisted that we attend the opera that night at nine. I demurred. "Mrs. Chou, you have to understand. We've had almost no sleep for two days."

"But it is major cultural event. *The Legend of the White Snake.* From Ming Dynasty." The woman's eyes flashed. "You are honored guests; you are expected. I have reserved whole row near stage."

The set of Comrade Chou's jaw told me we would go or create an international embarrassment.

We went.

As we took seats, I wondered what the US Environmental Protection Agency would think of the dust from the dirt floor mingling with cigarette smoke in thick clouds above us. Mrs. Chou sat between Sue and me to translate the story of a snake transformed into a beautiful woman whose husband's trust is poisoned when he learns she's a serpent. Right there, I knew I needed toothpicks to prop up my eyelids.

In the second hour of *White Snake*'s keening soprano, I began to nod off despite the racket. Mrs. Chou diligently continued her translation as she tried to ignore my head nodding within inches of her shoulder.

Finally, I went "lights out." With my head plunging headlong for Mrs. Chou's shoulder, Sue saw the disaster in the making. She leaned across Mrs. Chou's lap, gave her a wink, and rammed her elbow into my ribs. After the jolt, I stayed awake the rest of the way, enjoying *White Swan* and protecting my torso.

Mrs. Chou and Sue were the best of friends for the rest of the trip.

Our trip occurred during increased tension between China and the USSR. In every meeting, government officials warned us about war with the Soviet "Bear." In the most important governmental meeting of the trip, Tan Zhenlin, one of the vice chairmen of the Standing Committee of the People's Congress, declared war with the Bear "inevitable."

The vice chairman was fifty years my senior. He might have thought this thirty-six-year-old in front of him belonged in day care. But I rebutted. "War, I suppose, is possible," I said. "That's different than 'inevitable.'"

The old Communist cut off his translator and insisted on "inevitable."

I dug in. "*Inevitable* means 'preordained,'" I said. "Let's not forget free will. Not too many years ago, many would have said war between China and the United States was inevitable. Look at us now—we're building ties of friendship."

Hegemony also ranked high in our hosts' political liturgy. The memory of the foreign subjugation following the Opium Wars remained an open sore. During that era, European powers exploited the economy and seized territorial concessions. Chinese officials frequently told us the region should be free from the hegemony of any nation. Duly tutored, we still would not have guessed that the People's Republic would take up arms against Vietnam, a Moscow ally.

But it did.

Our departure was abruptly delayed in the southern city of Guilin, when the People's Liberation Army invaded neighboring Vietnam to "teach it a lesson." The Vietnamese transgression was its invasion and occupation of Cambodia, a Chinese client state. Henry Kissinger would write that Chinese leader Deng Xiaoping saw Hanoi's occupation as a Soviet attempt "to extend its evil tentacles into Southeast Asia"[11] and would not let it stand.

After two weeks of official meetings, random encounters, and private observations, we left the PRC during that invasion. I harbored the sense that China would not hesitate to risk global disapproval to protect what it saw as its strategic interests. Sure enough, ten years later, global abhorrence did not stop the People's Liberation Army and its tanks from massacring unarmed Chinese students in Beijing's Tiananmen Square. What threat did the young people pose to the country's interests? Young people had peacefully gathered for days outside the Forbidden City, demanding democratic reforms. To the Politburo, it was treason.

Ambassador Han Xu paid a hurried visit to my office as many members of Congress joined much of the rest of the world in denouncing the bloodbath. In a rare move, Mrs. Han accompanied him. I expect that as a party member, she was there to witness how her husband handled the meeting.

"Please do not be too critical of China," Han said. "We must not strain our countries' friendship."

"But my friend, how can I not criticize your government for slaughtering unarmed citizens of your own country?"

"Western propaganda exaggerates the situation," he replied.

I pulled a copy of *Newsweek* from a drawer in my coffee table and flipped through graphic color photographs of the carnage. "Propaganda, Ambassador Han? These photographs don't lie."

The ambassador said nothing. His wife kept her gaze on me.

"My friend," I said. "I know you don't approve of this slaughter. But you can't say so, can you?"

Slowly, the ambassador rose. With his wife, he left quietly. I would never see him again. When they vanished, despite my revulsion over Beijing's action in Tiananmen Square, I knew I had lost a friendship that could have survived Tiananmen. I had caused Han to lose face—or *mianzi*—one of the worse things that can happen in Chinese culture. *Mianzi* can be defined as dignity or prestige, but no translation completely covers its meaning. Loss of face can make an enemy for life and is at the root of many conflicts.[12]

My reproach of Han obviously provided no remedy for the Tiananmen Square crime.

Nothing could.

I do not regret my revulsion at the Tiananmen Square massacre. But what I learned about *mianzi* would make a good lesson for swaggering US policy makers who need to exercise care in disagreeing with the Middle Kingdom. Donald Trump, for example.

Trump's tariff war with China has only made trade solutions more elusive. So have his infantile accusations that Beijing trade practices are committing "the greatest thefts in the history of the world."[13]

China will continue to rise. Trump's "America First" policy will turn the United States inward. It would be the height of irony if, in the span of decades, China and the United States trade places, and the Middle Kingdom becomes the preeminent global power and we, the insular, isolated nation like the one I found on the Chinese mainland in 1979.

32
Checkmate

As my ninth term began in 1991, I had become a member whose voice mattered on both national and regional issues. On the Appropriations Committee, I produced major capital investments in every part of Oregon. I'd turned the First Congressional District Democratic blue, having vanquished the best candidates Republicans had put up against me. My legislative aides were among the most able teams in the House. Staff turnover was practically nonexistent. At the time, only one cloud hung over the immediate political landscape.

President George H. W. Bush and his Gulf War.

Within weeks, the president would invade Iraq, lifting his approval rating to 89 percent. Despite jingoistic opinion in Oregon and the nation, I objected to the war. With my Defense Subcommittee, I had inspected US troops massing on Kuwaiti's southern border during Operation Desert Shield, a major prewar military exercise in Bahrain. I took seriously the warning of CIA analysts who felt it was perilous to weaken Saddam Hussein without knowing how to prevent the Islamic Republic of Iran from filling the geopolitical void. There was no stopping Bush's go-to-war bandwagon, though. By 2016, twelve years after the first and then a second Iraq war, sure enough, Greater Iran had become the most dangerous power in the Middle East.

Before the vote in 1991, several House colleagues confided that they knew better but would stand with Bush. It was painful to watch the abuse of a flag-waving moment. In the Oregon delegation, Bob Packwood was the senior Republican to support the war. Hardline conservatives Denny and Bob Smith aligned with him, but no one else. Packwood would have surprised me if he had resisted the war. I couldn't remember the senator risking his neck or political capital by opposing a single US military adventure or Pentagon megaweapon. In this, he was the antithesis of Oregon's senior senator, Mark Hatfield, a towering advocate for peace.

As a politician, Packwood also was the mirror opposite of Senator Wayne Morse, the legendary senator he had ousted in 1968. Morse's credo had been "Principle above Politics." Standing the principle on its head may explain how Packwood got a reputation for switching positions so promiscuously.[1] "Sometimes I'm a whore," he once admitted to three environmental lobbyists over a glass of wine in his office.[2]

It's hard to argue with self-definition.

Packwood was alternatively an environmentalist and an environmental traitor, a women's rights defender and a sexual harasser, a tax-break defender[3] and a tax-break reformer.

My policy differences with him would boil over during the northern spotted owl crisis, which unfolded before, during, and after the Gulf War. Hatfield and I had been laboring virtually nonstop with others in the Northwest delegation to protect the endangered owl, an indicator species of forest health,[4] while saving timber jobs. I can't recall Packwood taking part in these sessions. Then, with little advance notice, he called for the repeal of the Endangered Species Act. Most rural Oregonians loved the move. Packwood did not tell them his idea had no chance of surviving a congressional debate, much less a Senate filibuster. Nor did he disclose that the court injunctions banning logging on Northwest federal forests were based not on the Endangered Species Act, but a Forest Service violation of the National Forest Management and National Environmental Policy Acts. Thus, even if the senator's idea had passed, it would not have made a scintilla of difference for timber workers. That wasn't the point, though. The point was that Packwood, already running for reelection, chose to frame the conflict as a case of which matters most—humans, or some damned bird. As political theater for timber workers, it was boffo. As policy, it was bunk.

Someone needed to unseat this man in his reelection eighteen months away. But who? My friend Congressman Peter DeFazio of Springfield mulled a candidacy before confiding that he would opt out. I had considered the Senate's superior platform for national leadership, better in all ways to that of the House. I was also growing tired of the House's every-two-year campaigns. On the other hand, I would have to abandon my seat in the House and on the Appropriations Committee, where I had accomplished a lot for Oregon, arms control, and a host of other issues. The race also would be a war. Packwood was a gut fighter, a shrewd strategist, and a strong debater. He had to be; among Oregon voters, his support was always thin. Those thin margins ensured that he would use his chairmanship of the powerful Senate Finance Committee to raise a campaign chest four or five times richer than any challenger, including me.

In the end, I felt compelled to run, not knowing, of course, that the race would become one of the most bizarre and controversial campaigns in modern Senate history. I did know I faced long odds, but I ran anyway. I was fighting for nuclear arms control, and Packwood wasn't. I resisted American support of right-wing dictatorships, and he didn't. I was for universal health care, and he wasn't. I supported "trickle-up" economics to help the middle class and poor. He supported "trickle-down," which favored the rich.

In the run-up to the 1992 election, analysts predicted that Packwood would have one of the toughest seats to defend in an election year that didn't look to favor Republicans, given a deep economic recession that slashed once-popular President Bush's public approval mark. Between July and August, Bush's favorable rating fell to 29 percent. He would go on to lose his re-election bid with the lowest percentage since William Howard Taft in 1912.[5] Nonetheless, state and national media billed my pending matchup against Packwood as an epic fight. Major national journalists regarded the senator, though weakened, as one of the nation's "most powerful elected officials" with "extraordinary political instincts."[6] I had been described by the state's largest daily newspaper, the *Oregonian*, as "the most powerful congressman in Oregon and one of the most influential members from the Northwest."[7]

It was shaping up as a scene from *The Gunfight at the OK Corral*, which, as the challenger, was fine by me.

Hellfire over the Nonbank Bank

Then came the first political earthquake. It shook the Capitol to its foundation and left me dumbstruck, a politically tongue-tied version of myself, from which I've never recovered.

It all involved a small nonbank bank that was a House members' co-operative. For 150 years, the House Bank granted no loans, paid no interest, offered no credit cards, and had no overdraft protection. Its sole purpose was to be a place where House administrators deposited individual paychecks. Members could write personal checks covered entirely by the pool of members' salaries.

On September 18, 1991—thirteen months before Election Day—a Government Accountability Office (GAO) audit showed that hundreds of

House members had multiple overdrafts on their individual accounts. Every payee, however, received full payment. Overages, many amounting to a few dollars, were drawn from the pool of other members' funds.

But in what was already a blistering anti-incumbent year,[8] the GAO audit created a tidal wave of outrage against what looked, wrongly, like the worst rip-off yet by untrustworthy, privileged pols who voted themselves pay raises, doled out pork-barrel goodies, and junketed around the world at taxpayer expense. In the frenzy, few voters differentiated between human error, deliberate deception, the nonbank nature of the bank, or what turned out to be its egregious management practices.

The *New York Times* editorialized that the "hysteria" over the Bank was fueled by three major misconceptions. "To begin with, few checks actually 'bounced,'" the editors explained:

> The House Bank generally honored the checks even if the members had too little money on deposit to cover them. Members were routinely allowed to write overdrafts up to the amount of their next month's pay. Once the overdrafts exceeded that level, the bank typically called to ask for a deposit. No taxpayer funds were used to cover the checks members wrote on insufficient funds. The bank used money from the accounts of other members, who were in effect making free loans to their colleagues, at no cost to themselves.[9]

Bank policies also were revealed to be lax. Deposited checks sometimes sat for days before being processed. Sue's deposit of $61,000 to our home re-modeler, Anthony Gatewood, took four days to go on the books. Gatewood banked it in one. On slow business days, the bank closed early. Overdrafts inevitably occurred. Some members deliberately abused the system, but they were few in number. Most overdrafts were caused by bank laxity or inattention or mistakes by members. The bipartisan House Ethics Committee singled out twenty-two members of Congress, some with more than nine hundred overdrafts in one year. Ultimately, four were convicted of crimes involving felonious activity with the help of their bank accounts. Lost in the fury over these sinners was a GAO finding that they were the exception, not the rule.

The bank scandal swept across the country like a scythe through prairie grass.

Had I known how poorly the bank was managed, I would have avoided it altogether and done our family banking in our neighborhood. It is impossible, however, to know what you don't know. Once the GAO released its audit, the damage had been done, no matter how faithfully Sue and I had followed the bank norms that had been explained to us when I arrived in office.

When the news first emerged, I asked the House sergeant at arms, Jack Russ, to tell me the exact number of my overdrafts. As a Democratic officer of the House, Russ was in charge of the bank. I wanted to be completely transparent about the condition of my bank account. "Seven," the sergeant at arms reported, each of which, he said, had been covered within four days. I didn't realize the defensive Russ had given me a false, de minimis figure. He wanted to minimize the story in every way he could. I also could not have known he was a crook. A month after careers were ruined in the general election, Russ was convicted of embezzlement, fraud, and false financial reporting and sentenced to two years in prison.[10]

Dutifully, I broke the news of my overdrafts to DC-based reporters covering my race. Even seven checks were treated like political dynamite. It took very little time until I was depicted as being a "check bouncer," unfit to deal with the federal budget deficit or the public trust. It was a harsh indictment. But with only seven checks in question, I could manage it.

Later, with my support, the House voted to disclose the overdrafts of all members. Everything quickly went nuclear.

To my horror, I discovered that Russ had lied. Over the course of seventeen years in the House, Sue and I had written eighty-three overdrafts. The Pacific Northwest media went wild. Not only had I reportedly bounced checks, but I had been dishonest about my misdeeds. In this little house of horrors, I could have strangled Jack Russ.

My staff and I watched videotapes of public opinion focus groups. These gatherings of everyday people reflected a scientific sample of Oregon voters. After seventeen years of faithful representation, I flinched to see voters turn on me, using epithets like "extortionist," and "liar," and "political crook who's in it for himself." One woman thought my overdrafts had siphoned taxpayers' money from the Treasury.

Not that truth mattered. I couldn't get anyone to listen to me. As a final resort, Sue and I held a press conference in downtown Portland during which we sat for several hours, answering question after question with our checkbook and our accountant until the reporters had nothing left to ask. Our honesty and candor did no good. After a life of rectitude, I continued to be pilloried by voters as a crook who papered walls with funny paper. It was a hell I'll never forget.

How to Wreck Democratic Unity

To defeat the well-funded Packwood, I needed to have the support of a unified Oregon Democratic party. It was important to save my campaign's financial resources until the critical final weeks of the fall General Election. Harry Lonsdale, a multimillionaire "outsider" from Central Oregon, shattered both goals by filing against me in the Democratic primary to be held in May. He charged that my role in lifting the logging injunction put me in the pocket of the timber industry. The irony was supreme: the industry was backing Packwood; it had targeted me for defeat.

Lonsdale had never held an elected office. Two years earlier, in a bare-knuckles brawl, the biotech entrepreneur nearly knocked off Oregon's popular senior senator, Mark Hatfield. He accused Hatfield—who had done more for Oregon than perhaps any other senator in modern history—of being a corrupt puppet of lobbyists, influence peddlers, and special interests.

Financing his campaign primarily with his personal wealth, Lonsdale was a model candidate in what the Pew Research Center called the "Year of the 'Outsider.'"[11] With no record to defend, he could concentrate on the attack. He charged that as a "congressional insider," I, like Hatfield, was out of step with Oregon. Worse, he declared that my PAC contributions proved that I was corrupt. As a man of moderate means, what was I to do—match his millions with bake sales? Lonsdale's holier-than-thou attitude infuriated me. So did his presumption that his lack of political experience was superior to eighteen years of achievement. I sputtered to an aide, "Who made Saint Harry God and didn't give us the memo?"

Then the race took another otherworldly twist.

Sensing blood, Republican Packwood put me in a cross fire by intervening in the Democratic primary with an anti-AuCoin TV attack ad. Lonsdale must have loved it. In a parody of the game show, *Jeopardy*, a voice stated the answer, "This Oregon congressman bounced 83 checks for over $61,000. Question: 'Who is Les AuCoin?'"[12]

My eight-point lead over Lonsdale evaporated. Sue and I watched primary election–night returns until well past midnight, with me trailing by some two hundred votes. It was a stinging rebuke from Oregon Democrats with whom and for whom I'd worked for twenty-four years.

Sue counseled, "Honey, you were shouting into a hurricane." Before turning in, we shared an emotional embrace with Kelly and Stacy. Stacy had organized college campuses across the state. Kelly had come up from his acting job at the Oregon Shakespeare Festival to watch the returns with us. My reasons for running had been buried in a mudslide. I didn't want to think about what I'd say in the next day's concession speech.

In the middle of my sleep, my bedside phone jolted me up.

"Yes?" I asked.

It was Kelly. He was in the motel lobby, waiting for his ride to the airport for the flight back to Ashland. "Dad!" he said. "You're ahead!"

"What?" I mumbled.

"A new batch of ballots came in. You're now up by 248 votes."

I thought I'd fallen through the looking glass. Overnight, I had inched ahead by a margin so slim that an automatic recount was required by law. There would be no damned concession speech. Not now!

That afternoon, our friends Ed and Mindy Leek, talented veterans of the 1968 recount between Wayne Morse and Packwood, volunteered to run my recount team. A month later, I was certified as having won by 330 votes. Ed and Mindy ensured there were no errors.

Suddenly, I was the Democratic nominee. My campaign, however, was flat broke. Packwood had over $4 million in the bank, having continued to raise money while I spent a month in purgatory.

With no lift at all from the primary, I went back to the daily fund-raising lists, calling donors across the country who couldn't pronounce my name.

More Political Theater

It wasn't a campaign that needed more epic drama, but the spotted-owl crisis provided it anyway. Over the summer and fall, anger in rural Oregon over the second successive logging injunction in two years drove political hysteria to a boiling point I'd never seen. Protests had broken out. Logging trucks convoyed, 434 strong, through downtown Roseburg, one of Oregon's top lumber towns. More than a thousand loggers protested in Portland's Pioneer Square. Most members of the Oregon and Washington delegations doubled down on our search for a solution that would restore jobs without harming either the owl or its old-growth habitat.

Packwood, in turn, doubled down on that bill of his to repeal the Endangered Species Act. He seemed to enjoy flying solo.

At outdoor rallies throughout rural Oregon, he ridiculed the ESA as excessive environmentalism that ignored human beings. He would stomp on an outdoor stage and say, "There! I'm sure I must have just killed three or four 'endangered' bugs." Audiences roared their approval. Logging companies previously in support of my reelection campaigns were now in thrall with Packwood's sophistry. They donated heavily through their PACs to his reelection. Not that he was desperate for money. Few senators were better at raising PAC funds than Packwood. He told Oregon voters he would no longer accept money from pro-Israel PACs, then used the mailing list of those PACs to send out a series of fund-raising appeals. One shameful letter began: "Dear Friend, please forgive the informal nature of this letter, but it is late in the evening, and my secretary already has gone home. What I want to discuss with you is Israel's future. It simply could not wait until morning . . ."[13]

Packwood would outspend me by $5.4 million in a general election decided by 5.6 percent of the vote.

The Issue That Couldn't Be Told

With Lonsdale disposed of, I had the one-on-one opportunity against Packwood that I'd hoped for so many months earlier. Moreover, I learned that white hot magma churned against Packwood just below the level of voter awareness, waiting to erupt.

Since spring, we knew that a freelance writer for *Vanity Fair* had interviewed twenty-two women, including some of Packwood's former staff aides who claimed to be victims of sexual harassment by the senator. In September, the writer took the story to the *Washington Post*. The *Oregonian* made a timorous attempt to catch up. However, when its reporter, Holley Gilbert, left the paper over the summer, no editor reassigned her project.[14]

I couldn't imagine an issue with greater potential to alter an election. However, my campaign strategists and I were of one mind: so long as Packwood's conduct remained below the surface, we couldn't and wouldn't touch it. After a controversial primary in which editorial writers criticized my team and me for airing hard-hitting, negative TV ads, such a move would have blown up in my face. Besides, we were certain the *Post* would run the story prior to the November election.

We soldiered on, continuing to be out-raised and out-spent, keeping our focus on issues directly impacting the state and the nation. The *Washington Post,* after all, had brought down Richard Nixon for his crimes. When it laid bare Packwood's abuses, I wanted to be sure that I had offered my case for national leadership. I disdained the idea of rising to high office solely on another man's tawdry ethics.

Organized labor had lost a lot of clout by 1992, but its volunteers and donations could still be decisive in a close race. Like most state affiliates, the Oregon AFL-CIO normally listens to candidates at its state convention but waits until after the national convention to give general election endorsements, paying heed to its national officers.

Packwood had tied up support of national union leaders so tightly he didn't attend labor's Oregon convention in August at the Inn of the Seventh Mountain near Bend. With the support of several local unions who knew my strategy, I stunned Packwood by winning the convention's endorsement. I had turned the convention around with a podium-pounding reminder of all the litmus-test issues I had shared with them over my career. The endorsement moved us forward, but several international unions donated to the senator despite their Oregon members' preference for my candidacy.

Big-name Democrats came to Oregon to help me—Senate Majority Leader George Mitchell, Illinois senator Paul Simon, Arizona governor Bruce Babbitt, and Delaware senator Joe Biden all did their part. Ted Kennedy and his wife, Vicki, attended my major fund-raising receptions in Washington. Long after Bill Clinton had locked up Oregon's electoral votes, he returned to lend me his coattails. It all helped at a time when I was paddling upstream and taking on water.

In September, two months before the general election, the US Department of Justice confirmed in a letter my innocence of any wrongdoing at the House Bank. The Associated Press ran my response. "That's what I've said from the beginning," I announced. "No taxpayer dollars were involved; my checks did not bounce. This ends it." Except, of course, it didn't. The public's mind was set. Only a television-advertising blitz could possibly have made a difference. By then I didn't have enough money left in my campaign kitty to try to turn it around.

Throughout this wicked campaign, Sue consistently brightened our way. In the fall, she was on a surrogate speaking tour, being driven by Stacy, when I had to back out of a key debate in Bend. The Defense Appropriations Bill was scheduled for floor action on the same day I was scheduled to debate Packwood before the Oregon Homebuilders' Association. I had to remain in Washington to protect my arms-control provisions. I called Sue, who was campaigning in Madras, north of Bend.

"Honey," I explained, "It's a lot to ask, but would you stand in for me at the Homebuilders debate?"

Without missing a beat, she replied, "Tell the staff to cancel my appearances, send me briefing books, take me off schedule for three days, and I'll do it." She boned up in Tumalo, at the home of her sister, Ann. Every report from the debate said she mopped the floor with Oregon's junior senator. Ironically, as a young page in the Oregon Legislature, Sue had dated him a few times when he served in Salem.

Sue shone again in October during the preparations for the debate at the Portland City Club, the state's most prestigious venue. In our nightly tracking polls, we were running neck and neck. The questions I would ask Packwood during the candidates' question period needed to be sharp and powerful.

As we went around the table, gathering ideas from my strategists, one suggestion after another seemed hackneyed. Nothing zinged.

Then Sue spoke. Knowing that Packwood had been trying to distance himself from the unpopular George Bush at the top of the ticket, she proposed this as my opening salvo: "Do you support President Bush, and if not, why not?"

Silence in the face of inspiration. As heads snapped toward her, Sue leaned forward with that laugh that wrinkles her nose. Everyone cracked up and applauded.

At the debate, I opened with Sue's question, and it brought down the house. The national media ran with it the next day. In congressional life, many wives hit the stump with their political husbands. Few have Sue's rapier sense of irony. Fewer still are willing to debate a Senate committee chairman, much less win. I've always counted on Sue's daring and courage.

As the campaign entered the home stretch, the *Post* sent its investigative team back to Oregon for a final round of interviews. Packwood had put them off until five days before the election. Confronted by the reporters,

Packwood categorically denied the allegations and attacked the credibility of his accusers in a series of written statements sent to the newspaper. His denials caused Leonard Downey Jr., the *Post's* executive editor, to hold the story until his reporters gathered more information. Meanwhile, nightly polling showed the race virtually deadlocked. Packwood responded with what in politics is called a telephone "push poll"; a campaign ruse masked as public opinion research, it imparts defamatory information about one's opponent to voters trying to decide whom to support. Timed at the end of the campaign, it leaves a targeted candidate no time for rebuttal.

Packwood's callers asked voters who they were supporting in the race. If the response was "Packwood" or "AuCoin," the caller would terminate the call and move on to the next voter. An "undecided" response, however, drew a follow-up question: "If you knew that Congressman AuCoin was under a federal investigation for writing bad checks on the House of Representatives Bank, would that effect your choice?"

The Packwood campaign spent $90,000 to spread that falsehood, weeks after I had received and made public a Department of Justice letter exonerating me.

After having held roughly even for weeks, my nightly poll numbers went into a tail spin. Election Day arrived, and neither the *Washington Post* nor the *Oregonian* published the results of their investigations.

I went to bed knowing that I would lose the first election of my career. Worse, the loss did not turn on any of the issues that caused me to run.

The next morning, a victorious Packwood announced in his press conference that he would recommend me to President-elect Clinton as Secretary of Interior, an agency that is the guardian of federal forests and rangeland. His comment gave ambidexterity new meaning. During the campaign, he had called me an environmental extremist.

If one must lose a Senate race, it helps to know that voters will soon be overcome with buyer's remorse. That is exactly what happened. When the *Post* broke the story three weeks later, Packwood's 52.1–46.5 percent victory[15] turned to ashes. The general public was furious.[16] The *Oregonian* ran a front-page apology, acknowledging that it had "failed to pursue the story aggressively enough, and to devote the time and resources needed to delve into the rumors, which had swirled around Packwood for years."[17] *Oregonian* editor William Hilliard said the paper was hesitant "to ruin a man's career."[18] In another Orwellian twist, some facts turned out to have lurked under the paper's nose all along. Among the senator's victims was a sixty-four-year-old *Oregonian* correspondent on whose lips Packwood had planted an unwanted kiss following an interview in his Washington office.[19]

Angry protesters picketed Packwood when he returned to Oregon.[20] Some 250 citizens,[21] led by former Oregon Supreme Court Justice Betty Roberts, petitioned the Senate Rules Committee to refuse to seat the senator because he had "defrauded the voters." The petition was denied.

However, on September 5, 1995, the Senate Ethics Committee found Packwood guilty of sexual harassment and misconduct and voted unanimously to expel him.[22] Three days later, to avoid being ousted, the senator announced he would resign.[23] Almost three years had elapsed since I awoke in Portland to concede my defeat.

With Packwood's announcement, more than a few Oregonians wanted me to run again. I considered why I had run in the first place. The issues were as valid as ever. Then I remembered the price I'd paid—hours of cold calls, begging for campaign bucks from strangers; the media's inability to report facts hidden in plain sight and a general failure to sort fact from sensation; and novices who proposed to turn my years of hard work into a political liability for being a "Beltway insider."

I decided I had but one life to give to my country and that I had given it. I also had gotten reacquainted with Nature and her ways, so rational compared to the human comedy the stars had watched over for ages. My career had let me live dreams beyond the imagination of the boy who grew up behind Redmond's Piggly Wiggly grocery store. I had done some good. My broken hopes would mend. Camping in the wild, gazing at the astral river above the great firs, I thought about what John Steinbeck wrote:

"Somewhere in the world there is a defeat for everyone. Some are destroyed by defeat, and some are made small and mean by victory. Greatness lives in one who triumphs equally over defeat and victory."[24]

That became my resolution.

Afterword

Outside of Oregon, I cannot think of another state in which someone like me could have made it to the top of national life. I am grateful. Retirement pulled Sue and me to Bozeman for ten years, where our daughter and two granddaughters lived exactly one block up the street from us, a dream come true. We watched those preschool girls grow up to be young women, a gift we'll never forget. Now we are home again in Portland, where on a clear morning we awaken to a view of Mt. Hood in the east, can dig for clams at the coast in ninety minutes, and relish Deschutes trout water in two hours. At seventy-seven, I may have lost some accuracy with my fly rod. But no matter; on the river I'm in my cathedral. And I am at peace with myself and the deep family love I spent a lifetime seeking.

My fellow House reformers will remain in my heart and memory forever. Strangers at first, we banded together in 1975 to turn a hidebound tugboat of a House into an exhilarating, agile vessel. The effect was like tacking a sailing boat sharply into the wind. The jolt seizes the vessel and fills it, mast to keel, with reawakened energy, singularity, and purpose.

The reformers gave all legislators rules that offered more freedom to act on both conscience and constituent needs. Armed with an idea to improve the commonweal, one no longer had to kiss the ring of some czar to file a bill. They just wrote the thing and dropped it in the hopper! We also forced the House to conduct the public's business in broad daylight. Under new rules, committees held hearings and voting sessions open to the press and the public. No more voting behind closed doors.[1] Floor amendments, once rare, became commonplace again; any member from any committee could try to alter a bill. Recorded votes could be requested by even the most junior House member. The days of secret voting had vanished.[2] By eliminating seniority as the absolute guarantor of committee leadership, committee chairs could no longer inherit their position by simply outliving or outlasting others on a committee. We also opened the institution to live cable television coverage, a move that would have dumbfounded bosses of yore who preferred working the shadows. Two years after the Nixon impeachment, we reasserted the institution as a more coequal branch to the executive. Committees vigorously investigated and exposed wrongdoing in the executive branch.

It was in many ways a golden era. I was fortunate to be part of it.

But it did not last.

Starting with the Newt Gingrich speakership in 1994 and cresting in Congresses led by Republicans Dennis Hastert, John Boehner, and Paul Ryan, partisan power brokers seized the reins of power again. The "world's greatest deliberative body" no longer deliberated. After months of induced stalemate, a few bosses habitually wrapped multiple appropriations bills and other measures into a single package and bought it to the floor in a clump, an "omnibus bill." Some of the packages resembled the unabridged version of the Oxford English Dictionary, in size if not in wisdom. Members had mere hours to study such bills before voting. Amendments were disallowed. These malign legislative hodgepodges presented members with a take-it-or-leave-it choice. Sometimes managers cut deals to insert previously defeated proposals inside these catchall bills. Like Lazarus, the toxic provisions arose from the dead to become law with no public hearings or a separate vote. The all-or-nothing nature of an omnibus bill often means accept-it-or-close-the-government because defeat means the elimination of funds to run the government. Since 1976, the government has shut down twenty-six times for this very reason.

It's impossible to imagine serving in this modern Congress. The return of a Democratic House majority in 2018 may remedy some abuses of recent Republican regimes. But I suspect not all of them. Gingrich and his acolytes seized power by weaponizing the openness created by the 1974 reforms, making congressional sessions an extension of the permanent partisan campaign that voters abhor. I doubt that the Democratic majority in 2018 will permit a return to the open days of 1975, which, despite the era's inherent virtues, created a strategic gateway for revanchist conservatives who show greater loyalty to power than to the institution in which they serve.

In 1992, the House Bank tempest and my loss to one of the Senate's least-upstanding humans was almost as shattering as the collapse of my parents' marriage that devastated me so many years earlier. In response, I looked for a new way to make a difference. My brief work as a lobbyist, which I had said I'd eschew, and as the CEO of a major Portland foundation turned out to be, in turn, excessively self-serving and bureaucratic. Then I found my second love.

In 1998, I accepted the Glenn L. Jackson Professorship of Government and Business Ethics at Southern Oregon University in Ashland. Watching a student's face respond to an "aha" moment gave me a rush second only to when I passed legislation in Congress. SOU students voted me "most popular professor" on campus. The SOU chapter of the national Phi Kappa Phi honor society named me "Professor of the Year" in 2004, my final year on the faculty. Those awards adorn my home office as proudly as plaques and honors for my congressional years.

I will never fall out of love with Oregon. Wherever I've resided, my iPhone operated on an Oregon number, a measure, however small, of continuity and a link to my roots. My former students around the globe correspond with me still. Many of my former congressional aides live in Portland and continue to enjoy socializing together. They care for each other like a family. When we lived in Montana, Sue and I loved seeing them again at someone's home when we returned to Portland.

We still attend these gatherings. They always draw a full house.

Notes

PREFACE

1 Foster Church, "Future Redistricting Troubles Dampen AuCoin's Triumphs," *Oregonian*, Portland, Oregon, June 18, 1988.

CHAPTER 4

1 From an unpublished memoir about the final Morse senate campaign by the late Ron Abel, a former Oregon reporter and Morse campaign aide. Abel gave it to me during a reunion in Portland a few years before his death on February 11, 2012.

2 Among the organizers were Steve Schell, John Gustafson, Joe (R. P.) Smith, Hardy Myers, and John Gould. Donors included Monford Orloff and Ken Brody, president and vice president, respectively, of Evans Products Company in Portland.

3 Obituary, Kenan Heise, *Chicago Tribune*, November 14, 1989.

4 In 1976, Bob Crane won the New York Newspaper Guild's Page One Award for conceiving of and writing most of the articles in a series about New York City's financial mismanagement. The series was titled "Save the City."

5 A paraphrase of Marine General Lewis "Chesty" Puller, when his troops were surrounded by Chinese soldiers in the Korean War.

6 Jim Kadera, "Democrat, 28, Does 'Impossible' in GOP's Suburban Stronghold," *Oregonian*, Portland, Oregon, November 8, 1970.

CHAPTER 5

1 While the university had matriculated a few black theology students, it would not admit its first class of black undergraduates for two more years (1964). "Celebrating Change: Courage, Determination, Inclusion," Vanderbilt University, https://www.vanderbilt.edu/celebratingblackhistory/look-back/

2 Henry Hampton and Steve Fayer, eds., *Voices of Freedom: An Oral History of the Civil Rights Movement from the 1950s through 1980s* (New York: Bantam Books, 1991).

CHAPTER 6

1 "A Sea Change in Oregon Politics: 1973 Legislative Session," Fortieth Anniversary Exhibit, Oregon Political Leadership Archive, College of Urban and Public Affairs, Portland State University, 2013.

2 Representative Stafford Hansel, speech on HB 2003, June 13, 1973, Oregon Archives, Floor Reel 26, Side B.

3 Hansel.

4 Hansel.

5 "House Reduces Pot Penalties," *Capital Journal*, Salem, Oregon. June 21, 1973.

CHAPTER 7

1 Stephen Kafoury introduced the gay rights bill in every subsequent legislative session until retiring in 1999. Each time, it lost by one vote in the house.

2 "Our Story," PFLAG (Parents, Families, Friends of Lesbians and Gays) website, Portland, Oregon, https://www.pflagpdx.org/about-pflag-pdx/our-story.

3 Sidney Bazett served from 1961 to 1973. He died in 1983.

4 The Oregon Equality Act was signed by Governor Ted Kulongoski on May 9, 2007, it went into effect on January 1, 2008.

CHAPTER 8

1 McCall served two years of a four-year term as Oregon Secretary of State and two four-year terms as governor. He held no other office and died in 1983.

2 Born in Egypt, Massachusetts, McCall was the grandson of Samuel Walker McCall, a Bay State congressman and governor.

3 Tom McCall's speech to the Oregon Legislative Assembly, 1973, Oregon History Project of the Oregon Historical Society, Tom McCall Papers, Mss625.

4 Paul W. Harvey Jr., "Oregonians Vote Defeat of Tax Plan," *Daily Chronicle*, Centralia, Washington, May 2, 1973.

5 The Oregon Constitution bans the legislature from affixing an emergency clause on any tax bill, thus moving the effective date to the following January 1. The delay allows time for citizens to gather petitions to put the tax on a referendum ballot.

6 Many legislators on both sides of the aisle suspected that McCall had encouraged the rumors.

7 To my knowledge, there is no known reference to this private letter in any history of Tom McCall. It may be the most candid account of the seriousness with which McCall contemplated changing political parties for what some thought might be a run against freshman US Senator Bob Packwood. I located a copy of it among my political papers as I prepared to write this work. I have sent a copy of the letter to the Oregon Historical Society in Portland, Oregon.

8 Oregon law requires the regulators of several industries to be members of those industries. In a state vaunted for its progressive governance, it is an anachronistic irony.

9 Robert E. Gangware, "HUD Aides Lauds City's Housing Plan," *Statesman Journal*, Salem, Oregon, November 9, 1973.

10 "McCall Praises Holbrook Ability," *Statesman Journal*, Salem, Oregon, December 11, 1973.

11 Tamara Avant, "Examining the Mob Mentality," *South Source* 1, January 2011.

12 Robert E. Gangware, "Legislature Repeals New Subdivision Law," *Statesman Journal*, Salem, Oregon, January 25, 1974.

CHAPTER 9

1 We were a disparate group, despite our common zeal for reform. Our numbers included a housewife from Kansas, a union house painter from Rhode Island, a

Shakespearean scholar from Texas, a former member of (Ralph) Nader's Raiders, the former first lady of New Jersey, and a crusading young editor of a weekly paper in Illinois. Many of us seized former Republican seats.

Some old-guard pols and pundits gave us the sobriquet, "Watergate Babies," implying that we were young, impetuous, and naïve. But Norman Ornstein, a scholar at the American Enterprise Institute, deemed our class as "the most consequential Congress in modern history. The record would suggest that Ornstein was correct. Newcomers provided the critical votes existing reformers needed to open up a largely secretive, insular institution that had ceded inordinate authority to the White House. House and committee votes were now recorded, committee hearings were opened to the public, and the hidebound seniority system was upended, ending the hammerlock on chairmanships held by conservative Democratic chairs who were aligned with the Republicans. Floor debate was opened to encourage amendments and free-flowing debate.

2   Nicholas Confessore, "Koch Brothers' Budget of $889 Million for 2016 Is on Par with Both Parties' Spending," *New York Times,* January 26, 2015, https://www. nytimes.com/2015/01/27/us/politics/kochs-plan-to-spend-900-million-on-2016-campaign.html.

3   Seth Cline, "Sheldon Adelson Spent $150 on Election," *U.S. News & World Report.* December 3, 2012.

4   Nathan Guttman, "How Sheldon Adelson's Bet on Trump Made Him 2016 Election's Biggest Winner," *Forward,* January 9, 2017, https://forward.com/news/national/356644/how-sheldon-adelsons-bet-on-trump-made-him-2016-elections-biggest-winner/.

5   According to campaign-finance watchdog OpenSecrets.org, https://opensecrets. org/overview/cost/php.

6   Editorial, "The Flaw in Buckley v. Valeo," *New York Times.* February 8, 2000, https://www.nytimes.com/2000/02/08/opinion/the-flaw-in-buckley-v-valeo.html.

7   In 1986, my campaign raised $958,023, according to the Federal Election Commission.

8   Sinita Rada, "Americans Don't Show Up at the Polls, but Neither Do the Swiss," *U.S. News & World Report,* November 2, 2018.

9   Paul Waldman, "How Our Political Campaign Finance System Compares to Other Countries," *American Prospect,* April 4, 2014, https://prospect.org/article/how-our-campaign-finance-system-compares-other-countries.

10 Danielle Kurtzleben, "2016 Campaigns Will Spend $4.4 Billion On TV Ads, But Why?" *It's All Politics* (blog), National Public Radio, August 19, 2015, https://www.npr.org/sections/itsallpoliti cs/2015/08/19/432759311/2016-campaign-tv-ad-spending.

11 Dana Goldstein, "How to Inform a More Perfect Union," *Slate,* February 2, 2017, https://slate.com/news-and-politics/2017/02/can-schools-help-americans-do-a-better-job-separating-fact-from-fake-news.html.

12 Norah O'Donnell, "Are Members of Congress Becoming Telemarketers?" *Sixty Minutes,* CBS, April 24, 2016.

13 Brooks Jackson, *Honest Graft: How Special Interests Buy Influence in Washington* (Washington, DC: Farragut, 1990). Chronicling the years from the 1970s to 1986,

the author, a Wall Street Journal reporter, describes the legal quid pro quo relationship between special tax breaks and deregulation and political donations.

14 "Declining trust in government is denting democracy," *Economist*, January 25, 2017.

15 Robert Kennedy delivered his "Ripple of Hope" speech at the University of Cape Town on June 6, 1966.

CHAPTER 10

1 George H. W. Bush coined the term voodoo economics when he ran against Reagan in the 1980 New Hampshire primary. Bush was against "trickle-down," supply-side economics then. That was before he was for it as Reagan's vice-presidential running mate.

2 John le Carré, "The United States of America Has Gone Mad," *Times* (London), January 15, 2003.

3 A condition of slow economic growth and relatively high unemployment—economic stagnation—accompanied by rising prices, inflation, or inflation and a decline in Gross Domestic Product (GDP).

4 Douglas A. Hibbs Jr., "President Reagan's Mandate from the 1980 Elections: A Shift to the Right?" *American Politics Quarterly* 10, October 1982, 387–420.

5 "A History of Fed Leaders and Interest Rates," *New York Times*, December 16, 2015.

6 Glenn Kessler, "Does Obama have the 'worst' record of any president on the national debt?" *Washington Post*, December 8, 2014.

7 James Fallows, "The Spend-Up," *Atlantic*, July 1986.

8 David Stockman, *The Triumph of Politics: Why the Reagan Revolution Failed* (New York: Harper & Row, 1986).

9 Mike Patton, "U.S. Debt Is Heading Toward $20 Trillion: Where it's Been, Where It's Going and Why," *Forbes*, March 28, 2016, https://www.forbes.com/sites/mikepatton/2016/03/28/u-s-debt-is-heading-toward-20-trillion-where-its-been-where-its-going-and-why/.

10 Christopher Chantrill, "What is the Deficit?" US Government Spending (website), http://www.usgovernmentspending.com/federal_deficit.

11 Jonathan Schwabish and Courtney Griffith, "U.S. Federal Budget: A Closer Look at Discretionary Spending," US Congressional Budget Office, April 2012, https://www.cbo.gov/sites/default/files/cbofiles/attachments/BS_Mandatory_print.pdf.

CHAPTER 11

1 "Labor Force Statistics from the Current Population Survey," Bureau of Labor Statistics, https://data.bls.gov/timeseries/LNU04000000?periods=Annual+Data&periods_option=specific_periods&years_option=all_years.

2 "Unemployment Rate in Oregon," FRED Economic Data, Federal Reserve Bank of St. Louis, https://fred.stlouisfed.org/series/ORURN.

3 Tri-County Metropolitan Transportation District of Oregon, "Making History: 45 years of TriMet and Transit in the Portland Region," 2015, 32.

4 This subcommittee had jurisdiction, among several agencies, over the Department of the Interior and the US Forest Service. As such, it was an important panel for issues in the American West.

5 Bob Young, "Highway to Hell," *Willamette Week*, Portland, Oregon, March 8, 2005.

6 Zach Rosenberg, "Why Portland's Mass Transit Rocks," Wired (blog), November 16, 2009, https://www.wired.com/2009/11/portland-trimet-mass-transit/.

7 "World's Top 25 Cities," *Monocle* 9, no. 85, July/August 2015.

CHAPTER 12

1 My caseworkers specialized in cutting through bureaucratic red tape to unsnarl problems between federal agencies and constituents.

2 William G. Robbins, "Oregon Donation Land Act," *The Oregon Encyclopedia*, a project of the Oregon Historical Society. This law, foreshadowing the Homestead Act of 1960, legitimized 640-acre claims "with the proviso that white male citizens were entitled to 320 acres and their wives were eligible for 320 acres. . . . To gain legal title to property, claimants had to reside and make improvements on the land for four years," https://oregonencyclopedia.org/articles/oregon_donation_land_act/.

3 History.com editors, "Manifest Destiny," A&E Television Networks, April 5, 2010, https://www.history.com/topics/westward-expansion/manifest-destiny.

4 David Lewis, "Confederated Tribes of Grand Ronde," *The Oregon Encyclopedia*, a project of the Oregon Historical Society, https://oregonencyclopedia.org/articles/confederated_tribes_of_grand_ronde/.
     "The tribes were the Kalapuyans, which included the Santiam, Tualatin, Marys River, Yamhill, Yoncalla, Winefella, Mohawk, and Long Tom; the Chinookans, which included the Clackamas Oregon City, Watlala, Multnomah, and Cascades; the Molala Northern, Santiam, and Southern; the southwestern Oregon tribes, which included the Rogue River, Cow Creek Umpqua, Takelma, and Chastacosta; and a few people of other tribes like the Shasta, Klamath, and Klickitat. The name Rogue River refers to a number of tribes in the Rogue River area, mainly the Dakubetede and Chastacosta (Athabaskan), the Shasta (Hokan), the Takelmas, and some neighboring tribes or bands."

5 In 1953 Congress adopted an official policy of "termination," declaring that the goal was "as rapidly as possible, to make the Indians within the territorial limits of the United States subject to the same laws and entitled to the same privileges and responsibilities as are applicable to other citizens of the United States." (House Concurrent Resolution 108, August 1, 1953, https://www.govinfo.gov/content/pkg/STATUTE-67/pdf/STATUTE-67-pgB132-2.pdf, B132.

6 Larry L. Naylor, *American Culture: Myth and Reality of a Culture of Diversity* (Westport, CT: Bergin & Garvey, 1998).

7 E. A. Schwartz, *The Rogue River Indian War and Its Aftermath, 1850–1960* (Norman, OK: University of Oklahoma Press, 1997), 260.

8 Testimony by Tribal Chair Mark Mercier at the field hearing on the reservation bill, Grand Ronde, Oregon, August 10, 1987.

9 In the Chinook trade jargon of Pacific Northwest native peoples, skookum means very strong, fearsome, or brave. In the Grand Ronde culture, powerful Skookum spirits reside on fog-shrouded Spirit Mountain. The term has evolved across cultures to mean awesome, impressive, or excellent. Walter Shelly Phillips, *The Chinook Book*, (Seattle: R. L. Davis, 1913).

10 Kristine Olson, *Standing Tall: The Lifeway of Kathryn Jones Harrison* (Seattle: University of Washington Press, 2005).

CHAPTER 13

1 A lame-duck session of Congress in the United States occurs whenever one Congress meets after its successor is elected but before the successor's term begins.

2 Aunt Mary died in 1987. Martha had earned her master's degree in education at Harvard University in 1992; she died in 2004 of pancreatitis.

CHAPTER 15

1 I witnessed Weinberger's testimony in a classified hearing of the House Defense Appropriations Subcommittee in 1983.

2 Bernard Weinraub, "Reagan Asking $4.2 Billion For Buildup of Civil Defense," *New York Times*, March 30, 1982, https://www.nytimes.com/1982/03/30/us/reagan-asking-4.2-billion-for-buildup-of-civil-defense.html.

3 Lester Stone II, "What Would Happen in an All-Out Nuclear War?" History News Network, August 9, 2010, https://historynewsnetwork.org/article/129966.

4 Lawrence S. Wittner, "The Nuclear Freeze and Its Impact," Arms Control Association, December 5, 2010, https://www.armscontrol.org/act/2010_12/LookingBack.

5 Stephen I. Schwartz, "The Real Cost of Ballistic Missile Defenses," WMD Junction, *Nonproliferation Review*, Middlebury Institute for International Studies at Monterey, California, April 13, 2012.

6 Robert Bridge commentary in *RT*, Russia's English-language news channel. "When does a defensive missile system become offensive?" *RT*, March 26, 2010.

7 George Field and David Spergel, "Cost of Space-Based Laser Ballistic Missile Defense," *Science* 231, no. 4744, March 21, 1986.

8 Philip M. Boffey, "Dark Side of 'Star Wars': System Could Also Attack," *New York Times*, March 7, 1985.

9 I'll never forget this conversation with Abrahamson in California when I visited Hughes Aircraft Company, where, retired, he was a senior executive. He remained a believer in SDI.

10 Game theory is the mathematical framework for discussing experiments with an outcome that is uncertain. Niels Richard Hansen, "Probability Theory and Statistics," Lecture Notes, University of Copenhagen, November 2010.

11 Leslie Stahl, CBS Evening News, March 31, 1983, https://tvnews.vanderbilt.edu/broadcasts/289456.

12 Reagan's second State of the Union Address, January 25, 1984.

13 Hans M. Kristensen and Max Korda, "Russian Nuclear Forces, 2019," *Bulletin of the Atomic Scientists* 75, no. 2, March 4, 2019, https://thebulletin.org/2019/03/russian-nuclear-forces-2019.

14 William J. Perry, "The Risk of Nuclear Catastrophe Is Greater Today Than During the Cold War," *Huffington Post*, January 20, 2016, https://www.huffpost.com/entry/nuclear-catastrophe-risk_b_9019558.

CHAPTER 16

1 *Congressional Record* 137, no. 130, September 19, 1991, S13337.

CHAPTER 19

1 Steve Forrester, "Wilderness Bill Moving Fast," *Register-Guard*, Eugene, Oregon, December 10, 1982, 11A.

2 *Congressional Quarterly Almanac* (Washington, DC: CQ Press, 1985), 313–317, https://library.cqpress.com/cqalmanac/document.php?id=cqal84-1152976#.

3 Packwood's role in the delegation's work on timber issues—wilderness, contract relief, or, later, the spotted owl—was limited. His October 1990 amendment to remove the northern spotted owl from the Endangered Species Act was tabled by the Senate. In April 1990, his amendment to restrict log exports off private lands cleared the Senate. The House took no action on the measure.

4 Matt Blitz, "Visit the World's Most Amazing Old-Growth Forests" (travel blog), *Smithsonian*, August 4, 2015, https://www.smithsonianmag.com/travel / amazing-old-growth-forests-world-180956083/.

5 Linnie Marsh Wolfe, ed., *John of the Mountains: The Unpublished Journals of John Muir* (Madison, WI: University of Wisconsin Press, 1979), 313.

6 Kathie Durbin, *Tree Huggers: Victory, Defeat and Renewal in the Northwest Ancient Forest Campaign* (Seattle: Mountaineers, 1996), 39.

7 Randal O'Toole, "Are Region 6 Forests Being Overcut?" *Forest Watch*, May 1987.

8 100th United States Congress, Second Session, "1989 Budget Explanatory Notes for Committee on Appropriations," US House Appropriations Subcommittee on the Department of the Interior and Related Agencies, Appropriations for 1989, Part 2: *Justification of the Budget Estimate* (Washington, DC: United States Government Printing Office, 1988), 1255.

9 Debra D. Warren, "Production, prices, employment, and trade in Northwest forest industries, third quarter 1993" (PDF), United States Forest Service, 107.

10 Much of this volume would be enjoined by a federal judge, as the reader will soon see, due to administrative failures by the Forest Service.

11 O'Toole.

12 After I had retired from Congress, the Northwest Forest Plan determined the allowable cut in Northwest Forest Service lands should be 1.1 billion board feet per year, an 80 percent reduction from earlier estimates of sustainability.

13 *Congressional Quarterly Almanac.*

14 Conference Report on H.R. 2788, Department of the Interior and Related Agencies Appropriations Act, 1990, *Congressional Record*, October 2, 1989, 22674.

15 Except that the rider would apply to Section 318 sales until their harvest was complete, sometimes requiring more than one year to be completed.

16 United States Supreme Court, Robertson v. Seattle Audubon Society (1992), No. 90-1596.

17 Dan Postrel, "Activist: Old Growth is National Issue; He Says Oregon Lawmakers Can't Cope," *Stateman Journal*, Salem, Oregon, March 8, 1990, 19.

18 Durbin, 193.

19 Durbin, 108.

20 Durbin, 107.

21 US District Court for the Western District of Washington, Seattle Audubon Society v. Evans, 771 F. Supp. 1081 (W.D. Wash. 1991).

22 Craig Welch, "Old-Growth Logging Nearing a Standstill in Dramatic Shift," *Seattle Times*, April 11, 2004.
23 Timber sold should not be expected to match the amount of timber cut during any time period. This is because timber sold may not be harvested for several years.
24 Steven E. Daniels, Corinne L. Gobeli, and Angela J. Findley, "Reemployment Programs for Dislocated Timber Workers: Lessons from Oregon," *Society and Natural Resources* 13, no. 2–3 (2000), 135–150.

CHAPTER 20

1 Richard Lessner, "Religious Tenets Guide James Watt," *Arizona New Republic*, August 8, 1981.
2 Colman McCarthy, "James Watt and the Puritan Ethic," *Washington Post*, May 24, 1981, L5.
3 Cotton Mather, *The Wonders of the Invisible World* (London: John Russell Smith, 1862). Project Gutenberg online edition, 2009, http://www.gutenberg.org/files/28513/28513-h/28513-h.htm.
4 Lessner.
5 Statement made in 1981, quoted in "Words Cited By Watt Critics," *New York Times*, October 10, 1983, D10.
6 "News Summary: National," *New York Times*, September 22, 1983, B1.
7 Associated Press, "James Watt Draws a Fine But Not Jail," *New York Times*, March 13, 1996, A16.

CHAPTER 21

1 Sensenbrenner was an heir to the Kimberly-Clark fortune. One decade later, he would be a leader in the impeachment of President Bill Clinton.
2 Steven V. Roberts, "Boland Is Center Stage, Like It Or Not," *New York Times*, May 1, 1983.
3 General Augusto Pinochet, the Chilean dictator, was responsible for gross human rights abuses during his reign, including murder and torture of political opponents. According to a government commission report that included testimony from more than 30,000 people, Pinochet's government killed at least 3,197 people and tortured about 29,000. Two-thirds of the cases listed in the report happened in 1973, the year of the US-backed coup d'état. Monte Reel and J. Y. Smith, "A Chilean Dictator's Dark Legacy," *Washington Post*, December 11, 2006.
4 Paul M. Rodriguez, "A Letter from the Editor," *Insight on the News*, October 1, 2002.
5 For a revealing report on this, I recommend Raymond Bonner's "Time for a U.S. Apology to El Salvador," *Nation*, April 15, 2016, https://www.thenation.com/article/time-for-a-us-apology-to-el-salvador/.
6 Robert Parry, "Reagan and Guatemala's Death Files," Consortium News, September 5, 2011, https://consortiumnews.com/2011/11/3/reagan-and-guatemalas-death-files/.
7 The school, still operated by the US Department of Defense, was renamed in 2000 as the Western Hemispheric Institute for Security Cooperation. Barbara Starr, "Controversial 'School of the Americas' Closes," ABC News, December 15, 2000, https://abcnews.go.com/International/story?id=81917&page=1.

8 School of Americas Watch (website), https://www.soaw.org/.

9 David Johnston, "Bush Pardons 6 in Iran Affair, Averting Weinberger Trial; Prosecutor Assails 'Cover Up,'" *New York Times*, December 25, 1992.

10 Kenneth J. Cooper, "Contra Victim's Kin Get Partisan Hearing," *Philadelphia Inquirer*, May 14, 1987.

11 Louis Jacobson, "David Axelrod Calls Newt Gingrich 'the Godfather of Gridlock,'" Politifact.Com, December 5, 2011, https://www.politifact.com/truth-o-meter/statements/2011/dec/05/david-axelrod/david-axelrod-calls-newt-gingrich-godfather-gridlo/.

12 *Congressional Record*, May 8, 1984, 11421–11427.

13 John Nichols, "ALEC Exposed: Rigging Elections," *Nation*, August 1–8, 2011, https://www.thenation.com/article/alec-exposed-rigging-elections/.

CHAPTER 22

1 Mckay Coppins, "The Man Who Broke Politics," *Atlantic*, November 2018.

2 Mario Cuomo, "The Last Liberal," *New York Times*, March 11, 2001.

3 Clyde Beatty (no relation) was a famous circus lion tamer in the 1950s and '60s.

4 Boland was O'Neill's closest friend in the House. For twenty years, they had roomed together in Washington before Tip became House Speaker and Millie O'Neill joined him in the capital.

CHAPTER 23

1 George Crile, *Charlie Wilson's War: The Extraordinary Story of How the Wildest Man in Congress and a Rogue CIA Agent Changed the History of Our Time* (New York: Grove, 2003).

2 In my first race for the Oregon House in 1970, I ran for an open seat. In my second in 1972, redistricting put another incumbent and me in the same district. In 1974, my first race for Oregon's First Congressional District seat was open due to the retirement of the incumbent, Wendell Wyatt.

3 Daniel W. Lehman, "Murphy's Staten Island Gambit," *Village Voice*, November 6, 1978.

4 Michael Dobbs, "'Koreagate' Figure Tied to Oil-For-Food Scandal," *Washington Post*, April 15, 2005.

5 The FBI's term is short for Arab Scam.

6 Richard Langworth, ed., *Churchill by Himself: The Definitive Collection of Quotations* (Philadelphia: PublicAffairs, 2008), 572.

7 Stanton E. Samenow, "The Criminal's 'Superoptimism,'" Inside the Criminal Mind (blog), *Psychology Today*, March 14, 2016, https://www.psychologytoday.com/us/blog/inside-the-criminal-mind/201603/the-criminals-superoptimism.

CHAPTER 24

1 Uninfluenced, that is, until the 2016 general election produced a Republican House and Senate with Donald Trump as president. Senator Lisa Murkowski was the deciding vote on Trump's $1.5 trillion tax bill. The price of her support

was an extraneous but reprehensible amendment that opened the refuge to oil and gas drilling, a stinging defeat for environmentalists who had successfully protected the lands for decades. Murkowski's "midnight amendment" had not received a single public hearing.

2 From the text of the Wilderness Act of 1964 (Pub. L. 88-577).

3 Steven Mufson, "Trump administration takes another step toward oil drilling in Arctic National Wildlife Refuge," Health & Science (blog), *Washington Post*, December 20, 2018, https://www.washingtonpost.com/national/health-science/trump-administration-takes-another-step-toward-oil-drilling-in-arctic-national-wildlife-refuge/2018/12/20/5fb93f40-0469-11e9-b5df-5d3874f1ac36_story.html?utm_term=.300f9e17d00e.

CHAPTER 25

1 Charles M. Blow, "Checking My Male Privilege," *New York Times*, October 29, 2017, https://www.nytimes.com/2017/10/29/checking-my-male-privilege.html.

CHAPTER 26

1 Gabe Rosenberg, "A Bill Banning Most Abortions Becomes Law in Ohio," National Public Radio, April 11, 2019, https://www.nhpr.org/post/bill-banning-most-abortions-becomes-law-ohio#stream/0.

2 This is my best recollection of the article read to my colleagues; the original article remains elusive.

3 United States Supreme Court, Webster v. Reproductive Health Services, 492 U.S. 490, No. 88-605 (1985).

4 United States Supreme Court, Roe v. Wade, 410 U.S. 113 (1973). The Supreme Court ruled unconstitutional a state law that banned abortions except to save the life of the mother. States were forbidden from outlawing or regulating any aspect of abortion performed during the first trimester of pregnancy, could only enact abortion regulations reasonably related to maternal health in the second and third trimesters, and could enact abortion laws protecting the life of the fetus only in the third trimester. Even then, an exception had to be made to protect the life of the mother. See Alex McBride, *Supreme Court History: Expanding Civil Rights: Landmark Cases*, Public Broadcasting System, 2007, https://www.pbs.org/wnet/supremecourt/rights/landmark_roe.html.

5 William Dannemeyer, House floor speech, *Congressional Record*, September 22, 1983.

6 "Required Reading: Abortion and the Debt," *New York Times*, September 27, 1983, A28.

7 Peter Bollen, *Frank Talk: The Wit and Wisdom of Barney Frank* (Lincoln, NE: iUniverse, 2003), 92.

CHAPTER 28

1 "Morse Voices Gun Control Opposition," *Register-Guard*, Eugene, Oregon, May 19, 1972.

2 Les AuCoin, "Confessions of a Former NRA Supporter," *Washington Post*, March 18, 1991.

3 Osha Gray Davidson, *Under Fire: The NRA and the Battle for Gun Control* (Iowa City: University of Iowa Press, 1998), 245.

4 Davidson, 247.

5 Indeed, Heston would later become president of the National Rifle Association.

6 In the Oregon House delegation, only Congressman Ron Wyden joined me in support of the bill. Republican Bob Smith opposed it, as did Democrats Peter DeFazio and Mike Kopetski.

7 Criminal Justice Information Services Division, *National Instant Criminal Background Check System (NICS) Operations 2017* (Washington, DC: Federal Bureau of Investigation, 2017), iv.

CHAPTER 29

1 Nigel Jaquiss, "1982," *Willamette Week*, March 8, 2005, https://www.wweek.com/portland/article-4181-1982.html.

2 James Kelly, "Unemployment on the Rise," *Time*, February 8, 1982.

3 TreasuryDirect, Reports, "Historical Debt Outstanding—Annual 1950–1999," https://www.treasurydirect.gov/govt/reports/pd/histdebt/histdebt_histo4.htm.

4 "Reagan Unwraps His 1983 Budget, Without Ribbons," *New York Times*, February 7, 1982, 4004001, https://www.nytimes.com/1982/02/07/weekinreview/reagan-unwraps-his-1983-budget-without-ribbons.html.

CHAPTER 30

1 In the US House, members of the committee that brings a bill to the floor have preference when seeking recognition to speak. The Speaker Pro Tempore will not recognize other House members to speak, regardless of seniority, as long as one member of the committee of jurisdiction seeks recognition. This meant I would never again wait up to an hour or more before addressing the House on defense spending measures.

2 Gregory M. Lamb, "US Jews protest treatment of Soviet dissidents, refuseniks," *Christian Science Monitor*, February 7, 1983.

3 Robert Kushen, Herman Schwartz, and Abner J. Mikva, *Prison Conditions in the Soviet Union: A Report of Facilities in Russia and Azerbaidzhan* (Washington, DC: Human Rights Watch, 1991), 4.

4 As a Foreign Ministry official and diplomat, Churkin survived through the reigns of several Soviet and Russian Republic leaders, including Gorbachev, Yeltsin, and Putin. He served as Russia's ambassador to the United Nations from 2006 until his death in February 2017 of an apparent heart attack in New York City. He was one of six high-ranking Russian officials to die, some by assassination, in a four-month period starting December 2016. Charlotte England, "Unexpected deaths of six Russians in four months triggers conspiracy theories," Independent, February 27, 2017.

5 Both Russia and China tested ASATs—Putin's Russia in 2015 and the Peoples Republic of China, in 2007, 2013, and 2014. The United States, alas, is in the act too. With my appropriations rider having lapsed in May of 2015, Congress added more than $32 million to the air force's space budget to study anti-satellite technology, including offensive and active defense capabilities. It also instructed the Pentagon to

"conduct a study of potential alternative defense and deterrent strategies in response to the existing and projected counterspace capabilities of China and Russia." George Leopold, "Antisatellite race heats up with China, Russia," Defensesystems.com, May 1, 2015, https://defensesystems.com/articles/2015/05/01/antisatellite-race-china-russia.aspx.

6 "Whoever destroys a soul, it is considered as if he destroyed an entire world. And whoever saves a life, it is considered as if he saved an entire world." Mishnah Sanhedrin 4:9; Yerushalmi Talmud, Tractate Sanhedrin 37a.

CHAPTER 31

1 Researching this memoir in 2017, I asked Heather Thomas, then a staff member of the US House Library, to check on him. I had only his first name and the year he worked for me, 1978. Within days, Heather had not only his full name but also his current telephone number. When I phoned, he was filling his gas tank at a Portland service station. With advanced degrees from MIT and Stanford, Micallef is now an entrepreneur, business executive, author, and lecturer on management, foreign policy, and military affairs.

2 George Ball, testimony on HR 8196 before the House Committee on Banking, Finance, and Urban Affairs, Subcommittee on International Trade, Investment, and Monetary Policy, January 26, 1978, *Congressional Record* (Washington, DC: US Government Printing Office, 1978), 16–17.

3 Gary Conkling, "Reflections on China," unpublished notes, February 12–24, 1979.

4 My traveling party included Lloyd Anderson (director of the Portland of Portland) and his wife and future Multnomah County Commissioner, Pauline; Ken Lewis (president of a shipping line) and his wife, Carol; Robert Dwyer Jr. (head of a timber trading company) and his wife, Lynne; Michael Hollern (president of a wood products company) and his wife, Sue; and Mel Peters (a heavy machinery manufacturing broker). Everyone lived in Portland, Oregon, except the Hollerns, who resided in Bend, Oregon.

5 Shanghai Pudong International Airport, Travel China Guide, http://www.travel-chinabuide.com/cityguides/shangai/pudong-airport.htm.

6 Philip P. Pan, "The Land that Failed to Fail," *New York Times*, November 18, 2018, https://www.nytimes.com/interactive/2018/11/18/world/asia/china-rules.html.

7 "China GDP: How it has changed since 1980," *Guardian*, England, March 22, 2012, https://www.theuardian.com/news/datablog/2012/mar/23/china-gdp-since-1980. (In 2016, the same newspaper estimated China's GDP at $8.5 trillion.)

8 World Shipping Council website, "Top 50 World Container Ports," 2016, http://www.worldshipping.org/about-the-industry/global-trade/top-50-world-container-ports.

9 Conkling.

10 Conkling.

11 Henry Kissinger, *On China* (New York: Penguin, 2011), 346.

12 Kwang-kuo Hwang, "Face and Favor: The Chinese Power Game," *American Journal of Sociology* 92, no. 4 (January 1987), 944–984.

13 Veronica Stracqualursi, "10 times Trump attacked China and its trade relations with the US," ABC News, November 9, 2017, htpps://abcnews.go.com/Politics/10-times-trump-attacked-china-trade-relations-us/story?id=46572567.

CHAPTER 32

1 Editorial, "Bob Packwood pulls a flip flop," *Statesman-Journal*, Salem, Oregon, July 12, 1985.

2 Andy Kerr, "The Browning of Bob Packwood," *Cascadia Times* 1, no. 6 (September 1995), 8–9.

3 Karen Tumulty, "Catching a 'Chameleon': Senate Wrestles With Packwood," *Los Angeles Times*, November 3, 1993.

4 Editorial, "Bush No Help in Timber Crisis," *Statesman-Journal*, Salem, Oregon, May, 22, 1990.

5 Jim Meyers, "George H. W. Bush Poll Numbers Swung Wildly During Presidency," NewsMax, August 12, 2014, https://www.newsmax.com/thewire/george-hw-bush-presidential-polls/2014/08/12/id/588216/.

6 Timothy Egan, "Packwood Is Leaving As a Pariah In His State, *New York Times*, September 5, 1995, 8.

7 Foster Church, "Future Redistricting Troubles Dampen AuCoin's Triumphs," *Oregonian*, Portland, Oregon, June 18, 1988.

8 Walter Burnham, "The Politics of Repudiation 1992: Edging Toward Upheaval," *American Prospect*, Winter 1993, https://prospect.org/article/politics-repudiation-1992-edging-toward-upheaval.

9 Editorial, "Overdrafts and Overkill: Capitol Punishment for the House Bank?" *New York Times*, April 16, 1992, https://www.nytimes.com/1992/04/16/opinion/overdrafts-and-overkill-capitol-punishment-for-the-house-bank.html.

10 William J. Eaton, "Ex-House Sergeant-at-Arms Sentenced to 2 Years," *Los Angeles Times*, December 18, 1993, https://www.latimes.com/archives/la-xpm-1993-12-18-mn-2999-story.html.

11 Donald S. Kellerman, Andrew Kohut, and Carol Bowman, "The People, the Press & Politics: Campaign '92, Year of the 'Outsiders,'" Survey VII (PDF), June 16, 1992, https://www.people-press.org/1992/06/16/year-of-the-outsider/.

12 Packwood cited the face value of my bank-protected overdrafts, not the difference between the face value of the instruments and funds on hand in my account. The actual amount that had to be covered was negligible.

13 Richard H. Curtiss, "Senate Call for Packwood Expulsion Ended Protection of Israel Lobby," Washington Report on Middle East Affairs 21 (October–November 1995), 101–102, https://www.wrmea.org/1995-october-november/senate-call-for-packwood-expulsion-ended-protection-of-israel-lobby.html.

14 Cheryl Reid, "A Newspaper Confesses: We Missed the Story," *American Journalism Review*, January–February, 1993, https://ajrarchive.org/article.asp?id=2101.

15 Packwood outspent me $8 million to $2.6 million. No senator raised or spent more that year. Don Hamilton, "Packwood Sets '92 Campaign Spending Record," *Oregonian*, Portland, Oregon, May 25, 1993, B4.

16 "Packwood Accused of Sexual Harassment," *Washington Post*, November 22, 1992, A1.

17 Richard C. Paddock, "For Many, Packwood Case Has Extra Sting of Betrayal," *Los Angeles Times*, December 6, 1992, https://www.latimes.com/archives/la-xpm-1992-12-06-mn-3565-story.html.

18 Reid.

19 Rachel Gorlin, "Why politicians got away with sexual abuse for so long," *Washington Post*, November 10, 2017, https://www.washingtonpost.com/outlook/why-politicians-got-away-with-sexual-misconduct-for-so-long/2017/11/10/4bb1ecc6-c4d8-11e7-aae0-cb18a8c29c65_story.html?utm_term=.3440eb9d6174.

20 Associated Press, "Packwood Moves Luncheon After 350 Protesters Show Up," *Los Angeles Times*, January 31, 1993, https://www.latimes.com/archives/la-xpm-1993-01-31-mn-1058-story.html.

21 Helen Dewar, Public Airing Set in Packwood Case," *Washington Post*, April 30, 1993, https://www.washingtonpost.com/archive/politics/1993/04/30/public-airing-set-in-packwood-case/2efa8110-f460-48da-bea6-5296ebe41cfd/?utm_term=.c9089984a552.

22 "Resolution For Disciplinary Action," Senate Ethics Committee, September 5, 1995, S. Rept. 104–137.

23 Paddock.

24 John Steinbeck, *The Acts of King Arthur and His Noble Knights* (Boston: Avenel, 1982).

AFTERWORD

1 Except in sensitive cases such as issues of national security.

2 Marjorie Hunter, "First Recorded Teller Vote is Taken in the House," *New York Times*, March 4, 1971.

Index

Note: Photographs are indicated by an italicized page number. Endnote material is indicated with an italicized "*n*" followed by the note number and its sequence on the page (when there are multiple same note numbers on the page).